# THE SECOND CITY
## UNSCRIPTED

MIKE
THOMAS

# *The Second City®*
## UNSCRIPTED

REVOLUTION AND REVELATION AT
THE WORLD-FAMOUS COMEDY THEATER

VILLARD
NEW YORK

Published in the United States by Villard Books, an imprint of
The Random House Publishing Group, a division of Random House,
Inc., New York.

VILLARD BOOKS and VILLARD & "V" CIRCLED Design are registered
trademarks of Random House, Inc.

ISBN 978-0-345-51422-6

Printed in the United States of America on acid-free paper

www.villard.com

9 8 7 6 5 4 3 2 1

First Edition

Book design by Liz Cosgrove

*For Sandy, Grace, and Audrey*

# AUTHOR'S NOTE

With only a few exceptions, the quotes from those who speak in *The Second City Unscripted* come entirely from interviews with the author. Bill Murray's words on page xi are from a twentieth-anniversary celebration he emceed at Second City in 1980. Jim Belushi's stories about his brother John, on pages 126 and 146, are excerpted from an interview he gave on a former Bravo series called *Second City Presents . . . with Bill Zehme.*

# CONTENTS

# PROLOGUE

**Jim Belushi, cast member**

The Second City grounded me, taught me everything about acting, comedy, writing, directing, music, rhythm. The comic rhythm. The timing. It resonates in everything I've done. To be honest, I don't know how other people do it who haven't done Second City.

**Stephen Colbert, cast member**

I was there for five years, and it was everything to me. At a certain point, I gave up doing other theater, and I went, "If I'm going to be good at this, I have to do nothing else." And so I went, "Okay, I'll find out what this has to offer me." And it had a great deal to offer me—and still does to anybody who wants to take their stupid seriously.

**Bonnie Hunt, cast member**

It definitely humbles you, because there are times when you go out there and you fail and you've got to brush yourself off and start all over again. It's kind of like being a Cubs fan. I think what I learned at Second City was that it was okay to take risks, to fall flat on my face and get back up and learn about myself. And I definitely learned to embrace the honesty of my own vulnerability.

**Tina Fey, cast member**

Being in that company, in some ways you lose your fear of failure. Because there are always nights in that set when you're developing a show where everything tanks, or where you're just bombing, and you come out the other side of it, and you survive it. And that's such a great thing to get rid of—that fear of failure.

**Bill Murray, cast member**

It's given many great performers their start, but more importantly, it's killed thousands of barely talented people and it's put them to death, and they're now doing the jobs they're built for. It's because they couldn't meet the rugged standards. I used to work at this place, and they paid me poorly and miserably, but they let me drink free, and I've never forgiven them for that.

On a snowless and seasonably mild Wednesday night in mid-December 1959, the Second City opened for business at 1842 North Wells Street, on Chicago's Near North Side. By all accounts the satire-centric, improvisation-steeped theater—housed in the former Wong Cleaners & Dyers Chinese laundry and later described as "a caucus room, fit for politics and poker and vote-swapping"—was a smash success from the start. Fifty years on, with a long and luminous alumni list that includes John Belushi and Bill Murray, Steve Carell and Chris Farley, Stephen Colbert and Tina Fey, it remains a top-tier comedy crucible—the Harvard of ha-ha.

For those fortunate enough to earn a residency there, Second City has long been a noble end in itself as well as a potential springboard to fame. Without the skills it teaches (chief among them collaboration), the confidence it instills, and the failure it allows, much of the comedy (and, to a lesser extent, the drama) we have seen and continue to see on screens big and small—from *Caddyshack* and *Ghostbusters* to *Curb Your Enthusiasm* and *30 Rock*—would be either distinctly different in tone or simply nonexistent. And it's a good bet *Saturday Night Live*—whose first season starred no fewer than three Second City–trained actors (John Belushi, Gilda Radner, and Dan Aykroyd)—would have struggled to lift off. Instead, it soared into the stratosphere.

Of course, like most good ideas, Second City didn't appear from out of nowhere. Its previous and less polished predecessor, the University of Chicago–rooted Compass Players, featured Mike Nichols, Elaine May, Shelley Berman, Barbara Harris, Severn Darden, and several other skilled actor-improvisers. Founded by David Shepherd and Paul Sills, the ensemble—which Shepherd hoped would appeal to the working class—was a big hit among hipsters in Chicago and St. Louis from 1955 to 1958. The Compass's precursor (if only in a general theatrical sense), Playwrights Theater Club, mounted twenty-four dramatic productions in two locations on Chicago's Near North Side between 1953 and 1955.

When Second City set up shop, Chicago was riper than ever for smart satire and cabaret-style entertainment. Though not yet the regional theater mecca it would become four decades later, the town was home to an increasing number of happening nightclubs, including Mister Kelly's and the Gate of Horn, where flourished a new generation of well-informed wits such as Shelley Berman, Mort Sahl, and Lenny Bruce. The revolution was further stoked by Chicago-based *Playboy* mogul Hugh Hefner, whose trailblazing magazine published hip humor pieces, and whose television program *Playboy's Penthouse* provided a nationally syndicated showcase for budding talent—Second City talent included. Guest stars could often be found mingling with barely clad babes at Hefner's swank North State Parkway manse, a swinging joint in its own right.

Mere blocks away, Second City was fast becoming a place—for many, *the* place—to see and be seen. With shows at nine and eleven P.M. every night but Monday, and an additional one A.M. performance on Saturdays (plus a postperformance improv set, which could stretch to three-thirty A.M. on Saturdays), it catered to night owl sophisticates—or those who merely fancied themselves such—and helped spur a theatrical renaissance in a city that's now rife with stages, teeming with stage actors, and host to an ongoing influx of big-budget productions.

"There was much less improvisation there," former Second City actor Omar Shapli told author Janet Coleman of the theater's first incarnation in her 1990 book *The Compass.* "Scruffy people came to Compass—university students in battle fatigues. Thin ties were worn by men in suits at Second City. Women dressed up for their dates. It was a red and gold atmosphere. It was meant to succeed."

Nowadays the satirical stronghold that once bought used bentwood chairs and leftover carpet, that purchased bar and kitchen supplies from a bankrupt restaurant, that forwent (and still forgoes) elaborate costumes and expansive sets, reaps millions of dollars annually from its various ventures. With a long-running sister site in Toronto that launched Dan Aykroyd, Mike Myers, John Candy, Martin Short, and Gilda Radner (among several others); constant TV, film, and Internet projects in the works; three popular training centers that offer an array of comedy-based workshops; multiple touring companies; busy corporate divisions; floating revues on seven ocean liners; and three resident theaters (two in Chicago and one in Toronto), Second City is (as it long has been) a bona fide institution and a widely revered funny farm.

Shortly after *Saturday Night Live* debuted on NBC in October 1975, talks began at Second City Toronto to devise a competing program. *SCTV* was the result, and at first it drew heavily from Second City's Canadian casts. Its ratings and popularity never approached those of *SNL,* but the meticulously honed and parody-rife sketch show had a profound impact on viewers—some of whom, such as *Tonight Show* host Conan O'Brien and movie star Ben Stiller, cultivated high-profile careers in comedy. The show was executive produced for its entire run by current Second City CEO Andrew Alexander and co-owner Len Stuart (Bernard Sahlins shared producing duties for seasons one and two), scripted by a staff that included Harold Ramis, Eugene Levy, Joe Flaherty, and Dave Thomas. In a flash of inspired irony, it was set at a small-time television station in the fictional town of Melonville. Debuting on Canadian airwaves in 1976, *SCTV* eventually appeared in syndicated reruns and original episodes (on NBC and Cinemax) in the United States. During a sporadically scheduled but frequently gut-busting six-season run, it gave millions of viewers their first peek at becowlicked übernerd Ed Grimley (Martin Short) and beer-chugging hosers Bob and Doug McKenzie (Rick Moranis and Dave Thomas)—all bound for international prominence. John Candy's sniping superstar Johnny LaRue, polka phenom Yosh Schmenge, and quivering cowboy Yellowbelly ("the biggest coward in the West") stood out, too. So did Eugene Levy's humorless Vegas comic Bobby Bittman and his brittle-brained newsman Earl Camembert, Andrea Martin's flashy station manager Edith Prickley and her disco queen Melba, Joe Flaherty's horrible horror host Count Floyd and his wheelchair-wielding ("for respect!") station owner Guy Caballero, Catherine O'Hara's Lola "I want to have your baby!" Heatherton and her blue nightclub comic Dusty Towne. And on and on.

This book is the product of more than 170 interviews and covers the first half century of Second City's existence. And though it is a celebration of the theater's influence and longevity, this uncensored oral history also delves into darker corners of a vibrant past. Present-day and former cast members, artistic directors, musical directors, producers, and stage managers recall onstage hilarity, backstage buffoonery, and offstage tragedy. Eminent outsiders weigh in, too. Their accounts are by turns funny, sad, angry, touching, and occasionally stomach-churning.

To their great credit, most of those interviewed summoned detailed memories of events and people as well as of-the-moment emotions. Moreover, many were candid about peccadilloes and shortcomings of their own that emerged at Second City. It should be noted, however, that tales told and feelings expressed herein are largely of an era. What people thought and who they were then—at a deeply formative and intensely competitive stage of their lives—aren't necessarily what they think and who they are now.

Despite publication over the past five decades of several Second City tomes and countless newspaper and magazine articles, the majority of stories in these pages have never before seen print. Even the familiar ones are more fully fleshed out than before. As for the storytellers, whether famous or obscure, a great many of them have this in common: abiding admiration for their alma mater—the comedy college that schooled them in satire, paid them to fail, nurtured their talents, and launched their careers.

Here, then, in the words of those who know it best, is the Second City unscripted.

# THE SECOND CITY
## UNSCRIPTED

# 1

## Coffee and Comedy, Hanging with Hef, and the Birth of a Sensation

1959–61

**Alan Arkin**
**Barbara Harris**
**Paul Sills**

**AMERICA WAS IN THE MIDST** of a comedy revolution when Bernard Sahlins, Howard Alk, and Paul Sills conspired in 1959 to open a bohemian coffeehouse for recreational smoking, erudite discourse, and satirical theater. Considering the times, it seemed destined for success—or miserable failure.

Alk and Sills had formed a professional bond working together at Chicago's famed folk den the Gate of Horn, where Sills house-managed and Alk ran lights. At that point, the business-oriented Sahlins was a budding producer and a devoted theater enthusiast. In addition to sharing a vision for what would become the Second City, another thing all three had in common was a diploma from the elite University of Chicago. A successful thirty-something entrepreneur, Sahlins had graduated in 1943 and went on to run a lucrative tape recorder manufacturing business. Alk entered the school in 1944 at the age of fourteen. Subsequent to his short-lived involvement with Second City, which ended in the early sixties, he became a respected film editor and cinematographer. In 1950, former military man Sills became a director with University Theater—which staged literary productions on a campus that had no formal theater program—and joined the student drama group Tonight at 8:30, where he worked with Mike Nichols, Elaine May, and several others who'd follow Sills to future endeavors.

Having already met during Sills's University of Chicago directing days, Sahlins and Sills initially hooked up professionally in the early fifties to produce dramas (Brecht, Chekhov) at and to sit on the three-member board of the highbrow but ragtag Playwrights Theater Club, which Sills co-founded with comrade Eugene Troobnick and a Socialist populist Harvard man named David Shepherd. For training purposes, Sills steeped the Playwrights cast in spontaneity-enhancing theater games developed by his mother, Viola Spolin. A Los Angeles–based improvisation teacher, Spolin also taught drama at Chicago's Hull House in the 1930s. Its Recreational Training School, founded by social worker Neva Boyd, was part of the U.S. government's Works Progress Administration. The Playwrights Theater Club featured a stable of young actors that included Ed Asner and Barbara Harris and operated at two locations on Chicago's Near North Side before the group folded in 1955.

That same year, Sills and Shepherd co-founded the Compass Players, which began performing extended scenario-based improv shows (essentially a modern version of the age-old Italian form called commedia dell'arte), shorter "blackout" scenes, and spur-of-the-moment material based on audience suggestions in the Compass Tavern near the University of Chicago campus in Hyde Park. The inventive ensemble was wildly popular among in-the-know intelligentsia types, and eventually migrated several miles northwest to the Argo Off-Beat Room. After leaving the fold, several Compass members—Shelley Berman, Mike Nichols, and Elaine May in particular—vaulted onto the national stage. Berman became a chart-topping stand-up (who mostly sat down), and Nichols and May formed the hottest social satire duo in recent memory, with best-selling albums and a triumphant run on Broadway.

But while the Compass drew capacity crowds night after night (the offering of then-rare Michelob beer may have played a role as well), it eventually hit financial bottom and folded in January 1957. Another incarnation opened in St. Louis shortly thereafter, but that branch dissolved before long, too. As of early 1958, after a roughly three-year run, the Compass Players was kaput. But the concepts upon which it was founded—a symbiotic actor-audience relationship and ensemble-based satire created through improvisation—were not. With that sturdy foundation already laid, Alk, Sahlins, and Sills began to build in the summer of 1959.

Little did they know that the result of their labors would become an instant hit. Sahlins, who'd produced plays in 1956 at the handsome and historic Studebaker Theatre on South Michigan Avenue, initially invested six thousand dollars, and the new organization's defiant handle was reportedly conjured by Alk in ironic response to a snotty 1952 New Yorker magazine feature-turned-book by A. J. Liebling (Chicago: The Second City). Original members—many of them Compass and/or Playwrights holdovers—included Roger Bowen (later Lieutenant Colonel Henry Blake in Robert Altman's film *M\*A\*S\*H*), Severn Darden, Andrew Duncan, Barbara Harris, Mina Kolb, and Eugene Troobnick. Allaudin (then William) Mathieu tickled the ivories as musical director. The opening night opener, sung by the magnetic Harris and part of a revue called *Excelsior! And Other Outcries,* was an especially apt tune called "Everybody's in the Know."

And they were. That shared sense of insider savvy coupled with an appreciation of and a hunger for smart satire—always in two acts—kept people coming back. So did cheap tickets ($2.50), flowing booze, beefy burgers, a soon-opened outdoor beer garden next door for summer sipping, and a red-velvet-curtained venue in which to absorb tar-tinged toxins. On many evenings in the months that followed, 120 educated and cultured patrons (University of Chicago types were prevalent, naturally) grinned and chortled and laughed themselves silly at scenes that referenced Kierkegaard, Eisenhower, and Greek mythology. Onstage, actors played at the top of their intelligence (an edict ever since), skewering people, politics, people in politics, and, as one early cast member put it, "almost all the foibles of everyday living from suburbia to fallout shelters." The post-intermission portion was improvised using audience suggestions. New scenes were born thusly, and eventually new shows. The formula—diluted though it became when writing nudged out improvising as the primary method of invention—would serve Second City well in decades to come.

And then, only three months after it began, in March 1960, none other than *Time* magazine praised the fledgling theater as a place where "the declining skill of satire is kept alive with brilliance and flourish"—lofty plaudits indeed for a tiny Midwestern outfit that boasted no national stars, a scant budget, and something of an inferiority complex. The fact that it remained afloat a few months out was—at least to the founders and early cast members—a small miracle. "For many months after that first performance we remained certain that our luck would run out and that no audience would appear the next night," Sahlins wrote in his 2001 memoir *Days and Nights at the Second City.* "Even if it was a brutally cold Tuesday in February, one empty seat convinced us it was the beginning of the end."

While tough times ahead would continue to cause concern, the beginning was more auspicious than anyone had imagined. From night one, even as the budget carpet was still being installed, there were crowds in the lobby and lines out the door to witness the birth of a sensation.

### Bernard Sahlins, co-founder and former owner, producer, and director

I had sold out of my business, which was manufacturing tape recorders. And I had been involved with Playwrights Theater Club as a business director. And when everybody was free—Paul Sills, Howard Alk, Barbara Harris, Eugene Troobnick, Andrew Duncan—we decided that since this was the beat generation, we would start a coffee shop. And we looked around and found this old Chinese laundry and hat shop on Wells Street, and we rented it and went to work fixing it up, not realizing we were going to do a show until a month or two after we started working on it.

But we started to do a show and were a bit uncertain as to what shape it should take. We knew we wanted to do political sketch comedy, but whether it was to be disparate scenes or linked by theme or what, we weren't sure. So we called Mike Nichols in before we opened, and he said, "No, leave it the way it is. One of the joys for the audience is in seeing an actor in so many different roles, exhibiting a diversity of talents." We listened, and he was right.

We sent for a man named Jimmy Masucci. He was a sort of primitive genius, able to take a rag of bone and a hank of hair and make a palace out of it. And he had done a lot of work in St. Louis, where they had a phenomenon called Gaslight Square, which was like Old Town. And everybody was deep into Victoriana, and Masucci would do all the designing. When he came to us, he purchased a lot of old telephone booths with glass panels, lined the walls with them, and put prints inside the glass panels. And lo and behold, we had a decorated nightclub. Everything was budget. We bought the chairs at auction for a dollar apiece—bentwood chairs.

### Dennis Cunningham, bartender and cast member

There were two storefronts next to each other, the southernmost one smaller, with an entrance and a lobby and a coat check, and in back was the kitchen. The bigger place was the showroom. The stage was in the middle of the long north side and was narrow in the middle and big on the sides. There were banquettes around the outside, and it was intimate. It was large enough to be successful by being full, and small enough so that everybody could hear and see and feel.

### Sheldon Patinkin, former manager and director and current artistic consultant

The woman who did the design for the Second City logo was a girlfriend of mine, Selma Quaitman. That's how I found out about the possible names. I thought Second City was a good one. It was snotty. It was an F-you to *The*

*New Yorker* magazine and to A. J. Liebling and to the idea that we were second in everything, including quality and culture.

### Bernard Sahlins

A. J. Liebling came in. And he got a great kick out of the fact that we called it the Second City. I said, "You're gonna change your mind." He said, "I already have!"

### Richard Christiansen, former *Chicago Tribune* chief theater critic

They did have a following, but remember that [Playwrights and the Compass] were failed efforts. The Second City was not a failure. It suddenly clicked, and it was attracting more than the core audience that they had brought over from the Compass as time went on. And most importantly, it began to be noticed by newspaper reviewers. You would get top-line reviewers—Claudia Cassidy, Sydney Harris—they would come and review the opening night of Second City. So it was considered a major entertainment event even in those early days.

### Melinda Dillon, cast member

Opening night, I was collecting coats. They didn't have a coatroom yet. I was just collecting the coats and putting them in the ladies' room. Once we got the coatroom built, which was pretty soon, the gangsters started coming with all their molls and their girlfriends and giving me huge tips. I was doing very well in the cloakroom.

### Bernard Sahlins

After we opened, a very tall and sort of menacing guy came in and said he was there to help us. He was dressed respectably and just oozing B-movie menace. I said, "In what way?" He said, "Well, you can either put us on the payroll and pay us so much a week, or give us a lump sum. But we'll help you see that there's no trouble." So I said I'd think it over. And when he left, I called the alderman and the police, and the police came down and identified the guy. I don't remember who he was. And we didn't hear any more from him except about a month later. Through our plate glass window came a stink bomb, which shattered the glass and sprayed foul-smelling stuff all over. And then a month later, another one, and that was it.

### Sheldon Patinkin

Here's the thing about that first place. Try this now: the box office was a card table set up in the lobby open to the air, to the front door, to anybody who wanted to come in and rob it. It was only set up before the show and during the show, but with the cash box right there. And it was never held up. Never.

### Richard Christiansen

Second City never had any kind of advertising budget, but they did have Irv Seidner, who was the perfect public relations guy for them. Very serious, very intense, glasses and so on. Button-down, the whole thing. He was very, very efficient and good at publicizing the company. So they did attract the prime reviewers of the time, and the word spread because of that. And you would get not only the aficionados, who remembered the brilliance of some of the Compass programs, but also new people who came and were attracted to that same kind of hip, sophisticated material that Second City presented. And it became, in those days, *the* thing to do—go to Second City. People thought it was smart to do, to be able to talk about the latest Second City show and to have been there and to recognize the personalities in the cast.

### Paul Sand, cast member

We were just having a great time. Some people would say to us, "What do you guys do in the daytime?" Because we were just playing all the time, playing with the work. Something clever would come up that night, and we'd work on it the next day and turn it into a scene. Or if we saw a movie, we'd do an Italian movie. It was wild. It was almost ancient. It was like *The Golden Coach* or something—a wild band of players. And the newspapers, they called us geniuses. We were stars in Chicago. It was like being extremely popular in high school.

Then again, popular high schoolers rarely draw interest from famous adventurers and Hollywood big shots. Not long after its inception, Second City began selling out nightly and hosting such notables as mountain climber Sir Edmund Hillary and movie star Anthony Quinn. "The waitresses fought to get his table," remembers Patinkin, who joined the fold as manager in November 1960 and soon took over as artistic director.

Over the next few years, Second City expanded operations locally, nationally, and internationally. There was a new venue for drama next door, fronted by ornate Louis Sullivan–designed arches from a razed theater downtown. There were stints on and off Broadway, and forays into England and Canada. There was even an appearance on *Playboy* magazine mogul Hugh Hefner's new nationally broadcast television program *Playboy's Penthouse,* which earned the cast an invite to the pajamaed one's palatial residence mere blocks from Second City.

### Bernard Sahlins

We went on the show and there was a clean-shaven, kind of diffident young man with us, a comedian, named Lenny Bruce. Totally different than the

Lenny Bruce we knew subsequently. And I don't even remember what we did. I do remember Severn Darden wandering around the mansion, with his jaw agape. We taped the show, and then there was a party. There was swimming. It was not the kind of thing that we loved. We were the University of Chicago. This was low-life.

## Hugh Hefner

I have always had a strong feeling that the whole postwar era after World War II—the late forties and throughout the fifties—was a very conservative time. Socially, sexually, politically. And the changes that took place that led then to the social-sexual-political changes [of] the sixties really began not in political forms, but in the most unusual places. They began on comedy stages with Mort Sahl and Lenny Bruce and others. They began in the pages of *Playboy*. They began on the stage with rock 'n' roll. And it was these voices that changed the world.

I practically lived at Second City. I took [cartoonist and playwright] Jules Feiffer to see Second City. He was completely blown away by them. He was already doing work for me, and I realized that what he was doing on paper was the same stuff that Second City was doing on the stage. That kind of improvisational theater was truly unique and innovative and very exciting. You never knew from night to night what was going to happen.

## Melinda Dillon

I was keeping my eye on the show, and Barbara Harris got sick one night, and they were going to have to cancel the whole show and give everybody their money back. It was a weekend, and it was going to be a big thing to go out there and say, "We just can't do the show." Because there were no backups—there was nobody but me. I was just doing it on my own. And I went up to them and said, "Excuse me, but I know the show." Bernie and Howard and Paul were the three owners and producers, and they were in this little huddle having a heated discussion.

So Bernie just said, "Get out of here." He was right, too. Bernie was right about me, because I knew nothing about current events. I was ignorant, I was slow, I wasn't funny. I was all of those things that you don't get up on the stage at Second City. But I knew that show and I could sing and I can sing. And Barbara had some songs and things, and they had an opera in gibberish, and I knew it totally. So Paul just said, "Let's go; let's do it. She's doing it. She'll do the first show, and if it's a total bomb, we'll give everybody their money back for the second show." And I went on, and it was just a huge success! Barbara was told [about it] and came back for the second show, and I was back in the cloakroom.

### Sheldon Patinkin

Barbara was beautiful; she was funny. You couldn't take your eyes off her when she was onstage. She was really a wonderful presence. She wasn't the world's greatest improviser, but it didn't matter. She didn't come up with ideas, but she came up with responses to ideas.

About six months after Second City opened, a Brooklyn-born folksinger named Alan Arkin (his band, the Tarriers, had a top-five hit with their version of "The Banana Boat Song") came on board—reluctantly at first. Arkin was in a bad way after the breakup of his marriage, and his outlook was bleak. Professional woes contributed greatly to his festering funk. Having made a less-than-successful go of it in New York, the seat of theatrical success, he'd resigned himself to the fact that he might die in obscurity in Chicago. It didn't happen, of course—there'd be hit movies and big money and gleaming award statues down the line—but it took a while for things to click.

### Alan Arkin, cast member

I was at a crossroads. I'd just gotten divorced, and I was upset about that. And I just felt that I needed work, which I wasn't getting in New York. And I went to Chicago thinking it was going to be the end of any kind of career of any size, and I thought I'd be at this crazy place they called Second City for the rest of my life for a hundred bucks a week, but I didn't care.

### Sheldon Patinkin

When Dostoyevsky is your reading choice for your mood, then you know you're not in very good shape. It seemed to help him a little bit in that it made him feel that there were other people who were in even worse shape than him. Lord knows there are in *The Idiot* or *Brothers Karamazov*. He played the guitar a lot, sang a lot. And he introduced me to folk music and jazz. He was living across the street at Emma's, which was a really depressing rooming house. It was also where Joan Rivers lived, depressed.

### Alan Arkin

[Second City] was my haven in every conceivable way when I got there. I was there from the time I got up in the morning till midnight every night. Then, after the last show and everybody calmed down and had a couple of beers, Sheldon Patinkin and I would walk down to the Clark Theater and see foreign films until three or four o'clock in the morning, and then walk back, talking about them and analyzing them. Then I'd go to bed and wake up and go back to [Second City]. So it was a twenty-four-hour-a-day learning experience.

**Joyce Sloane, former associate and executive producer, current producer emeritus**

I was afraid to talk to Alan then. I really was. He was this moody, brilliant guy, and I never had long conversations with him.

**Melinda Dillon**

Oh, I remember how beautiful he was! Oh, God, he was so gorgeous! And he and Barbara Harris fell in love, and there was this romance going on.

**Alan Arkin**

It started in Chicago, but it was just before we went to New York. It didn't go on terribly long.

**Melinda Dillon**

Alan could do anything and everything—sing and play his guitar, and he was funny, and he had all these characters he could do, all these accents he could do. And he was always at home on the stage. To me, he never seemed to be uncomfortable. Ever. He never had an awkward moment on the stage, and most of us do. He was very confident, and he had such a bag of tricks.

**Alan Arkin**

I didn't feel funny as a person at all. In fact, I didn't touch my own personality. I never got into using myself at Second City. That was the one thing I never did was play myself. I didn't know if there was anybody home.

I thought I was going to get fired initially, because I wasn't funny at all for about a month. I was waiting patiently for Paul to fire me. And then, after about a month, I found a character that worked. Whatever I did in that character was funny. And I hung on to that character like a lifeline, and everything I did for a while was in that character. I don't remember what character it was, but a series of characters followed shortly after that.

**Sheldon Patinkin**

There was more of a willingness to fail then, because we all knew that was the only way you were going to find the good stuff. That's true of Chicago theater. You can fail in Chicago and still get work.

**Alan Arkin**

First and most important, Second City gave me a place to go; it gave me a place to function. That was the main thing. And the second most important thing, which was very, very close to the first, was that it gave us a place to fail. Which doesn't exist in this civilization anymore. There is no place to fail anymore. And failing at something is crucial. You don't learn from anything unless you fail. And we were not only allowed to fail, but almost encouraged to take chances every night onstage. We knew that twenty, thirty, sometimes forty percent of what we were doing wasn't going to work, and Sills never said anything about it, Bernie never said anything about it, and the audience didn't mind. They knew that two things would fail and the next thing would be glorious.

## Sheldon Patinkin

One of the things that has changed is, if the actors don't get a laugh right away, they get scared and they start falling back on tricks and dirty words. There were sketches then where the audience never laughed at all, that were terrible. You take out a scene at Second City on a laugh, usually, or on a nice down ending. And it's up to the stage manager who's running the lights, or the pianist, to decide "Okay, that's the end of the scene" by either hitting the lights or starting the piano or both. There was one night during an improv between Barbara Harris and Alan Arkin that went on for forty-five minutes without the stage manager or the pianist being able to find a laugh. Just awful. We were all waiting for something to happen. It wasn't really forty-five minutes, by the way. It just felt like it. It was probably about twenty.

Arkin and Harris performed a now legendary scene called "Museum Piece," in which they played diametrically opposed characters (he a guitar-strumming beatnik, she an uptight art aficionado) who engaged in awkward yet revealing conversation at an art gallery. Arkin nailed the role of a free-spirited ne'er-do-well, and Harris's alluring vulnerability was on full display. "It's the same kind of vulnerability that Marilyn Monroe exhibited," Patinkin says, "but without that added oh-I'm-so-sexy part."

## Alan Arkin

That was the only scene the two of us did together that really worked. It was very endemic to the time. It was very much about the sixties. It was very much about the clash of consciousness in the sixties between all the young people coming up with kind of a new sense of freedom and openness and peace and confusion, and the old guard, which Barbara represented.

## Bernard Sahlins

That was as perfect and brilliant a performance as has ever been done on our stage. Absolute fidelity to truth, to character, to the work itself.

Another early Second City favorite, Severn Darden, was the child of privilege and was a bona fide eccentric. Bright and bearded, he appeared older than his years and was a born improviser. Among his most beloved characters was a know-it-all professor named Dr. Walter von der Vogelweide. As many in the well-educated audience probably knew, he was named after a prominent medieval German poet who penned odes to the importance of living a harmonious life. Darden also stood out in another audience favorite—a reprised Compass original scene called "Football Comes to the University of Chicago," wherein U. of C. brainiacs are schooled (unsuccessfully and often hilariously) in gridiron basics.

### Sheldon Patinkin

Among other things, Severn as his German professor would take a college subject from the audience, do a fifteen-minute lecture on it, and then do a Q&A.

### Paul Sand

Severn's brilliance was sort of jaw-dropping. If you had a cold, he'd come into your room and grab your cough syrup and drink it down in one gulp. He knew if someone had a cold they'd have cough syrup. He'd be stiff-arming you with one arm and chugalugging whatever that cough syrup was. He was delicious, this guy. Just astonishing.

### Alan Arkin

Severn was there when I got there. I enjoyed working with him, but I didn't hang out with him for two minutes in two years of work together. I just didn't get him at all as a person. I just thought he was like a martian. I couldn't find him emotionally at all. I used to relate to people emotionally, and I think he was very much in his head, and I didn't particularly relate to that.

Neither could Arkin fully comprehend Second City's original and still influential artistic godfather, Paul Sills. He wasn't alone. Never a master communicator—not in the traditional sense, anyway—the deep-thinking but plainspoken Sills had frequent trouble getting his points across. Oftentimes he yelled. Sometimes he hurled furniture. Even so, he was by all accounts immensely talented and intensely devoted, and his no-bullshit approach was ultimately beneficial in big ways. He also relished the writings of Austrian-Israeli philosopher Martin Buber, who authored the treatises on interpersonal relations *Between Man and Man* and *I and Thou.* In the latter, Buber declared that "All real living is meeting." While Sills's mother, Viola Spolin, schooled actors offstage in the art of improvisation, her son molded them onstage in rehearsals and performances. Besides overseeing the revues at Second City, he also directed dramatic works next door (1846 North Wells) at a newly built and larger venue christened Playwrights at Second City. Opened in 1961, the theater was named in an homage to pre-Compass years. It was a "colorful and exciting night club with a spacious, smoothly flexible stage that holds the promise of fine things," as one journalist described it. Nonetheless, the more serious Playwrights struggled to fill its 225 seats. When the burgeoning Second City needed new digs, the two theaters traded spaces. Despite the downsizing, however, Playwrights folded in 1963. That August, Second City began screening silent films after dark in its outdoor Roman beer garden. When the weather turned cold, the films migrated to the bar area inside— a value-added attraction for the pre- and post-show cocktail crowd.

### Mina Kolb, cast member

One time, Paul had called us all together and we were all onstage, and he was giving us some instructions about something, God only knows what. And Barbara was standing at the back of the stage reading a newspaper. And he got so mad that he jumped up and knocked the paper out of her hands because she wasn't paying attention. Paul got down off the stage, and she came after him like a flying saucer, jumped on his back, and knocked him down. And right after her came Andrew Duncan. He dragged her off of Paul, and— Oh, god, it was marvelous!

### Paul Sand

I was in the audience. I wasn't in the scene, so I was sitting there, and Paul got really mad at her. They knew how to drive each other crazy because they were lovers and married and everything, so they knew all the buttons to push. They were already divorced or separated. So there would be these invisible flash fires. You didn't know where they came from. So he went up and screamed at her, and then one of the other actors—I won't mention his name—he gets up and he slaps her. It was like, "What is that?" It was astonishing. It was so weird. That put a freeze-frame on the whole moment. It was like, "Whoa." It was too deep for me.

### Sheldon Patinkin

There were arguments. There were major arguments. There were occasional fistfights—usually about the work. It was usually at night, planning the set or after the set. There weren't that many physical fights. Paul would throw chairs every once in a while. He never hit anybody, by the way. He'd just throw them. He almost clipped Mina one day. Alan was in the company by then, and he walked up to Paul afterward and said, "If you ever talk to me like that again, I'll kill you." And I believed him.

### Alan Arkin

A chair went whizzing by my head one day. Paul was very, very vocal. It was very loud, that's all I remember—very loud and incomprehensible. I could understand the swear words, but the rest of it I couldn't understand at all. It didn't make me particularly happy, since I had an enormous amount of respect for him and I felt like I was working my ass off there nonstop. It was only directed at me once, but I didn't understand it at all because I felt like it was not warranted. I took the work there very seriously.

### Mina Kolb

Arkin didn't like people telling him what to do. He kind of figured that Paul was not any smarter than he was—that kind of thing. I'm sure Paul fought with everybody. He even made me cry. He made everybody cry. He had to break you in with a few tears.

### Sheldon Patinkin

Paul was very volatile. Partly out of the frustration of not being able to find the language he wanted. Most of the anger that I know of was about the work. It was rare to get mad at an audience. What's the point? It's just that night's audience.

### Paul Sand

The day after I arrived, Paul said to come into the theater, so it would just be him and me. And I was standing up on the little stage and he was sitting there in the empty cabaret room, and he started asking me to do certain things, and then all of a sudden he insulted me. And I don't know where it came from, because I'm not a violent man, but I picked up a chair on the stage and I threw it across the room, aiming it at him. And I saw him duck and smile at the same time. Then I said to him, "If you want me to be great, don't hurt my feelings." Because Paul had a way of insulting when he was directing, which could be just devastating unless you sort of made a joke out of it or something.

### Dennis Cunningham

He hated actors. He hated the actor mentality that would get in the way a lot.

### David Shepherd, Compass co-founder

I found Paul very direct and responsive to what was happening, and he pushed constantly for energy and pace that I think were the keys to his success, because he directed hundreds of plays. He also had a lot of contempt for acting that was not sincere, that was not real. At Compass, when we would do a show three times in one night, it would come out limper and limper and limper, and he would be furious with us because we hadn't recreated the same sensitivity and vitality that we had in the first show. So eventually we gave up doing three shows a night and we did only two a night.

### Bob Dishy, cast member

He felt a moral responsibility to the choices that you make in an improv. Now, of course, that's not on a day-to-day basis. He was also pragmatic, and he knew he had to do shows. But he was pained, physically pained, by what he considered cheap laughs. I mean, they would drive him up the wall. He'd come backstage and yell, "Stop it! What are you doing?!" Because he had these high standards, which was great. I found it so enlightening.

### Sheldon Patinkin

Every once in a while Paul would need help getting things organized. I spent a lot of time with him over the first couple of years I was at Second City, learning from him and then working with him on running orders for shows and things like that. I also learned not to throw chairs.

### Dick Schaal, cast member

Paul was vague. It was never something that cleared up eventually. We were doing his *Story Theatre* on Broadway, and we were just about to open, and he's all pleased and he's kissing Paul Sand and raving, "This is terrific! This works, that works." And he turned to me and he said, threateningly, "Schaal, you better get this." I didn't know I didn't have it. I didn't know what he meant. But I understand it now. What a genius thing to say, "You better get this," and then it's up to you. So I started thinking, I started working like crazy trying to find out what he meant.

### Paul Sand

There's nobody else. Everybody else elbowed their way in. And Paul was sort of cheated out of money and things by a lot of people. He was the genius originator who ended up needing some money. He didn't strive for fame, because something else was on his mind. It wasn't that he didn't want it. He was really busy being the creator, and those kinds of people need a business partner so they don't get screwed. He is the only one. He is Second City.

### Dick Schaal

I remember one time I had been working with Viola all day. I'd been doing space work a couple of times a week and then going on a stage and doing space work six nights a week. The bar was downstairs at the old place, and the theater was upstairs. So as usual I went downstairs and ordered a Heineken from Benny the bartender. I gave a high sign—he was way at the other end of the bar. And then I was kind of preoccupied, and I found myself pouring the space of a bottle of beer into the space of an empty glass, and all of a sudden I realized, "Oh, my God, what am I doing?" And my hands collapsed and I looked around nervously to be sure that nobody noticed the level of insanity that I had finally reached. So I went right to Paul and told him what just happened. I said, "I'd better get away from this." So he gave me a couple of weeks off and I went to Mexico. But that's the level of the work. It just moved in.

### Dennis Cunningham

Viola Spolin was amazing. She was like no one I'd ever been around. All that improvisation stuff was new to me, and that was my real introduction to it, the workshop. She was acerbic to a degree in doing that stuff, and she knew what she wanted and she worked hard to get it, and she worked you hard to try to do it and respond and understand it. And she was really dedicated and very glad to be participating in the enterprise as a whole. There was probably not 100 percent agreement that it was the best thing to have that workshop and have her be attached to it, but it was, and they needed it. They definitely needed it to get people to understand some of the same stuff so that they could work together onstage. And it wasn't that easy to understand, what she was saying or what she meant or what it really was, or to really tell if you were doing it or not doing it or to know what she meant when she said somebody got it or somebody didn't get it. But at the same time it was really rich and pithy. She would say, "No playwriting. You're in your head, and you've got to get out and let the game take you out or the exercise take you out, and you have to let your mind focus on the point of concentration." And there were a lot of those exercises that were really abstruse and mystifying, if not mystical.

### Sheldon Patinkin

I never found it mystical. I know that some people did, and I know that Viola sort of felt that way about it. I think it was more that when your job is to respond rather than to initiate, which is the rule in an improv—you don't know what your next line is until you know what just happened or what was just said—it gives you a kind of concentration that perhaps feels mystical to some people, but to me feels like human communication.

### Valerie Harper, cast member

It made my career. The work. I'm well over sixty and I'm using Viola's games to get at what I need to do. If you came out of her workshops and you weren't an actor, you weren't a failure. Your life would be better because her games unleash something in people that connects them to other people, that makes you observe more clearly, more keenly, be aware of the other over there. She used to say my performance isn't here in Valerie, it's over there in the other player. Look at them. How are they reacting to what I'm saying? Her work came out of such a pure, beautiful, inspired place, and it never really changed all through these decades.

# 2

# Big Apple Bound, Naked Sonatas, and the Reign of King David

**Robert Klein**
**Joan Rivers**
**David Steinberg**
**Fred Willard**

SECOND CITY'S FOUNDERS and early players had little confidence that this sudden phenomenon of which they were a part would last very long or go very far. Hence their subdued delight when celebrated theater producer David Merrick strode in one day early in 1961, stood at the back of the house during a sold-out performance, and pledged his support—financial and otherwise—if the company would perform in New York. Still ambivalent about proving their mettle in America's theatrical epicenter, Sahlins and Sills nonetheless traveled east to find a suitable space. No such luck—possibly, as Sahlins now muses, for lack of trying. But a second shot at taking Manhattan came mere months thereafter, and this time they were ready. After television producer Max Liebman of *The Sid Caesar Show* caught Second City in action, he invited the cast to open on Broadway. Following a triumphant summerlong stint at the Ivar Theatre in Los Angeles, Sahlins, Sills, and company brought a revue, *From the Second City,* to New York's comparatively cavernous Royale Theater on Forty-fifth Street. A replacement crew took over back home on North Wells, and things, it seemed, were looking up.

Second City's run on the Great White Way was artistically thrilling and critically lauded. "*From the Second City* is an informal, talent-laden revue that is saucy, sassy, hip, zooty and xiphoid," *Time* raved in early December 1961, "plus being more fun than two barrels of monkeys." But the venture soon proved financially infeasible, so the company moved to smaller and less vaunted Greenwich Village digs called Square East, at 15 West Fourth Street. There, New Yorkers continued to swoon, and shows were mostly well attended over the next four years. New York actor Alan Alda even joined the cast for a brief time. Future Emmy-winning television star Valerie Harper hung around the theater, too, and eventually performed with Second City outside of New York. Among the Chicago actors—those already in New York and those on the mainstage back home—ambition surfaced like never before.

### Alan Arkin

I guess I'd been [at Second City Chicago] about six months or so, and David Merrick came there after we started getting some national attention. And everyone was enormously protective of the group and the place. I guess it was a Saturday night, and he said, "I'd like two tickets." And they said, "We're all sold out." And he said, "You don't understand. I'm David Merrick." And they said, "Well, okay, we have standing room in the back for you." And he said, "I am David Merrick." They said, "Okay. Then we'll definitely give you standing room in the back." And that was it—he stood in the back, and we thought it was great.

### Bernard Sahlins

Everybody felt the work was important. Not where it was taking them, not for Hollywood, not for television, but for what they were doing on the spot at the time. There wasn't that much action in Chicago, and the actors were very happy to be working. Not that they weren't ambitious, but they kept that ambition tucked away in favor of the work.

### Sheldon Patinkin

[New York] didn't really affect anything much, until we moved from Broadway, which was a flop, and into Square East in the Village. At that point it was just struggling along until David Susskind put them on his local TV show and they did material and talked, and New York fell in love with them and business got great and they started getting picked up for other stuff, at which point they had to be replaced. That's when it started getting interesting. The reward [for Chicago casts] was, you get to play New York.

### Alan Arkin

We went there and we were just snooty as hell. We didn't feel like we needed [Susskind] particularly, and we sat there in a room listening to him talk about how great we were and how much he wanted us at the show. Nobody said a word. He finally got so nervous he showed us his Phi Beta Kappa key to impress us with the fact that he was smart.

### Bernard Sahlins

We were really friendly until Broadway came up, and then all of a sudden everybody was suspicious, paranoid that we were taking advantage of them contractually. That's when they started pulling away from Second City.

### Alan Arkin

One of my favorite moments the entire time I was at Second City was when we had just done *The David Susskind Show,* and immediately afterward we got a whole new kind of crowd. We were getting the uptown crowd, the mink coat crowd, for the first time, and I *hated* them. I *hated* them. Because they would laugh at any kind of reference, whether they understood it or not. It had nothing to do with the content; it had to do with the reference. And I came offstage one night from doing a scene and I was bitching, and I said, "Damn these people to hell! I hate them. They're snobs, Upper East Side crowd. Just mention the name Thomas Mann and you get a laugh." And my next scene was with Severn, and it took place in a clothing store. I was trying on a new jacket. Severn was the salesman. And I turned to Severn, which was part of the scene, and I said, "How do I look?" He said, "Oh, you look wonderful. You look just like Thomas Mann." And the whole audience fell apart. And I left the stage furious. I was furious at the audience and furious at Severn for turning the joke on me.

### Paul Sand

Second City was very simple. No one had any desires to do anything outside of it. There we were in Chicago really having a great time and getting noticed in magazines and things. And then we went to Los Angeles and Broadway, so we did go out into the world. But for about two years it was just completely isolated and wonderful. TV hadn't started tempting all of us at that time. We didn't have any ideas of "Let's do this and be movie stars or TV stars."

I think after we went to Broadway, it became more nationally known. And then all of us more or less stayed in New York. We'd do Second City there sometimes, but I started working off-Broadway, and there was a lot of TV and stuff.

### Bernard Sahlins

Once we went to Broadway in 1961, it subtly started to change from total attention to the work to some attention to where the work was taking them.

The Chicago replacements who stepped in for the Broadway bunch debuted their first revue and Second City's seventh, *Alarums and Excursions,* in late November 1961. Directed by Sills, the show's cast included

Bill Alton, John Brent, Hamilton Camp, Del Close, Melinda Dillon, Anthony Holland, Zohra Lampert, and Avery Schreiber—a Chicago-born classically trained actor who'd one day become famous as the Doritos pitchman for Frito-Lay. Like many of his mates, Schreiber (who subsequently developed a popular act with fellow Second City cast member Jack Burns) went on to join the New York gang at Square East.

Also in the replacement cast was a New York–bred comedienne-on-the-make named Joan Rivers. A strong solo player who preferred comedy bits to scenes (which irked some fellow performers), she never really fit in at Second City. Nonetheless, she long ago admitted in author and playwright Jeffrey Sweet's book *Something Wonderful Right Away,* the brief and often rocky experience there made her "whole career."

"The minute something became commercial, it became trash to a lot of them," Rivers says in Sweet's oral history. "When we were in Chicago, all of us at Second City were into Truth and Beauty, and they didn't want to take the next step because then it became commercial and anything commercial was not Art. We all believed this to a certain extent."

### Sheldon Patinkin

I don't think Joan and I have spoken since she left Second City. There's been no need to. There's been no opportunity to. We didn't not like each other. In fact, in her first book, she says I was the only one who was nice to her while she was in Chicago. Which isn't true. Well, it was totally sexist in those days. It's better now. Part of the problem was she was into showbiz. Like, she made us all go to *Cleopatra,* a disaster with Elizabeth Taylor. We had to see it opening day—all four fucking hours of it—at the State-Lake theater downtown.

Joan felt forced into being a loner, although she and Tony Holland became really good friends. She was able to do two-person scenes with Tony, and she was able to do two-person scenes with Bill Alton. She had no fears from Tony, who was gay, so the laughs went back and forth. And she had no fears with Bill because he was not aggressive. Bill basically always played the straight. And his wife was around a lot, so there was no worry about that as well. So was his ex-wife, by the way.

### Richard Libertini, cast member

She was never happy in that form. But you could tell. She's a stand-up. Whenever she had a chance to work it into a show, she would get off some jokes.

### Joyce Sloane

I liked her. I got along with her. But Jimmy [aka Tony] Holland was her only friend. They did a wonderful scene that I still remember passionately called

"The Tailor and the Model." She stands on a chair and he's fixing the hem on her dress, and she's saying she has to go to this family dinner. And she doesn't want to go, because she's going to be twenty-five and she's not married and her sister's married and has two children. And he's looking up at her, fixing the dress, and they discover each other. It was quiet, it was sweet. You couldn't get away with that now.

### Alan Myerson, director

Joan really was a short-timer from New York. I don't think she saw this as a major part of her life. This was a gig, and it had some real currency because of Second City's new celebrity. But I think she always saw herself as this sort of brash New York comedienne who would return to New York and kill 'em on the supper club circuit. And she would often try to develop stand-up material in sets, which I would usually try and knock down, because what she would do is take a scene and then she would turn it into a bit for herself rather than playing the scene. She got creamed by most of the other actors. Tony Holland was the only one who really— He adored her, and I think she him.

Particularly people like Del Close and Bill Alton were kind of ruthless with her. They would stiff her offstage a lot. After the show, people would go downstairs to the bar, and she would be with Tony, but she wasn't integrated into the group at all. And I'm not sure whether that was entirely the group's doing or whether that may have also been her preference. It was kind of a fractious group of people to begin with. First of all, it was a very misogynistic time, and the men were pretty misogynistic guys. And there were a number of them, like Del and Bill Alton, who were sort of snooty to anybody. They were gender-unspecific in that case.

### Melinda Dillon

When little fat Joan came to town, she was very funny and very fast, joking all the time, getting up there and doing these so-called improvs where she just told jokes and things. And Paul just loved her. It was summertime, and this was my only job. I had graduated, I think, and I had to have this job. And I was in the show. And I went down there for rehearsal one morning, and Joan was on the stage doing some improv thing, and Paul Sills came to me and he said, "You're fired." And Bill Alton was lying there in the window seat, and he said, "It's about time." And I heard all of this and I fled, and I went home and I was crying and I was on the phone, calling my father to ask him for a loan to tide me over. And a knock came on the door, and it was Sills, and he said, "Come on back." And I said, "What?" And he said, "Oh, come on back. We'll find something for you to do." So he had had a little change of heart. But it was quite openly hostile toward me. I was in the wrong environment there, and there was an anger about that, a hostility, which I can't understand, really. Years later Bill Alton came up and said, "I was wrong." But that was kind of unctuous and self-serving, I thought.

Del Close was a semi-trained fire-eater, a former member of the Compass Players (in St. Louis), and a stand-up comic whose 1959 album, *How to Speak Hip,* with John Brent, became a cult favorite. He also starred on Broadway that year in Tommy Wolf's beat musical, *The Nervous Set.* A well-read narcotics enthusiast who both acted and directed during the first few years of Second City's existence, Close was brilliant and abusive, a high-minded intellectual and a reckless junkie. After his first firing, at the end of 1963, he bummed around Chicago for a year or so before heading to San Francisco, where he immersed himself in the growing counterculture scene and hooked up with an edgy improv comedy troupe called the Committee. Now legendary in comedy circles, its first members included Alan Myerson and *WKRP in Cincinnati* star Howard Hesseman. Close would eventually return to Second City, demons and genius in tow, but not until early the next decade.

### Richard Libertini

Del and I would do Lenny Bruce routines once in a while. Del is onstage about to introduce something, and I rush on and say, "Hey, did you hear? Lenny Bruce got busted for obscenity at the Gate of Horn." And then Del says, "No shit?" And that was it. Very mild by today's standards. Bernie and Paul both hated that stuff.

### Mina Kolb

We had to dig him out of his house one time. He had overdosed, and they had to break in and get him because he was essential to the show. He had a lot of stuff to do. Del was funny. He was brilliant.

### Dick Schaal

Del was sort of stiff. It looked like he was in an emotional trap. On one occasion, Hamilton Camp and I went to his apartment, broke in, and saved his life. He was suicidal. He tried to do suicide several times. He didn't show up for the show that night—it was in a half hour—so we looked at each other and said, "Listen, he's not that far. Let's go over there." So we went over, and here he was on the floor.

### Bernard Sahlins

Del was not stable. Sheldon and I would pick him up at his mental rehab institute, take him to the show, and then take him back for the night.

## Sheldon Patinkin

Del had an analyst who used LSD for treatments. No kidding. I can't think of a worse analyst for anybody. He eventually got disbarred. Del tried to kill himself one night. Took pills about a half hour before curtain time so that we'd be sure to find him. I went over and found him and got Bernie, and we got him to the emergency room and got his stomach pumped. And they were going to put him in County, and we didn't want that to happen. And we knew that the husband of one of the lawyers in our lawyer's office had a small private sanitarium on the Near South Side. So we got him admitted there. That husband was the guy who used LSD for treatment. He called us after about a month and said that Del could continue doing the show again if either Bernie or I picked him up at the sanitarium, checked him out, brought him to the show, and brought him back afterward. And Bernie refused, so I did it every night, for about two months. Del once called me—he had taken LSD—to tell me he was being devoured by a spider king inch by inch. That was what I believe is known as a bad trip. He apparently had a lot of bad trips.

## Alan Myerson

There was a fight for power that resulted in Del getting me fired, actually. I don't think he wanted to do certain things particularly. I think he just wanted to be in charge. Del was an exceedingly bright man whose brilliance was matched by his arrogance, and he felt that he could do everything better than anyone else. He became much more mellow and generous toward other people in his later years, but in those years he was not generous toward anybody—including Paul. He gave Paul a hard time, too.

While the New York and Chicago operations forged ahead, there were side jaunts to Cleveland and London, England. A *Daily Express* story praised one of Second City's British invasions as "memorable entertainment from Chicago" that "has more hard things to say about the American way of life than two Mort Sahls or one Lenny Bruce."

Second City's initial foray into Canada—where a company played Toronto's Royal Alexandra Theatre for one week in 1963—came during its first few years as well. A resounding success, the excursion was followed by several more triumphant visits in subsequent years—foreshadowing good things to come.

In August 1963, with Paul Sills mostly in New York helming the action at Square East (he returned intermittently to check up on things and direct shows in Chicago), Sahlins appointed Patinkin artistic director. Possessed of a calmer and more nurturing demeanor than Sills, Patinkin made his directorial debut with a well-reviewed show called *13 Mino-*

*taurs, or, Slouching Toward Bethlehem.* "Happily free of vulgarity, far-fetched symbolism and hidden meaning, this bright revue should be a welcome night life beacon in Old Town for many months," one of the town's top critics praised. Having begun dabbling in television, Sahlins spent several months in England producing *Second City Reports* TV specials that aired in the fall of 1963, but otherwise he was an influential presence around the theater.

### Sheldon Patinkin

Paul stormed out of a rehearsal, saying, "See what you can do with them, Sheldon." And about an hour later I called Bernie and said, "I can't find Paul. He's really disappeared." He said, "He's on his way to New York. You're the director now." And that was it. And then I came in trembling and told the cast, because they didn't know, either. I think he just didn't want to be directing that company at that particular point. And he didn't want to be in Chicago; he wanted to be back in New York.

### Bernard Sahlins

Paul made it clear he was going to stay in New York, and so I had to appoint a different director. He came back and did at least two shows, including one called *My Friend Art Is Dead.* We printed little buttons: "Art Is Dead." Got requests from all over the country.

Several months later, as a shocked nation mourned the recent death of John F. Kennedy, a very young and very funny University of Chicago grad and former yeshiva student named David Steinberg joined Second City. His then comedy partner, Gene Kadish, came aboard, too, if only for half a year, before heading back to law school. Although they didn't open an original mainstage revue until January 1964, Kadish was present when, only a day after JFK's assassination, the show went on.

### Gene Kadish, cast member

The first night, we performed, and there were virtually no laughs at all. We did the same thing, and there was polite applause at the end and that was it. And it was like, "Wow. Did we bomb or what?" And afterward, you mingle with the audience, and people would say, "Great, really enjoyed it, such a tragedy, but we're glad to come here." And the next five or six days, people would chuckle a little bit. It was almost a continuum of people responding, until after about a week or so, it was back to what it had been before the event.

### Sheldon Patinkin

Just as it was right after 9/11, they were wanting to laugh, not wanting to think about what had happened. [When] asking for suggestions for the improv set, somebody called out "The assassination!" in an audience that had been trying to forget it for the night. And Del said, "Just what the fuck did you want to see, sir?" Really pissed off. Said "fuck" for the first time on the Second City stage. And the audience applauded.

Soon enough Steinberg had crowds clapping, too, but for different reasons. "A comedy star was born Tuesday night at Second City," *Chicago Daily News* critic Sam Lesner wrote in late January 1964. "His name is David Steinberg. A newcomer to the group, he dominates Second City's 14th revue, 'New York City Is Missing!' like the North Star in a clear night sky."

### David Steinberg, cast member

Gene and I had an act that was at a place called Old Town North, and later the Crystal Palace. It was a few blocks away from the old Second City, which was on Lincoln and Wells. Gene was a lawyer [in training], and I was just a student at the University of Chicago, floundering around. We might only have been in the business for three and a half weeks to four weeks at the Crystal Palace and someone reviewed us, saying, "Second City should see these guys." And the only reason I was doing anything was because of Second City. I saw them and I thought, "My God! This is something I think I can do! How do we do it? How do we get there?" So the act was my version of stuff that you'd do if you were two guys just doing a version of Second City.

### Bernard Sahlins

[David and Gene] were playing in the neighborhood. Somebody suggested we go see them. I liked David. I didn't think a lot of Kadish. But this was a team, so we took them.

### Gene Kadish

David started out slowly and started building up some characters and then came to the point where people were thinking that he was pretty obnoxious.

### Sheldon Patinkin

The first night that David Steinberg was in the cast, Del Close punched out the stage manager afterward because he was so upset about the way that David had stolen a joke of his by accident at the end of the set. But he didn't take it out on David. He took it out on the stage manager.

### David Steinberg

I broke a major Second City rule but got a huge laugh and endeared myself to maybe a third of the company who didn't care about the rules. We were doing an opera, and you had to know the style you were singing in. I knew nothing about opera at all. I knew Pete Seeger and the Weavers. I was so limited in the cultural depth these older guys who were in the company had. And so they did *Rumpelstiltskin.* And I remember Jack Burns was playing Rumpelstiltkin. And the plan was for him and maybe Mina Kolb at the time to sing this duet at the end. Everything is about guessing his name. But everyone took a character, and I didn't take one. So I just walked offstage. And I was watching them, and they were doing this number, and Jack was singing and everyone was carrying on, and the audience was going nuts for how skillful this group was. And I was so anxious to get out there, I put on a hat and a raincoat and said, "Hi, Rumpelstiltskin. How are you? Haven't seen you since college." It was the antithesis of what you do at Second City. You don't negate anyone's reality. I walked the plank that night.

### Sheldon Patinkin

David is perfectly willing to admit that he was impossible. He was very difficult. We screamed at each other a lot—disagreements about the work. But we also really liked each other. And it wasn't really screaming. It was just raised voices periodically.

### David Steinberg

I was very connected to the audience. I liked to hear the laughs, and I was able to get them. I thought I did these great characters, but basically, I just would put on a hat and a scarf and sound like I do now. So I had no range whatsoever. Even though I had my connection with the audience, I would still play the scene in a very strong way in the character, but it wasn't like you were seeing an incredible range there. It's no surprise that I would become a stand-up comic, where you only have to be yourself all the time. But I was connected to the audience somehow more than the actors, because the actors were connected to each other—certainly when I started out—through Viola and the games and what Paul was doing, [more] than I was, because I just didn't get it.

Those audiences at Second City were just amazing. They were smart and funny and they knew that they were onto something that no one was seeing anywhere else in the country. And so you got energy from them, and that's why the material was so good. What you took away from that is, if you try to hide any version of yourself, you're not going to be good. And be as smart as you want to be. Don't play to the dumbest person in the audience. Play to the smartest person in the audience. That seems like a little rule, but at the time it was a sort of revolutionary thing.

### Bernard Sahlins

It was difficult to get [David] to play ensemble. As was true of Joan Rivers. In fact, those two were probably the most difficult of people to work with, as far as I was concerned. Not that they were mean or hostile. It's just that they found it difficult to allow somebody else the limelight.

After a hop across the pond to England in the summer of 1965, Steinberg returned to the States and rejoined an overhauled cast that included some new players, at least a couple of whom had landed at Second City shortly before his leave of absence. Their names: Robert Klein (known as Bob) and Fred Willard. Plucked by Sahlins and Patinkin from a William Morris Agency cattle call audition in New York, they were very different personalities who complemented each other onstage and off. Klein (who was known to do fine impersonations of Chicago's iron-fisted mayor, Richard J. Daley, and President Lyndon Johnson) could be voluble and headstrong; Willard (a self-proclaimed "weird" guy) was more subdued and agreeable. Consequently, he got along swimmingly with BMOC Steinberg. Klein, not so much. Not at first. In the early going he regarded King David—by then Second City's box office hero—as a scene-stealer who could do no wrong in the bosses' eyes. Paul Sills's included.

### Robert Klein, cast member

I wanted so much to please Paul Sills, but he'd say, "The thing with the thing . . ." I'd see the index finger and the thumb together, trying to express what he meant. He was after the truth. And there wasn't an awful lot of praise coming from him. On the other hand—and I suppose it was heightened by this competition with David Steinberg, who was the reigning guy—Steinberg always seemed to please him. And he never criticized David for hogging the stage, or any of the other things.

### David Steinberg

You couldn't hog the scenes at Second City. You only got the scenes on by having the best scenes. And I didn't make the decision as to which ones went on. Bernie and Sheldon did. So it was sort of one-sided. In truth, I can't remember any harsh words with Klein at all.

### Sheldon Patinkin

David intimidated Bob Klein—seriously intimidated Bob Klein. He kept on making Bob feel inferior. Bob was a team player, and David would always set him up as the straight man. In fact, David would always set everybody up as the straight man. But Bob got intimidated by it. I don't think he ever lost it.

We talked it out. We talked it out a lot with Fred. [Bob] also tried out ideas for stand-up with Fred. He was starting to build that, so he had somewhere he thought he was going. David knew he was going there. And that was part of the intimidation. David wanted the laughs.

### Robert Klein

Steinberg was awe-inspiring. When I came there and saw him, the way he could gesture and take the stage, he was really such a fantastic stage performer, that he went into the wrong thing. Stand-up was not his thing, but he could have been a great comedy star in the theater. Steinberg commanded that audience brilliantly, and I was rough when I got there. And he told me, "Watch out for Sheldon." And Sheldon told me, "Watch out for Steinberg."

It was a wonderful and fortuitous thing that Steinberg went to London, because the pressure was off, and I was able to star. And then when he came back, I could hold my own. [It was] a respite to grow. I don't know what his motivations were. He had a big ego. He was a gigantic talent, but it wasn't helping me. It wouldn't help me to be someone's enemy onstage. You've got to feel relaxed. You've got to feel like you love the guy you're doing it with, or the woman, and relax and do it.

### Fred Willard, cast member

I didn't know at the time, but there seemed to be friction between Robert and David, which I was not aware of at all. Because Robert's very headstrong and very opinionated, and David was the star.

### Sheldon Patinkin

It never bothered Fred, who also just laughed at David's bullshit. And I don't think David ever even got angry with Fred. He respected how funny he was in his own way, and that it was a very different way than David was being funny.

### Robert Klein

One thing that Steinberg and I totally agreed on was that Willard completely cracked us up.

### David Steinberg

Fred Willard and I would get into stuff where I just couldn't stop laughing. He was so brilliantly funny, playing these offbeat unique characters all the time, and it was just hard to do a scene with him. But he and I did a lot of scenes together. Fred was totally unique. The trick to becoming an audience favorite was originality. He was totally original. You never saw anything like Fred. Weird characters. And Fred himself is offbeat, even to this day.

### Bernard Sahlins

Fred has the uncanny ability to see the truth in everything, and the comic truth. He never played Fred Willard. You knew it was Bob Klein. But Fred Willard was a character. Which is not a criticism, it's just two different styles.

### Judy Graubart, cast member

Fred was desperate to do a scene about a man who only wore gray. And gray was the theme. The furniture was gray. He was gray. His skin was gray. And that's all. So it was hard to build a scene on that.

### Fred Willard

One time I decided it was right for me to take ballet lessons. And somebody said to me, "Fred, why are you taking ballet lessons?" And Sheldon jumped in on my side. He said, "Because he's a New York actor, and New York actors feel they have to take ballet lessons." So I would get up on Saturday morning—we'd done two shows on Friday night—and I'd pedal my bike downtown, and I was always ten minutes late. I guess I must have had leotards on, and I'd walk into the class, and everyone else in the class was, like, a teenage girl. They probably thought I was some old pervert. And I would walk in and the teacher would stop what she was doing and give me a very dirty look. "Mr. Willard, take your place over there." And I would go through these ballet lessons. And after a while I said, "These aren't really helping me."

### Judy Graubart

Fred was sweet and very bright—if a little bit hard to fathom sometimes. And he was full of surprises because he was sort of inscrutable. I just remember once he wanted to know if I wanted to have dinner with him. And, oh, yes, I did. So we wound up having supper at the YMCA where he was staying. It was just sort of odd, you know? He didn't think it was odd. And each man for himself. It was platonic.

### Fred Willard

I moved into the YMCA at first because it had a gymnasium. And I'd work out at the gym and take my bike and I'd pedal up to Second City and park it outside. And then I got connected with one of these waitresses and I moved in with her, and that didn't last long, because her kids would wake us up at seven in the morning. So I moved over to a place called the Park Plaza, which is no longer there. I still had my bike and I'd get on and pedal over to the theater. And in the middle of the winter, I'd get on the bike and pedal home.

I was kind of the weird guy. The original Second City guys all had beards and sat around smoking dope, and I heard stories of when the thaw came in the spring, you'd go out in this garden next door, and there were all these hypodermic needles and drug paraphernalia there. But I was never into drugs.

### Bernard Sahlins

The early sixties company was a drug company, which I didn't know anything about. They were heavily into marijuana and things like that. I was not part of it. I didn't know anything about it. Nobody believes that I was as surprised as I was. I didn't know. I wasn't of that generation.

### David Steinberg

I always remember there was a little bit of coke around backstage. But no one touched it. No one would ever have taken too much coke, no matter how abusive you were. It was like getting drunk on the Drambuie. It had to register in the culture, which it didn't till five years later, for me or anybody else.

Besides, there were other activities to occupy the time.

### Fred Willard

We kind of paired up, when we got to Chicago, with different waitresses. I went off and spent time with one, and Bob went off with another. He was quite the ladies' man, which I really wasn't. I was more into the comedy.

### Judy Graubart

I noticed it later, shall we say, after we were in Second City—that part of [Klein]. I would see him with various lovely women.

### Robert Klein

I met a cellist through Sheldon, because Sheldon had been a piano prodigy when he was a child. She was sexy in a kind of peasanty Russian way. She had this thick head of curly black hair, and she was a little chunky, but not fat. And she played the cello well enough to be in the Chicago Symphony. I was bowled over! It was a wonderful experience. And she did play for me some of Bach's unaccompanied sonatas and partitas, naked. After or before or during, I don't know. And I don't think I asked her to play for too long.

### David Steinberg

When you're in a small area like Second City, you don't have groupies. You have waitresses you can date. So the quality was definitely coming up.

There's no question about it. No matter how much they say it was the football guys who were getting all the girls, I found out doing comedy was just fine.

In April 1966, Sahlins hauled his cast back to Square East in New York, where Second City had taken its last Big Apple bows late in 1964. A group of newbies fresh from workshop classes was left to stalk the stage back home, but their lack of experience showed. So Patinkin and Sahlins, with assistance from their William Morris Agency rep Tony Fantozzi, auditioned a few more replacements. Vaudeville-influenced comedians all, they definitely weren't cut from the Second City cloth.

### Sheldon Patinkin

We needed a funnier cast than the one that we had. It was before there was a touring company; it was before there were understudies. I was doing workshops, as was [improv teacher] Jo Forsberg. And Bernie took the entire existing company to New York and we didn't have a new company. I had to form one out of what we had, and it wasn't that great. So for a while, we needed to add some more people to it and get rid of some people in it. The ones we added were J. J. Barry and Marty Friedberg and Burt Heyman, because they were really funny.

### Ira Miller, cast member

I enjoyed working with Marty and J.J. and Burt. They were kind of set in their ways. They were stand-up comedians who knew comedy, knew comedy timing, knew funny, and weren't afraid to take chances. They were kind of characters in that J.J. had been doing burlesque in New York, and Marty Friedberg was a doorman and sort of the host of the Improv in New York. Burt Heyman had more experience. He had done some theater, and he was a little more polished in terms of theater. When J.J. and Marty got there, the first show they did was Paul Sills's last show, *The Return of the Viper.* That was in '67. It was this very weird kind of show that Paul put together, about an LSD acid trip. In '67, that was the rage. So it was pretty wild working with them with Paul. But Paul got a great show out of it. When the show opened, they all came out smelling likes roses and looking really good, and the show was very, very good, and got good reviews.

### Sheldon Patinkin

Over half of the first act was improv games and one very bad scene of Martin Harvey Friedberg, J. J. Barry [once described in print as "an upright hippo of a man"], and Burt Heyman playing ants, with a huge boiling pot on film [projected onstage] that they were trying to reach. Paul wasn't interested in doing any more scenes, because he did this LSD trip as the entire second half of the show, which was way beyond the knowledge of J.J., Marty, and Burt. They had to be fed what it was all about and what to say. It went back to Oedipus, which they didn't know anything about. It traveled history, none of which they were cognizant of, so they hated it.

By the time Paul Sills returned from New York in late 1966 to relieve Sheldon Patinkin, Patinkin had quickly "cobbled together" the makeshift mainstage ensemble from workshop classes to replace the group Sahlins had sent to New York. Because the actors hadn't the skills to sustain a show, the first official touring company was born in early 1967—partly to make sure Second City's talent pool stayed stocked in the event of individual or mass exodus. The touring company also generated extra revenue (Joyce Sloane handled bookings) and eliminated the need for repeated scouting excursions, which were growing tiresome.

Late that summer Second City vacated its home at 1846 North Wells and moved into bigger (but not always better) digs just south at the site of a former bakery—complete with transplanted Sullivan arches out front. And there it has remained—at 1616 North Wells—ever since. To celebrate the grand reopening in a by-now highly trafficked area full of watering holes and eateries and bong-filled head shops, David Steinberg returned briefly to appear in a "best of" revue and draw crowds.

The next year, 1968, saw the production of Second City's first film project, a quirky sci-fi satire called *The Monitors*. Produced in partnership with electronics company Bell & Howell, it starred a host of Second City players (including Avery Schreiber) and promptly flopped upon release in 1969—perhaps a victim, in some way, of increasingly dark and contentious times. As *Chicago Tribune* scribe William Leonard wrote in December 1969, the film "has caused very few observers to hail the coming of a renaissance of motion picture production on the Chicago scene."

In Chicago, around the country, and in far-flung regions of the world, tumult ruled. The Vietnam War and civil rights battles raged, Martin Luther King, Jr., and Robert F. Kennedy were assassinated, and shaggy-maned, acid-tripping youths took to the streets in sociopolitical protest. Close to home, race riots rocked Chicago in the spring of 1968, and, mere months later, the Democratic National Convention brought chaos and carnage of its own. When Mayor Daley's punk-pulverizing police clashed with mobs of marchers downtown and in Chicago's north side nature preserve, Lincoln Park, blood and righteous anger flowed. Amid the strife, Second City (whose former beer garden at 1846 North Wells served as a makeshift triage location for gassed and clubbed protesters) began a creative rebirth in the bohemian bustle of Old Town.

# 3

## How to Speak Hippie, Return of the Guru, and a Bowl Full of Fuck

**John Belushi**     **Harold Ramis**
**Del Close**     **Betty Thomas**
**Bill Murray**

1967-74

SECOND CITY HAD ALREADY BEEN struggling finan-
cially when it fell into an even worse slump following John F. Kennedy's
assassination in 1963. Things were destined to get better—much better—
but it would take time. And talent. Fortunately the latter was in increasingly abundant supply. In the late sixties, Chicago's theater scene was
expanding, and Second City had added depth to its bench with the for-
mation of the touring company. And so it was that seven educated, liber-
ated actor-improvisers were summoned for duty during the most turbulent
period in modern American history. Dubbed the Next Generation, they
eventually lived up to their prophetic name.

**Michael Miller, director**

Second City wasn't all that successful at that point. I just thought, "This is
the cast." I didn't go in thinking, "I've got to get a new cast." I had no idea,
because that wasn't my approach to things. My approach to things was, if
you didn't like something, direct it so you did like it. And they didn't know
what to make of me. I fuckin' had strobe lights and movies. And I'm not a
big laugher. Ira Miller says I have no fuckin' sense of humor at all. So I did
three or four shows and they got more and more successful and they were
not happy with me.

I was painting the place black and Sheldon thought I was completely
fuckin' nuts. I was turning it into a black box. And I said, "What about these

bentwood chairs?" I wanted to get rid of the bentwood chairs. And that's like telling the pope he doesn't need a cross. Oh, my God!

## Murphy Dunne, cast member

I remember one time Bernie came in and said to all of us, [*nasal voice*] "Tomorrow I want everybody to bring in some jokes. We'll add the satire later." Really, he said that. Which is apocryphal. So Martin Harvey Friedberg is up there on the stage with J. J. Barry, and we're all sitting around and we're putting a show together. It's a nervous time. And Bernie goes, [*nasal voice*] "Well, where are your jokes?" So Marty turns around and drops trou and goes, [*farting sound*]. "That's my joke. This one, [*farting sound*], is another joke. Bernie, you want a joke? [*farting sound*]." And I immediately raised my hand. "Bernie, Bernie, Bernie, Bernie? He stole my joke. Those are my jokes."

## Harold Ramis, cast member

After college, I moved back to Chicago and thought I wanted to be an actor and a writer, so I enrolled in workshops at Second City and went to see the show. This was '67. I loved what David Steinberg was doing. The rest of the cast was funny. And I had that feeling that so many Second City people have reported, or even entertainers: you look at someone onstage and go, "I can do that." Josephine Forsberg was teaching the workshops, and she also did a weekend children's theater at University of Chicago. We were all in the cast of *Peer Gynt*. I met some funny people there. And after twelve workshops, a spot opened up in the touring company and I didn't get it. Josephine picked someone else. They were dating. And I felt slighted. I thought, "I'm better than him." So I quit. In the meantime, I had started working as an editor at *Playboy* magazine. And also, Old Town Players was based in a church in Old Town right around the corner from Second City. I auditioned for a play, *The Importance of Being Earnest*. I really worked on my English accent, and the director told me I wasn't Dresden enough. But they liked me and they knew I'd been at Second City for twelve classes and asked if I wanted to teach an improv workshop there, so I did. I had eight students for several weeks, and we did a performance at the end of it.

   I was doing fairly well, advancing rapidly at *Playboy*. And I'd started as a journalist by freelancing for Dick Christiansen. He was at the old *Chicago Daily News* then, and he was their arts and leisure editor. So one day Dick called me and said that a friend of his had taken over as director at Second City—Michael Miller—and he knew I really wanted to be an actor, and he said, "If you want to audition, I can arrange it." So I called Mike Miller, and he said, "Yeah, come on in Saturday night, I'll put you in the set. So I went in on a Saturday, full house, after the eleven o'clock show. He said, "All right, go backstage and do something." Basically, "Make me laugh." I didn't know anybody, but I felt good about Ira Miller. He seemed welcoming. So I got into a couple of pieces that they were planning, and it was fun, it worked fine. I was a little nervous but it was okay. I got laughs and I felt comfortable. And then Mike said they were putting together a new touring company and would I be in it. So I said sure.

It was 1968; everything was changing. Second City was feeling more a part of the fifties than a part of the new future that everyone was seeing. [The touring company] had a different audience, it seemed. The theater was ours on Monday nights, and we kind of developed our own fan base, which seemed a little younger and hipper than the basic Second City audience. The material was more radical politics and drugs and hippie stuff.

### Roberta Maguire, cast member

I was in the park marching and getting mace in my face. I didn't do that until I saw on television that the police were hauling people into alleys and just beating the shit out of them. And I thought, "Wait a minute!" And I got motivated, as did everyone.

### Fred Kaz, musical director

I remember being out front of Second City and seeing some young kids being stopped by cops—against the wall, facing the wall, with everything spread. And the younger cop was tending to be careful and relatively polite. Certainly not beastly. But the older cop pushed him aside and had to show him what cops are supposed to be like. So the kids got beat around the ankles.

### Sheldon Patinkin

Second City was where the protesters ran toward when they were teargassed out of the park at eleven o'clock every night. We could smell the gas on the front steps. We could see them getting the shit beaten out of them across the street, against the wall of Walgreens drugstore. A couple of our people made the mistake of coming off the steps. They got hit. Paul Sills was starting what eventually became *Story Theatre* in the old beer garden that Second City had left when we moved to where we are now.

### Murphy Dunne

In '68, if memory serves, the mayor closed the park. It was an old curfew time, and he had it enforced—I think to the detriment of everybody, because the police chased the kids out, and they ran down North Avenue, and there were people leading the running by telling them to smash windows and things of that nature. And there was a cop who put a gun to my throat and put me up against the wall. I was in a suit and a tie, and I was going for a car around the corner. It was pretty frightening. I walked out of the building, and the cop just threw me up against the wall. And I also remember at one time finding a bug on my phone. There was a tap on my phone. I asked a friend of mine who was a cop. He said his guess was an off-duty cop was trying to get some information.

I don't know if we were radicalized. We certainly didn't paint the administration in a fine light. I remember one blackout I think I wrote was, a guy comes out from one part of the stage as a policeman, and I think I played the guy who was a member of the press. And he says, "Okay, you yippie, sit down here," and he starts beating me. I said, "You can't beat me. I'm a member of the press." So he pulls out a gun and shoots me. That was our particular point of view at the time.

### Ira Miller

We opened a show right in the middle of the convention in '68, during the riots, called *A Plague on Both Your Houses.* And it was a very political show. I played Lyndon Johnson in a lot of the shows. Opening night, the audience consisted of all these people from the press and the Chicago elite, and there was a lot of anti–Vietnam War rhetoric. Second City was very much anti–Vietnam War.

### Harold Ramis

I looked like I should be in the streets, but I was actually a well-paid professional. Life was pretty good. I had the touring company and was working at *Playboy* every day. It was cool. All my sympathies were with the people on the street, but I didn't do anything. Even Hefner did more than I did. I remember he went through Lincoln Park and got swatted by a cop, and that's when he was sort of radicalized and started doing more political articles in the magazine.

Thanks to Ramis's *Playboy* connections, the touring company was invited to party hearty at Hef's sprawling funhouse on North State Parkway.

### Joyce Sloane

I couldn't wait to get out of there. The nude girls and the pool—it just wasn't my cup of tea. I wasn't offended or disgusted. I just didn't want to be there.

### Harold Ramis

We were invited as a group. It was a very magical night, because I remember the entire cast of *Hair* was in the basement swimming pool naked, singing

"Let the Sunshine In." It was amazing. It kind of encapsulated the whole late-sixties experience for me.

### Joe Mantegna, actor

We used to get invited there all the time because we were the cast of *Hair*. And we were whacked out. Not all of us were aspiring actors. Some of us were, like myself, but a lot of them were just people who'd auditioned for the play who kind of were closer to that lifestyle than you would imagine. So we'd go to a party like that and we were used to taking our clothes off onstage for those nude scenes and it was the late sixties. It was like, who gives a shit? So our inhibitions were pretty low on the scale.

### Joe Flaherty, cast member

I started work as a stage manager. I went to Second City in January of '69. The convention obviously was over, but everybody was talking about it— the tear gas in the air and all that stuff. I watched the show the first night, before I started work. The stage manager I was replacing said, "Take a look, and just see what this is." And I watched, and I thought, "I love this! This is great! They're doing really funny clever stuff, and they're improvising, too." And I thought, "I'd love to do this!"

   And those guys had been there for quite a while. And they were not happy. They were going through that typical Second City thing of just not wanting to really be there, sort of wanting to get out and do something else. But at the same time, it was a steady job, and they were getting paychecks. But they were not a happy group.

### Eugenie Ross-Leming, cast member

I was still in college at the University of Chicago, and I got this job that Mike Miller was directing at Second City. So I was sort of still divided. I was really a full-time student. It was really hard for me to go back and forth. And it really wasn't a company I was comfortable with. It was kind of old-time comics. They were much older than me and they did stand-up, and it wasn't terribly political and I just really wasn't interested in it. So I probably didn't do my best work. So Michael fired me.

### Ira Miller

Marty Friedberg almost killed Bernie Sahlins by throwing a chair at him. As I recall, Bernie had said to us, "Come in with three blackouts each." And each one of us went and told Bernie our blackouts, and he got to Marty, and Marty had a violent temper—something set him off. I don't remember what it was. But he got very upset with Bernie, and picked up one of those cane chairs, and threw it at him, across the room. It didn't hit him, but we were all like, "What are you doing?"

### Joe Flaherty

Martin Harvey Friedberg got into a fight with Bernie. He was screaming at Bernie. Mike Miller was directing. Mike Miller sort of had one foot out, anyway. I don't think he wanted to keep directing there. He was ready to leave. And Bernie wanted to direct. And those guys knew Bernie is basically an accountant, so they were having problems with him directing. And I remember that he was giving them some direction, and Marty was furious. He said, "Bullshit, Bernie!" So they got into a scuffle. It was kind of a bitchy fight, but it was still a physical altercation. It was kind of a weird situation. So nobody was really happy. Everybody was kind of angry at one thing or another. And I was in the middle of all that stuff, trying to keep the actors happy as much as I could. But they were always grousing and complaining about something.

### Michael Miller

They were just like, "This isn't going to work. This is terrible. And you're out of your fuckin' mind." About the skits, the things I liked. I like dark things. I liked Burt Heyman, who is very dark. I would sit and watch the show, and then I sometimes would just sit and watch the audience from behind the rail. And if the audience was there and I was there, I thought, "This is all cool." Because from a theater point of view, the group didn't know what they were talking about. And I knew I had good instincts about that. I didn't know about comedy, but I knew if the audience was laughing, it was okay.

### Murphy Dunne

Bernie had made the choice to get those guys, and they were basically stand-up comedians. But they were kind of eccentric. J.J. was blustery. And Marty was very eccentric and tall and would take any kind of chances. I remember one night, he walked out and he said to the audience, out of nowhere, "I may be gay. I don't know. I had my prostate examination. I liked it." He did five minutes. So it wasn't as if these people were afraid to try things. They would try anything. And there was one scene we referred to as "Pirandello." The idea was that, in some Pirandello plays, you'd break down the wall between the audience [and actors]. And they had this scene where Marty and J.J. are talking, and Marty would stop, and he'd whisper to J.J., in front of the audience. He'd look out at them like something bad happened and say, "That's not the line." J.J. would go, "Well, I'm improvising. Just go with it." Marty would say, "That's not the fuckin' line. What are you talking about here? That's not what we are supposed to do." And you could see the audience's hair go up on the back of their neck, and they're going, "Is this really what's happening?"

**Ira Miller**

Marty Friedberg's style was angry sometimes. That was kind of his shtick. And J.J., to a certain extent. Not myself or Murphy. We were gentler and more satirical. Marty and J.J., in real life, used to have these huge arguments. They would scream at each other. It never meant much because they would make up ten minutes later. They were good friends and they loved each other, but they would go to town on each other. It was part of their shtick. And the "Pirandello" scene kind of came from that. It was pure anger, but I always loved it because the audience always thought it was a real argument. And the scene would end with Marty and J.J. stalking offstage, and about five minutes before that, Fred Kaz would leave the piano in complete disgust like he couldn't take it anymore, their arguing. And then the intermission would come right then, so the audience would be like, "What the hell happened?" I'd be out by the bar, and the audience would come up to me or Murphy and they'd say, "What happened? What happened?" And I'd say, "Come back tomorrow night. You'll see the exact same argument. It's part of the show."

The cast's work was well received, but not all the shows drew raves. In a review from May 1969, *Chicago Sun-Times* theater critic Glenna Syse tried to be generous. "I'm sitting here trying to think of something buoyant to say about the new revue at Second City, which calls itself 'Peace, Serenity and Other Possibilities, or, Eight Blocks from Tokyo Rose,'" she wrote. "But it's tough. It's sort of like describing yesterday's champagne. Flat. I could, of course, just ignore the whole thing and write lavishly and lovingly about all the talented people that Second City always manages somehow to gather round. I can, for example, have a perfectly marvelous time just watching their faces."

But Sahlins needed more than fabulous faces. In the fall of 1969, he sent the discordant group to perform in New York (his preferred method of cleaning house), where they were hailed by *New York Times* critic Clive Barnes as "subtly and superbly funny." In the same article, he declared: "The entire recent tradition of American theatrical satire can be summed up in three words, 'The Second City.'"

With an empty stage to fill in Chicago, Sahlins installed his tight-knit road-tested touring crew for an October show (Second City's thirty-seventh) titled, aptly enough, *The Next Generation.* Featuring Jim Fisher, Brian Doyle-Murray, Judy Morgan, Harold Ramis, Joe Flaherty, Roberta Maguire, and the late David Blum, it fizzled fast. "As it stands now, 'The Next Generation' as a whole is a pleasant little show with a good number of fumbles, and that is not the best of the SC tradition," the *Sun-Times's*

Syse appraised in mid-October 1969. Still, potential abounded. With their bell-bottoms and shaggy manes, their pot smoking and hippie slang, the cool and congenial bunch helped usher Second City into a transformative new decade.

### Bernard Sahlins

I got tired of the older casts. I thought they weren't reflecting what was going on. They had a different frame of reference and a different adjustment to the world. They were kind of old-fashioned.

### Judy Morgan, cast member

We were well-read and kind of had fingers on the pulse of what was going on. And we were, in a way, fortunate—1968, Chicago, the convention, the women's movement, civil rights. We had a lot to play with, and we had opinions about all of it because it concerned us offstage.

### Bernard Sahlins

They were connected to our audience in a way that the previous cast had not been. The director at Second City learns from the cast and the audience what's going on. They're generally young, and their preoccupations and the material they choose to do is a clue as to what's happening. If you as a director are trying to direct from your own sensibility only, you're slightly out of whack with the times.

### Harold Ramis

I think Bernie thought we were already on the right track. We were doing a lot of antiwar material and antipolice material. We looked like the people in the streets. But none of us were radical.

### Bernard Sahlins

When I installed Ramis and company, these were children of the '68 rebellion, and naturally their work reflected it, as well as what was interesting to the audience. These were people who had started the youth movement, so to speak. This particular company didn't feel a deep sense of protest, though. They were mirroring what was going on around them. And remember, you had Lenny Bruce and Dick Gregory and all those people starting to become rich and famous. It was the zeitgeist; it was in the air.

### Joe Flaherty

In '69, when I came in, that show was sort of nonpolitical, because two shows before that, *A Plague on Both Your Houses,* was very political. That show didn't do well financially. And I don't even know what the reviews were like, but something happens. You get so involved in the politics that there's nothing more to say.

### Sheldon Patinkin

[*A Plague on Both Your Houses*] was too angry. It wasn't funny enough. If you're doing satire and comedy, you have to figure out how to do it so that the audience will laugh at what you hate, rather than just get angry at it. If you can laugh at it, you can fix it.

### Jim Fisher, cast member

The first time we came out as *The Next Generation,* we suddenly *were* the audience. Up to then, de rigueur was thin narrow black tie, white shirt, black pants, black coat for guys, black dresses for girls, and that's what they always wore. And we were the first ones that came with our wonderfully tie-dyed shirts and long hair and facial hair. And we got creamed for it in the first reviews.

### Harold Ramis

We bombed. It was terrible. Our first show was not good. I remember someone reviewed us during previews and they slammed us. "If this is the next generation, bring back the last generation," or something like that. I got really angry and wrote a letter to the editor. And Bernie said, "Never reply to a bad review. It just makes it worse." We didn't have a lot of confidence in our director, a man named Cyril Simon. But Flaherty might have recalled nights when there were more of us than there were people in the audience. There were seven of us onstage and I think six people in the audience. And we kept trying to invoke an imaginary equity rule that if there aren't more people in the audience than on the stage, you don't have to perform. It was too humiliating. But somehow enough people would always show up.

As Ramis and friends played to sometimes sparsely populated houses in the fall of 1969, protest prince Abbie Hoffman returned to Chicago with seven (soon to be six) others to face charges for his alleged role in the Chicago Democratic National Convention riots of 1968. During the so-called Chicago Conspiracy Trial, which extended into the following year, Hoffman (reportedly accompanied by fellow rabble-rouser Jerry Rubin) sought out comic relief on North Wells. He'd been to Second City before, but this time he took part in the improv action—on at least one occasion playing (and mocking, as he frequently did in the actual courtroom) his potential jailor, Judge Julius J. Hoffman.

### Roberta Maguire

Abbie Hoffman not only came to our shows almost every night, but he stayed with me, and we were lovers at one point. For the trial. He'd go to the trial, and then he'd come at night and do the improvs with us.

### Harold Ramis

He played Judge Julius Hoffman onstage, and Jim Fisher played Abbie Hoffman, which was funny. Remember the Weather Underground? The Weathermen were in the streets, and we think Abbie might have been just using the stage as an alibi so three hundred people could see that he was not outside on the street. One day we were performing—I don't think it was when Abbie was there—and someone came in and said, "The Weathermen are smashing cars on Wells Street." And I went, "Yes!" And then I went, "Wait a minute, I'm parked on Wells Street." So I was ambivalent.

### Jim Fisher

They had always said the Illinois Bureau of Investigation was tracking Abbie, and so his thing was, he'd come in, and he'd do a couple of scenes that he could with us, and then he'd take off and down the stairs and out the back door before they could track down where he was. It was, "I wasn't there. I wasn't making fun of the judge. Wasn't me." He used to play him as a buffoon, and then he'd light out.

### Roberta Maguire

We were the lawyers, and we brought up people from the audience and made them the jury, and we said, "And now here's Judge Hoffman." And Abbie came out with a choir robe that he had found backstage, and a noose over his shoulder. And he ended up finding them guilty. I mean, how ironic was that?

Toward the end of 1970, Ramis took a leave of absence and headed overseas to Europe and Greece before rejoining the company in 1972. Eugenie Ross-Leming, a couple of years after being fired from the mainstage (a blessing in disguise, she now says) after a short stint with the Next Generation's older and more conflict-prone predecessors, returned to fill an opening left by the departed Roberta Maguire. Overall, the ensemble in its various incarnations meshed uncommonly well and created such immortal scenes as "Brest Litovsk" (wherein a hapless student tries to fake his way through a makeup history exam), "V.D." (wherein patients at a medial clinic encounter a judgmental nun who scolds them for contracting social diseases), and "Funeral" (wherein mourners stifle laughter at the funeral of a friend who died from getting his head wedged in a can of Van Camp's beans), for a string of new and increasingly well-received revues.

During this especially fertile stretch, acting teacher and former main-stage understudy Josephine Forsberg founded Players Workshop of Second City, where countless performers (including many future stars) were schooled in the ways of improvisation. A friend of Paul Sills's, and Viola Spolin's assistant in the sixties, Forsberg also directed children's plays at the theater on weekend afternoons. The promotional plug, sung as part of a longer musical number at the end of weekday evening performances in the cabaret: "Saturday and Sunday is the little bastards' fun day. Come in and see the Second City children's show."

### Richard Christiansen

At that point there was a huge concentration of talent in Chicago. This is during the Vietnam War, and it was a great time of passionate protest against the establishment and the factors that led us into the conflict. And there was a tremendous amount of youthful energy poured into that protest movement. Then when the Vietnam War ended, there was still that incredible energy, that need to express oneself. And what better outlet for it than going into the performing arts—theater, cabaret, and so on? I think that's probably one of the reasons that you had this amazing confluence of talent at the time. It's true not only of Second City, but of theater in general in Chicago. You get the feeling that in the early and mid-seventies there was just this tremendous flush of new groups and new people establishing themselves.

### Eugenie Ross-Leming

I really think we were all having such a good time being funny at someone else's expense—at the bad guys' expense—and getting laughs, that it was hard to be angry. I mean, you might be angry at your mother for not being good to you, or you might have some kind of Freudian issues, but in terms of the culture, we just had a lot of fun. We hadn't been beaten down yet. We hadn't been on the nightclub circuit, like the cast before us. We weren't actors who had failed at so many things and knew what rejection is like. And there wasn't a huge level of narcissism because we were all so young. I was literally just getting out of college.

### Dennis Franz, actor

I always had such great admiration for what they did at Second City. I thought, "My God, how do these people do it?" I was nervous for them. I'm good with scripted words and having it on paper, but to just get up there, cold and naked, and do it—holy cow. Even when I was in college theater classes, when it came to improvisation, it was something that I just sucked at. I'd get to a point and I would just shut up and leave whoever was up on-stage with me cold.

### Joe Mantegna

When I was a student at the Goodman Theatre, we'd go over to Second City. I even remember a few of us from my class went over there on a Monday, improv night. We did a little skit, and it was bad. I think the mistake we made is, we worked it out a little bit. We got up there and got a few giggles, but as we did, we realized, "Now what?" That was one of the first times I realized this improv stuff is a whole other ball game.

### Judy Morgan

We were blessed, we were gifted, because we all got along. And I think somehow that was different from casts that had gone before us. We worked together; we were good at improvising group scenes. To the best of my knowledge, that was rare up to that point. There were two-person scenes, there were three-person scenes, there were four-person scenes. But we had the compatibility for seven people to get onstage and come up with something. So that requires extreme listening and give-and-take.

### Eugenie Ross-Leming

When you go on the road, or when you work on a steady basis with a group of people like at Second City, you become their allies in this war. And I always felt like the wives who got left behind maybe didn't like us so much—the girls in the company. Because we shared something—and I don't mean anything romantic—but we just shared a camaraderie, an experience with their guys that they couldn't experience.

As he became more involved with the creative side of Second City, Sahlins did everything in his power to keep lowbrow laughs at bay. "Play at the top of your intelligence," or some version thereof, was his oft-repeated mantra. That bit of noble sagacity didn't always fly, though, particularly as Second City scenes took on an edgier and earthier sensibility. Sometimes, it turned out, there was nothing funnier than a steaming bowl of fuck.

### Roberta Maguire

Mike Miller was our director in the touring company. And then this guy whose name I don't remember was the first director [on the mainstage]. And then from that point on, Bernie directed us. And he knew nothing about theater or improv. He used to be puffin' on his cigar, and we'd be just lost up there, and he'd say, "Now say something funny!" And we would all freeze, and—ugh! For me it was a nightmare.

### Joe Flaherty

I look back at Bernie, and we would get so frustrated with him. He was not a theater person to begin with. And he never had a creative job until he took over directing. But what I liked about him was, he observed. He watched things. He watched and saw how things went and how scenes work and what helped make things work and what killed things. And so he started compiling his own philosophy.

### Jim Fisher

There was this whole University of Chicago background. He just would not let the level drop. We couldn't swear onstage. I remember we were allowed to say "shit" in a show once, maybe twice. It was like, "You can always find a more intelligent alternative than swearing."

### Harold Ramis

Groucho Marx saw our show in Chicago, and it didn't go well. I idolized the Marx Brothers and was so disappointed in our performance that I didn't even go out into the house to meet him. I went into the bar to hide out, and after a few minutes, Flaherty came out to look for me. "Groucho wants to see you," he said. "Groucho asked for me specifically?" "Yes," Joe said. "What did he say?" "Groucho asked, 'Where's the guy with the wig and the false nose?' " I did go out to meet him then, and he was quite old and not very pleasant. He teased me about my hair and nose again, but I guess I was glad that he actually showed some interest in me, however unpleasant it was.

### Roberta Maguire

We were just shitting ourselves backstage. It's like having God out there. "What are we gonna do?" Groucho had been at Northwestern University giving a talk, and the students thought it would be fun to bring him to Second City. And after the show, he stayed and talked to us, and they said to us, "By the way, he fell asleep during the show 'cause he's so old." And he was just standing there, kind of doing a routine, and he said, "Uh, you guys— you were good, but your material stunk. Why don't you use some of our old stuff?" You know, nobody's gonna notice. And there were always two women, and he looked at Judy Morgan and he said, "You were the prettiest." And he looked at me and he said, "You were next." I just went home and cried. I actually cried. I was so hurt.

In the first half of 1971, Second City got a much-needed shock to its system by way of a charismatic and oddly built Albanian lightning bolt named John Belushi. As a Chicago-area college student, he and pals Tino

Insana and Steve Beshakes were deeply inspired by the theater's work. They even performed Second City scenes with their own upstart outfit, the swaggeringly named West Compass Players. Not long after, a very young and theatrically green Belushi made his Second City debut in a June 1971 revue titled *No, No, Wilmette* (the theater's forty-first). His manic energy, terrier-like tenacity and dead-on impressions of Joe Cocker, Mayor Daley, Henry Kissinger, and Truman Capote lifted the Next Generation cast—and Second City itself—to a new level of local acclaim. Despite his almost immediate audience appeal and undeniable raw talent, however, the new guy took some getting used to among his peers.

### Joyce Sloane

John came running up the stairs and we auditioned him. Everything wasn't as formal then. "Okay. Bernie, I've got somebody that wants to audition. I think we should see him now." And he was just great. He always said, "You hit the stage like a bull; you don't just walk out." He was like a rocket going off.

### Tino Insana, cast member

We had been to Second City to see the shows. It was just the three of us on-stage, and Bernie was sitting down on the floor, at one of the tables, and I think Joyce was there, too, because she had brought us to the audition. And we were having a great time. We were prepared for the audition because we had been doing this stuff for a while, so we were bringing in our sketches. We were thrilled. We said, "Hey, this is great. Wait till he sees this stuff."

### Bernard Sahlins

I remember that John was the only actor I ever hired on the spot for the regular company. He walked onstage with his two buddies—hired. That was it.

### Richard Christiansen

When Belushi came along, that was one of the very first times that you could say "star material." This guy was going to make it big. And John was always on the lookout for ways to establish himself as a big charismatic personality. I did an interview with him—I think I was still at the *Daily News* at the time. And the interview went very well, and it appeared and was pretty good. So the next opening at Second City, I was sitting along the rail and John was working the house, and he came over and said hello and said he liked the piece and so on. And then he said, "Do you know Sydney Harris?" Sydney was then our chief theater critic at the *Daily News*. I said, "Oh, yeah." He said, "I'd like to get a story by *him* about me." He was always on the lookout for the next big thing.

**Judy Belushi Pisano, John Belushi's then-girlfriend**

I think he was a sensitive person in general, and I don't know that he ever much got beyond realizing that you're going to get good reviews and bad reviews. Taking one to heart means you've got to take them all to heart. And it's a lot more fun to have a good one than a bad one. I do recall he often had a favorite review in his wallet. And in fact, when we went to get married, he didn't have any identification, and we were trying to get the license. And they're like, "No, you can't get a wedding license without identification." And he pulled out his wallet and he pulled out this folded-up piece of newspaper, and he opened it up, and it had a picture of him, and it had his name under it, and his age, so he said, "Well, won't this do?" No. No, it did not do. We had to get a judge—we had to find a judge who would take his sworn statement that he was who he was, and give him an affidavit that allowed us to get the license.

**Paul Flaherty, guest musical director and John Belushi's roommate**

After the opening of one of the shows, the reviews came out. John waited up to get the early papers, and I was sleeping. And I could hear him talking to somebody. I opened the bedroom door, and it was John at the window, reading his review out loud. And the review was saying something like, "John Belushi is obviously going to be a star. His magnetic presence and his keen humor . . ." And I remember he read that phrase two or three times over. "John Belushi's going to be a star. John Belushi's going to be a star." And it was such a private moment. I shut the door and didn't want him to know that I had heard it. This was all new to him. And he was starting to realize that he had that kind of charisma. And that's what made me realize that it was going to be a little hard for him, being that young, taking on fame. Because you knew John was going to be famous. You just knew it. Everybody knew it. He just had that presence.

**Bernard Sahlins**

You know when you go to a wedding, and there's a bride there and the bride is beautiful? And the reason she's beautiful is she knows she's a bride? And she stands up there and she says, "Yes, I'm beautiful." And you say, "Yes, you're beautiful." Belushi was a bride. Always. He knew who he was. He knew he was good. He was in the present, totally in the present.

**Harold Ramis**

When I was gone, Joe Flaherty sent me a letter and said, "They hired a guy to replace you. He's a little Albanian and he's really funny." I didn't know if that meant he was just little or a little Albanian. He was all Albanian and really funny. I knew they'd replace me, but when I saw John, he was so funny and so good. And in fact, the interesting thing was he ended up taking over not just my parts, but the roles that I played. I had always played the long-haired zany guy, and John was the long-haired zany guy. And I remember the first time we improvised, I had a spot that I was kind of heading toward onstage. Everyone developed a little zone where they felt comfortable. I was heading for my little zone, and John was already in it. He didn't know that was my spot. We had the same power center. So I started doing things differently. I found something that I could do that complemented what he was doing, and we worked well together. John was very earthy, and I got more ethereal, more intellectual. In every improv I was Doc, Specs, or the professor. It was natural and easy. I became the Henry Poindexter, whatever that means, and that was fine. John was much earthier than me, always, so he kind of covered that territory. And John was bolder. He took chances that no one had yet taken with language. I believe he introduced the word "fuck" to Second City.

Or at least he was the first to utter it in supremely funny fashion.

### Jim Fisher

Of all the performers I've ever worked with, John had a connection with the audience that I have never seen before. People just laughed when he came onstage. I mean, he had no problem seemingly—they were in his pocket and laughing. Harold was brilliant mentally. He was an improviser, and he also knew jokes from working in the *Playboy* joke days. Flaherty was the guy I always went to if I did silly shtick. He could do silly shtick. Brian always wanted to be the actor, and always did heavy character stuff. If you wanted an acting scene with Brian, he'd do the acting scene. He was really versatile. And John was John. His personality was him—over-the-top and barging, crashing through.

### Bernard Sahlins

The company was mature. I don't mean in age, but in sensibility. They were able to appreciate Belushi, and also he was able to appreciate them. He respected them in a way that I don't think he respected subsequent companies that he was involved with. He was the new kid on the block, and he was bright enough to know it. So he contributed a lot, and he was very funny, and the public loved him. But he was not the subject of hostility from any of the others.

### Eugenie Ross-Leming

It was hard to be angry at him, because he just took such pleasure in what he was doing. And you can't be angry at someone who is not doing something to hurt you but just having a good time. I would get irritated. It's not like I'm saintly or anything. You know, we all have egos, too. But we were all so different as people that you couldn't confuse one for the other, so there was room for all of us. It wasn't like there were two tall blondes with big boobs, or two incredibly intellectual Jewish nerds or two burly jock-types. Everybody was really different and really a personality. And since you were generating your own material, you always brought your perspective and your point of view and your vocabulary and your voice to whatever scenes you were creating. So there really was room for everybody.

### Jim Fisher

One time John was late to rehearsal. I said, "I have an idea for a scene." At the time, *Dark Shadows* was the big hit soap opera, with vampires. And I remember thinking, "They're getting so desperate, I wouldn't be surprised if they turn to the Bible as the next source for a soap opera." So we decided to do this biblical scene. And John wasn't there. And I'm thinking, "Well, if I'm Joseph, that's got to be a juicy part." And Joe became Nicodemus, my best friend, and Judy was Mary. The only part left when John came was the angel. You know, "Deliver the news!" We were like, "We'll improvise that tonight." So we come up to the part, and here comes the angel. He puts the wings on from [a past scene called] "Swine Lake," and a red plastic aviator cap that we had back there for years, and that's where he developed the move where he made the wings flap that he used later with the bees on *Saturday Night Live.* His little moment stole the whole scene.

### Harold Ramis

I knew when to lay back. You had no choice. Once John was on a roll, he couldn't hear you or see you. He was going, and you either found a way to complement what he was doing or you got offstage. Or disappeared. We were all onstage, but in his head he was a solo. Or we were there as props. But it wasn't unpleasant. He wasn't obnoxious about it. It's just his natural instinct was to fill the void somehow.

### Eugenie Ross-Leming

John's zany was, like, sociopathic zany. Harold never had that. Harold was much more droll. Very droll, very dry. John would get messed up. He'd get sweaty. There was this one character he came up with. This would be a perfect example of why John could succeed in areas, say, someone like Harold or I could not succeed in. The character was the most obnoxious date in the world. So John is the date. He comes to meet the girl's parents, and—oh, my God. He was the grossest character alive. I mean, it was so repellent I could barely get through the scene, and there would be no way that Harold would ever have—one, thought of that part, but two, he could never have pulled it off. He would never allow himself to be as vile as John. And the audience did kind of wiggle and they squirmed. And they did laugh, but you couldn't believe anyone was that gross. You simply couldn't believe it, that an actor in polite society would utter those words. He'd say to the father of the girl he was trying to impress, "I have to go to the bathroom. Can I use your bathroom?" And then he'd be in there for a while, and you'd hear the toilet flush or something, and he'd come out and he'd say, "Wow! I just took a shit a foot long!" And he'd do the physical [image], with his hands. And the entire audience, they were stunned. I was stunned. I had a visual image of a foot-long shit. And he went on. He would elaborate on how it was uninterrupted—you know, it wasn't like there were pieces—and how hard that was to evacuate. I was aghast. And I can promise you Harold never would have done that scene. You bring to these scenes who you are. And even though we all have imaginations, [and] we play some things differently than we are in real life, nothing in Harold spoke to that behavior.

### Joe Flaherty

Harold certainly was the brain of the group. Very funny. Witty. Although he always claimed that he wasn't an actor, that he was just basically a head, a brain, walking around onstage. And he'd break up occasionally. I mean, he was easy to make laugh onstage. He was working at *Playboy*—he was the jokes editor over there—so he had this storehouse of jokes that he knew, that he'd just committed to memory, basically, and would throw them out whenever he got a chance.

### Eugenie Ross-Leming

He was an elegant thinker. Even though he had long hair, he had an educated demeanor. John could play a thug. I mean, John was just this beefy goofball. Now, John had a twinkle, and there was nothing malevolent or scary about him. And he could often play sweet characters or just goony characters. But they were, I would say, more antisocial than Harold's characters.

### Judy Belushi Pisano

John would do some pretty base stuff, which is often funny. But that was not so much appreciated. "Eat a bowl of fuck." It was something that began with Tino and Steve and John when they worked together. I'm not sure where it originally came from, but John made it work best.

### Harold Ramis

He was famous for that. I only heard him say it once, as I recall.

### Joe Flaherty

He would just walk out there and get laughs. Because physically he had a very interesting body. He had those short legs and that long torso. And the way he moved—he had that bearish kind of walk. Between that and the long hair and his face, which was a great face—I used to tell him, "Boy, you're a combination of Lou Costello and Marlon Brando," and it would piss him off. He liked the Brando part. He wasn't too happy with the Costello thing. But it was true.

### Tino Insana

John was friends with everybody in the neighborhood, and there was this local character whose name was Dr. Psychedelic. Say no more. We were gonna go home for Thanksgiving, and I was going to pick him up, so he told me where Dr. Psychedelic lived, kind of, and I pulled up and went to the back staircase and walked up. And some guy came out and said, "Who you looking for?" I says, "John Belushi. Is he here?" And he said, "Yeah, yeah. He's in there." So I said, "Okay." Went in. There was a gun on the table and a badge, and there was a cop. It was a drug bust. And I was searched, and there on the couch was Dr. Psychedelic and an albino guy, John, and a pregnant woman. In handcuffs. And John said, "He's in Second City, too!" So the cop took the cuffs off John and said, "Okay, you two can leave!" That was pretty amazing. And we ran out of there just like something out of *Animal House*.

### Joe Flaherty

Because we worked as a group all the time, we didn't have stars among us. We used to get ticked off, because we'd be doing a scene, and John wouldn't have anything to do in a scene, and then he'd start just doing something. Usually it was something like shooting up, or some kind of a dope thing back then, and he would always get laughs. Any kind of dope reference, drug reference, got huge laughs. He was always kind of getting into that stuff, off on his own in a corner somewhere. And all of us would hear this laughter coming from the audience, and you look over and you see Belushi looking real groggy. Right now it's not funny because that's ultimately what happened to him, but he really took off with that and ran with it.

### Jim Staahl, cast member

John was the only person I knew that would drop acid and then come out onstage and perform. He did that on a Monday night, and I went, "Holy cow! How do you do that?" There was no hint of heavy drugs.

### Joe Flaherty

He came in one night and did a show on PCP. Well, it was angel dust. I think that's PCP, isn't it? All I know is it was called angel dust and somebody said it was a horse tranquilizer. His timing was really bad and his performance suffered. But that was a onetime only thing with him. We were all joking about it the next day, saying, "Aw, geez, you were so bad you were funny out there." But, you know, that was the times, too. Everybody was experimenting with drugs and LSD and stuff like that. And our cast sort of eventually realized that you don't do shows on LSD. Even grass didn't enhance your performance that much. You find too many things funny. Everything's funny when you're on that stuff. So booze was sort of the only thing we would do. We would have a few—before the improvs, we'd have our drinks. And sometimes it was more than a few. But that was about it.

### Paul Flaherty

John fervently believed in drugs. He believed in them. That was the culture at the time. You remember Keith Richards with that big button that said, "Things go better with coke"? That's the way it was back then. And it was sort of a limitless frontier, as to where your mind could go.

In late 1971, Del Close relocated permanently to Chicago following a years-long stay in San Francisco, where he'd become acquainted with such counterculture icons as Ken Kesey's Merry Pranksters and the Grateful Dead. He'd also been part of the cutting-edge comedy troupe the Committee, co-founded by former Second City director Alan Myerson. He was already something of a Zelig-like legend among Second City insiders, and his searing intellect and rebellious nature quickly attracted disciples among cast members, including John Belushi. In addition to being brilliant and blustery and intermittently bearded, Close also used copious amounts of drugs, did several stints in rehab institutions, and lived in book-cramped squalor across from the theater. Returned now from his self-imposed West Coast exile, he was rehired by Sahlins to direct the forty-third mainstage revue, *43rd Parallel, or, McCabre and Mrs. Miller.*" It opened in March 1972 to rave reviews and marked the start of an up-and-down decade-long tenure during which Close made a deep and lasting impression on Second City and its players—for better and for worse.

### Jim Fisher

I always remember we almost sunk the theater. Our most successful show was *43rd Parallel.* All your career you always hear, "Well, it's not the old Second City. They're good, but it's not the old Second City." They're talking about Alan Arkin and back into those days. And *43rd Parallel* was the show where almost unanimously the critics said, "This is Second City! This is the old days!"

### Roberta Maguire

I went on a trip to Mexico with Betty Thomas in her van with a couple other women. We were gone for a month or two. Those Mexicans thought we were a traveling whorehouse, I'm sure. I was trying to decide if I could stay at Second City any longer, and when I got back, Bernie had fired me. And so he made it easy. Eugenie replaced me when I was gone. And I've never told anyone that in my whole life, because I was pretty unhappy about it, but it left me free to hang out with Del for about three years. I've spent the last thirty years teaching what he taught me. He really was a genius. And I sat there for about three years, in his classes, and hung out with him, and he was my best friend and my mentor and my teacher, and boy, did he ever have some amazing stuff coming through his brain.

### Harold Ramis

Del was impressive for a lot of reasons. His survival was impressive. And he was legendary for being crazy. "Hey, that's Del Close. They used to pick him up at a psych ward and bring him to the show and then bring him back to the psych ward after the show." These were the legends. And he'd done a prodigious amount of drugs. And he'd show you his track marks. He always wanted to be further out than everybody else.

### David Rasche, cast member

He came over to my house one morning with his face all scratched up because he'd tried to commit suicide with a plastic bag, but he scratched it off. But what a force. He had an engine that other people don't have. One thing you learned from him was to take care of each other as actors. His basic thing was, "If you take care of me, I'll take care of you. I will never let you fail. Don't let me fail." And that's the way he directed. And he really stuck to it. It was an outgrowth of the way humans should treat each other.

### Eugenie Ross-Leming

He was a veteran who had come back, so clearly he had a history. He had an autobiography that preceded him that lent him a great deal of credibility as a creative leader. And he was kind of respectful of the work. It wasn't boring working with Del. It was fun. I don't know if I would say he was our guru, but I certainly respected the fact that he'd been there before me and had walked the minefield and kind of knew, "Don't step here." So I would listen to him.

### Bernard Sahlins

Del was Del. He was a strange mixture of talent and self-destruction. And he had this distinct inability to accept kindness and love.

### Joyce Sloane

The amazing thing was that Del didn't like women, and I never had a bit of trouble with him. Every Christmas he'd come in with a box of fudge that his mother and his aunt sent him. He was great with me.

### Judy Morgan

I considered myself, on the stage, to be supportive. Therefore it was not unusual for me to feel like I was coming up and under somebody. There were other people that were better at handling the really funny parts. I would get laughs because sometimes I would just say things that were just so innocent that I think it was easy to like me. "Isn't she cute? She's harmless. She's sweet." We were work-shopping with Del at one point and the show was up and running. We were just getting together to kind of stay in touch. And he wanted to work with us to develop where he thought we were weak, what he never saw us do—a side of us he had not seen yet. So he had me go up onstage, and he came up with me and said, "You never dominate. You're very agreeable." He said, "I want you to dominate me on this stage." He had done similar things to the others. I was not being cornered in any way. I felt very comfortable with his direction. And I knew what he meant and I knew what he wanted, and I think it was time for me to stop being the good little girl. So I started very carefully and easily, like, "Did you do the dishes?" And then I went on and on and on, and he would play up and under that, like the humble servant. And by God, I rather liked it. I use it to this day.

### Harold Ramis

Del's whole crusade at Second City and after was to keep people in the moment. Del believed that the Second City games—he actually said this once—[are] just like life. Life is an improvisation. We're constantly discovering our character, we're constantly discovering everyone else's character, and we're in situations that are constantly evolving and changing. And the ultimate improv game—he called it the Game Game—is the game we'd play all the time. No one tells us what to say; we were always making up our own dialogue. So he wanted the stage to be as real as life in that sense.

### Eugenie Ross-Leming

Del would come up with an idea, and he wanted to work something out. And we'd be sitting around—we had headaches from the night before.

Drinking coffee. "Eugenie, get onstage. Try this out." Joe said I was like the lab rat. He would make me go onstage, and he'd say, "Okay, now stick your head in that bucket. Okay, John, what would you say?" And I'd have to hold my bucket or whatever the metaphor was, while other people experimented with stuff. This poor fool, like the court jester. But I was young enough that I could take whatever Del had to dish out. We all were.

### Harold Ramis

Del saw in John this force of nature. Del always wanted to revolutionize the theater, and here was John, the perfect person to lead the charge. And John had amazing respect for Del. And I know Del liked and respected me, but we were different. Del loved that John was so present in the moment, and I was known to be in my head. I was always "writing" onstage. And John was not a writer. He was not thinking abstractly about what's good for the scene. He was just there following some impulse of his. And Del admired that.

### Joe Flaherty

John worshipped him, basically. He loved everything that Del did. He loved Del's mind. And I think they were kindred spirits as far as drugs went. It was sort of obvious. I don't know if I forgive him for his, but Del would even say, "I don't find anything wrong with drug experimentation. I think it helps the creative process."

### Bernard Sahlins

He was very talented, no question about it. He was also very mixed up. Very neurotic, very prone to breakdown.

### Joe Flaherty

He'd come in and ramble. He'd just ramble. But the thing with Del is, he was brilliant. The man had a great mind. I loved the guy's mind—his viewpoint and how quickly he assimilated things and how he grasped complex ideas. He was always reading a book. Even when he was holding workshops, he'd be rifling through a science-fiction book or something. And so you were aware of that. You were aware he had a great mind, and artistically he had a sensibility there. So we were willing to try anything for him.

After Belushi split for New York to star in the National Lampoon play *Lemmings,* Second City began cultivating a new crop of actors on its mainstage. They included future TV star and comedy director Betty Thomas. Like her predecessor Eugenie Ross-Leming, the former art student and Chicago schoolteacher busted chops and held her own in a historically testosterone-stoked workplace that wasn't exactly female-friendly.

### Roberta Maguire

Bernie would say, "Call Jim and Joe and Dave and Harold, and the girls," was always what he said. And it was always five men and two women, and the women always had to wear dresses. So given that the people are seated below the stage, mostly what we had to do was remember to keep our legs together. It was like binding our feet or something. Oh, God! I just couldn't believe it. And when I tell people that, they're just stunned. "Oh, we thought Second City was this great place where everybody had fun, and everybody hung out together, and there was all this camaraderie." And there was that, too. I loved the people in my company.

### Eugenie Ross-Leming

The culture was still misogynistic pretty much. But if you have to be a misogynist, at least they were smart misogynists. And because they were satirists, you could make fun of them and they would get it. So it wasn't like you were dealing with Cro-Magnon Green Bay Packers or something. You were dealing with funny people who understood that there is no price too high to pay for funny, including self-humiliation. Yeah, Del was a misogynist, but he took a great intellectual pride in being able to stand outside of himself and say, "Yes, I'm a drug addict misogynist, but . . ." He wouldn't live the life, but he could talk the talk of an enlightened person. He just couldn't walk it.

### Jim Staahl

All the way through to the J. J. Barry cast, there were five men and two women. That was the standard formula for the show. The women always were a secondary role. They were the secretary, the wife, the girlfriend, the date, the mom, the grandma. And the men did the heavy lifting on the humor. The sensibility of the women was typified by Mina Kolb and Elaine May. They're a little ditzy, a little crazy, but benign. Judy Morgan typified that. Wafer-thin, likable, goes with the flow. Roberta wanted to do more, but knew she was up against it. Because of the tenor of the times, the drugs and war and everything, women's liberation began in front of our very eyes. Eugenie is in the cast, and she is a ballbuster. Eugenie is like, "Hey, I can handle any man's parts." I remember that was a line she used when she was improvising or something, and they worked it into one of the scenes in the show. She would stand onstage, and she was defiant. It wasn't like, "I'm the girlfriend. I'm the mom. I'm the sister." No. "I'm the fuckin' boss of you guys. I'm your equal." And she acted that out and she sort of championed what we were trying to do in the real world, women's lib. She lived it.

## Bernard Sahlins

I think what happened was that the women took a more prominent role in the work and asserted themselves in a way they hadn't asserted before. Even though they were bright and emancipated, they were still a bit handicapped by the times.

## Jim Staahl

Betty was a waitress [before getting cast], and I remember we would laugh at her, with this giant hairdo. And she didn't shave her legs. Hairier than Robin Williams—oh, my God. But see, she did that because this was a matter of principal for her. It's like, "Fuck you. I don't dance to anybody's fuckin' time." That's who Betty was. Betty was unflappable. And she was tall. If Fisher was onstage, she would block him serving people down in front, because she was so fucking tall.

## Ann Ryerson, cast member

She was a broad. She wasn't a girl or even a gal. She was a broad. She'd lived, she'd done some pretty wild things. And, of course, that's what we all liked about her.

What I personally loved about Betty is that she had such an incredible enjoyment of life and she was unashamed to show her enjoyment of life, and everybody else vicariously felt good about her and about themselves with Betty around. She really inspired me and changed my life. I remember she would sometimes go on kayaking trips. She'd just pack up her kayak and go kayaking. She was very adventurous and very self-sufficient. And she had a few boyfriends, I will tell you that. That's where I will just draw the line and I won't say any more.

## Betty Thomas, cast member

I remember one time Ann Ryerson was let go, and Del came to me and said, [*deep voice*] "Uhh, Betty, uhh, you have two weeks to get it together. Ann's been let go, and you'll be let go, too, if you can't get it together." I mean, it's hard when you first start. There were no two-women scenes. Eugenie and Roberta maybe did one, and it wasn't that fun. It just wasn't a classic scene, let's say. It might have been more meaningful, but it wasn't classic, and it didn't make people roll in the aisles. And I thought, "That's just messed up that there are only two women and there are five guys." Because then you only have the two of you to turn to, and if you're not perfectly suited to each other, you're always going to be doing a scene as the mother or the girlfriend or the virgin or the whatever—whatever the boys want to make you. And so I do remember sort of trying to get it together. And here was my way of dealing with that two-week thing: Every set from then on, I did a scene with the most powerful people in the company. Whether it was John Candy or Bill Murray or David Rasche, or maybe even Jim Staahl might have still been around. Or Tino Insana. But whoever had a good idea, I would latch on to their scene and get in their scene. And I think Debbie Harmon took over at that point, and Debbie said, "Do you want to try a two-girl scene?" And I said, "No, Deb, I don't. Not until I have power! When I have power, I will come back to you and we will be doing two-women scenes. And I'll see you when that happens!" Pretty fucked up. But it worked for me.

I know Rasche has some horrible stories about me not closing the bathroom door. But that's beside the point. They were always talking in the back room there, and putting our [improv] set together. I mean, you have to go to the lavatory between the show and the set. And you don't want to miss a single thing! You have to be able to shout out! I was kind of a hippie girl. That didn't have anything to do with it. What it was about was putting that damn set together, and being aggressive backstage, so that you got your scenes up on the board. Or you had to connect yourself to some scene that was going up there. That's the moment maybe they'll make a movie about someday. Those backstage moments where you're putting together the set are as important as being onstage. More, maybe. That backstage area was, in the beginning, really difficult. That was nothing like anything you had in a workshop situation. There's no way you could prepare yourself for that. If you didn't get your name up there on anything, you were like, "Aw, shit! I'm not doing this set," basically. "Now I'm gonna have to fit myself into three scenes." Very stressful.

It served me very well. People say that being a director, you have to make a decision about every half a second. And it's very simple for me. I don't need more than half a second. And that's a great trait to have as a director. "Should he wear this? Should that be there? Should that be over there? Do you want this?" "Yes, No, Yes, Yes. Let's go. Move that here." I would say that was the beginning of confidence and decisiveness.

## Jim Staahl

I remember we were doing some stupid-ass thing backstage, and people were arguing, and David Rasche was disagreeing with Betty about something. And Betty stands there and goes, "All right, I'm done with you. You think you're such hot shit. Okay, whip it out. Show me your dick." And then we're all looking around like, "Holy crap!" And I swear to God, Rasche unzips his pants, holds out his dick, and she's like, "You call that a dick?"

## David Rasche

I would do that today.

## Mert Rich, cast member

When you were a new guy, you had to show her your dick. Betty said it had to be done. "Come on. Show me your dick."

## Sheldon Patinkin

Betty walked around backstage completely naked. Before she got into her show clothes and after she got out of her show clothes. She wasn't looking for a sex partner—she just simply didn't like underwear. If you've been backstage at Second City, there ain't a hell of a lot of space to hide yourself. And she wasn't particularly concerned about hiding herself, because she didn't think it mattered. Not because she was trying to attract anything; it just didn't matter to her. And very quickly, it didn't matter to anybody else. Broadway Betty, she was called in those days.

## Betty Thomas

There was a writer in Chicago—sort of a local bon vivant guy who hung around there. I was in Chicago when I was nineteen. I got thrown out of Ohio University and I lived at the Lincoln Hotel, right across from the old Second City. And at the time I was sort of involved with a different group of humans. Not really a creative group. Creative in criminal ways, perhaps. But whatever that was, I remember this guy met me—and at the time, I had white go-go boots and I had been performing on Rush Street as a go-go dancer, and I had false eyelashes and wigs, and I was just having fun. He wrote a book about Lincoln Avenue—I don't know if it even got published—and called me Broadway Betty. And you know how people are, especially in Chicago. They love that nickname stuff, and it kind of stuck.

The younger brother of Brian Doyle-Murray, commonly known as Billy, had been hanging around Second City for years and was coming off a touring company stint in 1973. He, too, was a colorful character. Also, he was wary—if not downright disdainful—of authority figures, and a disarming charmer to boot. The confluence of those qualities, plus the fact that he was fiercely funny, made him a force to be reckoned with onstage and off. His self-written Second City bio gives some sense of his outlook at the time.

> Bill Murray, the fifth of nine children, is currently casting to replace himself in his family. Bill has lots of personal problems, most typically with his employer at The Second City. He is interested in organic foods, ecology, and human relations, but just doesn't have the time. Basically insincere, he hopes his experience in theatre,

movies, and television can perhaps get him work as a *Playgirl* center-fold.

## Harold Ramis

I met Bill as a teenager when he'd just graduated from Loyola Academy in Wilmette. He was Brian's kid brother to me. Brian introduced me to him on the Wilmette golf course, where Bill was running the ninth-hole snack bar. And then that winter I ran into him. He was selling hot chestnuts in front of Treasure Island [a grocery store] on Wells Street. And then when I came back, he was in the touring company and Bernie had asked me to speak to him right away because he had had some conflict with other cast members. He said, "I think he respects you because you're Brian's friend. Talk to him." So I sat Bill down and said, "I heard there was some bad blood with other company members." He said, "Yeah." I said, "Do you care?" He said, "No." I said, "Okay. Good talk."

## Michael Gellman, cast member

I thought Billy was a fricking genius. I would watch him every night to see how he evolved and changed material and characters. I thought he was one of the best people I had ever seen onstage. I enjoyed being his understudy. I learned more from watching Billy. I learned more from watching that cast. It was old-school.

## Joe Flaherty

He did more characters than Brian. Bill did a lot of sort of weird characters. Like that guy [Carl Spackler in *Caddyshack*] that talks out of the side of his mouth. And so I'd say he had a great stage presence, too. The audiences sort of just zeroed in on him. He had that kind of star quality.

## Jim Staahl

Billy had his own different style. But I think apart from that was, Billy was this antisocial guy, and he would do things that would piss people off, that he thought were funny. Or to be different. He just was antiauthority. And when you recognized it, you went, "Oh, I get it. Okay, I can live with this." But if you're not aware of that, and you don't recognize Billy's contempt for authority, then get out of the way, because that's Billy.

## Joe Flaherty

It's acting, and you've got egos on the line. A lot of people in acting have strong egos. And they're driven. But Bill, he had a bad temper. I mean, he wasn't that volatile. It wasn't like this happened a lot. But it would. He'd get into scuffles with his cast mates and stuff like that. None of that stuff was ever very serious, but you gave Bill a wide berth as far as getting him upset. He liked to mix it up.

### Ann Ryerson

You have to be an assertive person to make it on the stage at Second City. If you aren't an assertive person, you won't make it. So every single person was probably assertive in their own way, and that's why I can't single out Bill more than anybody else.

### Bernard Sahlins

The Bill you saw onstage was the Bill you saw in life—sort of a fetching bad boy.

### Joyce Sloane

We were touring at Wabash College. And we're leaving there and everybody's giggling, and I can't figure out what they're giggling about. Bill had taken it upon himself to take the Oriental rug from the president's home and put it in the back of the van. We drove right back. He was always doing something. When we played Notre Dame, I lost him for about a week. Saint Mary's [a women's college] is right there. I think he hitchhiked back. I don't even know.

### Betty Thomas

There's a charming assholeness to Bill, and it's how he really has gotten through life. When I knew him, that was kind of how I thought of him, as this charming, always seducing, assholey kind of guy. But asshole in the sense of old-fashioned asshole. Like, a jerk willing to make a fool of himself—willing to do *anything* in order to get the girl. And there's something admirable about that, and there's something that makes you want to punch somebody about that. I don't feel like I have that kind of passion, and in some ways I envied his ability to give it up, so to speak, in a *huge* way, whenever he wanted something.

### Ann Ryerson

Bill liked women, so in that way he was not difficult to work with if you were a woman. I think he actually got along well with women just in general. He would be much more volatile with men. He was not that way with women. You can just hope to learn half the tricks that Bill Murray has got in his repertoire and had in his repertoire then as a young man. Let me just tell you, there are many of them. He's a lady-killer. How do you describe a Don Juan? He looks at women and he knows how to say something, and he movies in and he's close to you, and he's very charming.

### Eric Boardman, cast member

Fred Kaz would sit down and start playing the piano, and Murray wasn't in the building yet. They would leave the street door open, down by where the stairway was, and Murray would come up the stairs, and he had a coat set, and he'd put his arms through the jacket and make his entrance. He was never there at fifteen [minutes to curtain]; he was never there at five. They would start the show, and Murray would always make the show.

Bill was very casual, but, God, there was a power to him. I didn't know anybody like Murray. He was really good with that distance humor, and the humor of irony that Martin Mull and David Letterman were going to take to a new level. He was mocking onstage, and he was fierce, and he was bold, and he was physical.

### Mert Rich

I had just moved up [from the touring company], so even though I'm a year or two older than Billy, it was like, "Yes, Mr. Murray." He'd counsel me. He'd give me notes. And he was a little intimidating because he was so fuckin' good that it really brought your performance up, because you were forced to go toe-to-toe with that.

### Fred Kaz

I think he tempted [the audience] to rebel, and then closed the gate he already had around them. Because he'll make you laugh at something, and then you'll realize it's yourself, and you'll want to say "No," but you can't. It's lovely.

### David Rasche

He did a scene with Tino called "Read 'Em and Weep." That was his Vegas routine. That's when that whole thing happened. That lounge singer started right there.

### Tino Insana

I was his assistant [Jackie Weep] that just did silly shtick. He was best when he did characters where we'd go, "What in the world was that? How would you make that choice?"

His skills sharpened by two years of comedy boot camp, Murray split for New York and a host of increasingly high-profile gigs late in 1974. Over the next decade he'd become one of the most beloved comic actors in the world.

# 4

## Livin' Large with Johnny Toronto, the Fury of Murray, and Taking Off in the Great White North

**1973–78**

Dan Aykroyd
John Candy
Eugene Levy
Catherine O'Hara

Gilda Radner
Martin Short
Dave Thomas

SECOND CITY HAD ALREADY MADE several successful treks to Toronto in the sixties. Planting itself there on a permanent basis, however, proved much more challenging—even with ample funding from Canadian backers and even with the abundance of talent that came forth to audition for the fledgling troupe.

When Bernard Sahlins, Joyce Sloane, and Del Close went scouting early in 1973, they had no trouble assembling a first-rate cast. Dan Aykroyd, Gilda Radner, and John Candy were among the finalists. While details were hashed out up north, Candy returned with his new bosses to star on the resident stage in Chicago. He remained there for six months before heading back to Toronto.

Knowing his latest venture needed guidance from Chicago veterans, Sahlins imported Joe Flaherty and Brian Doyle-Murray to school the new hires and, in Flaherty's case, round out the first cast. Fred Kaz handled musical duties, and Del Close was a semi-regular presence as well, doling out wisdom and abuse in equal measure. The first revue, a remounted Chicago show called *Tippecanoe and Déjà Vu*, premiered on June 11, 1973, in a sweaty cabaret at 207 Adelaide Street East.

### Bernard Sahlins

We had done the big theater, the Royal Alex, for a week at a time, a couple of times. And the leading critic there suggested that we should open in Toronto, and backers came.

## Joe Flaherty

One day Bernie came in and said, "We're opening a theater in Toronto. Does anybody want to go? Any volunteers?" And everybody said, "Toronto? What the hell's that?" Nobody knew anything about Toronto. And he said, "I'll tell you what. We'll book a show in up there, and you can take a look at the city." He says, "I think it's a great town." And he booked us at the University of Toronto, at a theater up there. So we went up and took a look at it and said, "Hey, this is pretty nice!" But I was the only one who volunteered, along with Brian.

## Dan Aykroyd, cast member

[My comedy partner] Valri Bromfield and I were advised by a publicist, Gino Empry, that Second City was coming to town with auditions. And for any of us in the underground theater and improvisational comedy world, Second City represented the foremost training center for improvisation. And at that time, John Candy and I and Valri were all hanging out informally, doing children's theater, underground theater, some radio, CBC work. We were just part of the comedy artistry brigade along with Gilda Radner, who was in *Godspell*. Dave Thomas was in *Godspell*. Martin Short was in *Godspell*. Eugene Levy was in *Godspell*. We all were associates in the comedy world, kind of supporting each other's work. We were all friends. We all hung out for the year before Second City had come to town. We all basically knew each other, and we were all kind of supportive of each other's career in theater. We used to hang around the stage door of *Godspell* and go to the parties afterward. 1063 Avenue Road in Toronto should have a plaque on it, because it was Eugene Levy's house. It was John Candy's house. And all of us partied there and sang there. It was just full of music and fun and comedy. Everybody did a turn. Everybody tried to top each other and make each other laugh.

## Joe Flaherty

We went up there thinking, "Can we find anybody who can do this kind of work? We're doing really good comedy. And we're improvising. Not a lot of people can do that stuff." So we were wondering if we could scrape a cast together. I remember Joyce had booked this church in the area, and Del, Bernie, and I went in to look at the assembled groups that came in to improvise. And in walked Eugene Levy, John Candy, Dan Aykroyd, and Gilda Radner.

## Joyce Sloane

Dan Aykroyd and Valri had come down to Chicago. They slept on my manager's floor. They did a set and they were really great. So when we went to

Canada, we called them immediately. Then we went to see *Godspell,* which we called the "Huggin' and Muggin' Show," and we hired everybody right out of *Godspell.*

## Dan Aykroyd

When Second City came to town, it was the place to go and audition. And everybody wanted to get in, because we knew it would be a lot of fun and it would provide the training that might lead to a professional career such as those who had gone before: Shelley Berman, Alan Arkin, Nichols and May. So we were all very passionate about it, and nervous. Valri and I and John Candy auditioned on the same day. And at the time, John was selling Kleenex for Kimberly-Clark to make a living. He had a route.

## Joe Flaherty

John was a young, heavyset kid with this real likable face. And, man, we were just really impressed! We thought, "Oh, shit, we got a cast!" And we did. Bernie wasn't real high on John because he was so young, but Del liked him a lot, so John actually went to Chicago for his first show.

## Tino Insana

John Candy came into the company when they were trying to get it going up in Toronto. We'd make entrances and exits through all the doors and different slots and nooks and crannies on the stage. And on John's first night, I made my entrance that I had been making for the two months of the run, and he made his exit, and we collided. Blam!

## Jim Staahl

The lights came up, and Tino was looking a little frazzled. Tino was looking like, "What the hell was that?" I go offstage, and there's John. He's out cold. Tino had hit him. Knocked him out. So we're getting ice and we're going, "Crap! John's knocked out! What are we gonna do?" "Well, do another scene." "He's in the next scene. We can't do that." "Well, do something else!" So we're calling the light booth like, "We've got a change in the running order." It was strange. He was the outsider, this kid from Toronto. He was kind of a sweet guy, and we were thinking, "Who the hell is this? Why did Bernie hire him? Why didn't he hire one of our friends? Why didn't he hire somebody from the touring company?" What was ironic about it was, in that moment, for some bizarre reason, it was like John was now welcome to the cast.

Of the original Toronto gaggle, Gilda Radner stood out for her caring nature and her uncanny ability to draw laughs even in scenes that fell flat. She was ambitious, too.

### Dan Aykroyd

She was sort of our den mother in Toronto when she was doing *Godspell* and we were all hanging around the back door. And she came into Second City with us and she fed us, she clothed us, she housed us. We were just living on the theater salary. She lent us her car. She gave us gas. She took us in. She nurtured and nursed our hearts and spirits, and she was just an amazing physical comedienne. Fantastic. You could throw her around excitedly, like a doll. And she had the biggest heart, and everybody fell in love with her. Joe fell in love with her, I think. Brian, me, Bill Murray, Marty Short—we all had massive crushes on Gilda.

### Eugene Levy, cast member

Audiences just loved her. She could do no wrong onstage. She could laugh her way through a scene, and the audience would laugh longer and harder. They loved her personality, and Gilda onstage was totally just her. It's not like she could become another character. That's why she could not fail at an improvisation. Couldn't fail. Always managed to get out smelling sweet and getting laughs even though she might not have been doing that much.

### Jayne Eastwood, cast member

Second City was collegial with a harder edge underneath it than I'd been used to before with these people. Because I think Second City can bring out the worst in you just because you're out there on the firing line every night, so it became like survival of the fittest onstage. That's what I was noticing. Maybe Gilda wasn't as patient with me as she had been before. I wasn't picking up the ball as quickly as she would've liked. I was a little slower. I think my defense mechanism was sort of clicking in, saying, "Well, really I'm a *dramaahtic ahctress*."

### Joe Flaherty

I only knew Gilda as a director/co-performer. I got a big kick out of her. But I think all the guys did. There was something appealing about her. And she played to that, too, by the way. She was funny. She had a great sense of humor. She knew Second City and had a good feel for it. I used to love working with her onstage. I found out later that some of the gals didn't particularly enjoy working with her. How can I say this? She was very competitive. She didn't like to be the gal in the show. It was as simple as that.

### Dan Aykroyd

She wanted to be an actress and she got into *Godspell,* and she starred in it. And she got into Second City and she fought for her stuff, and backed her stuff up. And, of course, she was a very strong performer. Really great will. If you want to get anywhere, you have to have some kind of faith in your own ability, and ambition is a part of it.

### Jayne Eastwood

In *Godspell* it was sort of a big happy love fest. And then I saw Gilda starting to work it more at Second City. I don't want to bad-mouth her, because I loved her, but Gilda was very competitive and I'm not, and I think that's the Second City dynamic that I'm not that crazy about. I think she sort of left her girlhood behind when she started Second City, because I think she knew she was getting into a bigger arena.

The Joe Flaherty–directed *Tippecanoe and Déjà Vu* ran for about two and a half months, from mid-August until late October. It was followed by *Terminal Two,* which marked Eugene Levy's Second City debut and lasted until late December. But problems arose even before it opened. While John Candy and his adoptive Chicago cast played on Wells Street with *Phase 46, or, Watergate Tomorrow, Comedy Tonight!* things got increasingly tough in Toronto. Blazing late-summer temperatures combined with no air-conditioning, mass refunds to perspiring patrons, and problems obtaining a liquor license. As a result, Sahlins and company were finally forced to shut down operations roughly six months after they'd begun rehearsals. Two revues and it was over—but not out.

### Joe Flaherty

The air-conditioning was out. It was one of the hottest summers in Toronto and we were doing a scene called "Hamlet," where we were all wearing sheets. It was a very physical show. And it was like a sauna. I mean, we were drenched in sweat. It was so uncomfortable. Brian Doyle-Murray went running backstage and chased Bernie around a desk, apparently, and took a swing at him.

### Joyce Sloane

[Bernie] and Brian had a big fight in Toronto. I was right there. Brian pulled him by his tie across the counter in the back because the air-conditioning wasn't working.

### Bernard Sahlins

It was the hottest September on record—over ninety—and we had no air-conditioning. Tempers were short, including mine.

### Joyce Sloane

Gilda called me and said, "Joyce, we're at the theater. We can't get in. The door's locked. What should we do?" The landlord had locked the theater because the brilliant young man that we chose to work with us up there stopped payment on the landlord's check.

### Eugene Levy

I think the last performance at that theater on Adelaide Street was a nonperformance. The cast was in the lobby, waiting to see who's going to show up for the show, kind of hoping nobody showed up, to be honest. And sure enough, nobody showed up. There were two people who walked in the door at five to eight or five to nine, whenever we went on, and we told them, "You're probably not going to enjoy the show, just the two of you out there, maybe you should go away and we'll give you two free tickets to come back." And the reason we were hoping nobody showed up was because the National Lampoon road show was in town. So we went over and caught the second act of the show with John Belushi and Chevy Chase and Chris Guest and whoever else was in that company. And I think that was the last week before they closed the doors and put up the sign that said, "We're closed." But what're you gonna do? Nobody shows up, so we just figured it was over, and it was over. And then we get a call a month or two later, after the theater closed, saying they wanted to open again.

Aid had arrived in the form of twenty-nine-year-old Canadian entrepreneur Andrew Alexander. Already a fan of Second City, he'd even worked for a time in Chicago and hung out at the theater on Wells Street to watch fellow Torontonian John Candy in action. Having become acquainted with Sahlins and Sloane during his Chicago residency, and while their new recruits rehearsed in Toronto earlier that year, he and some investor associates were positioned to help them regroup at a city-owned venue called the Old Firehall, close to the booze-free sweatbox the troupe had vacated on Adelaide Street. Not only was the Firehall air-conditioned, but Alexander had a liquor license, too. A deal was soon struck, and Second City rose from the proverbial ashes in March 1974—complete with native son John Candy, recently (if reluctantly) returned from Chicago.

Later that year, after Gilda Radner left Toronto for New York and was replaced by Catherine O'Hara (nowadays a mainstay of Christopher Guest's cinematic mockumentaries), Sheldon Patinkin was rehired to direct the Canadian company—a duty he shared with veterans Joe Flaherty, Bernard Sahlins, and Del Close. But while Patinkin had trained under Paul Sills and been involved with pre–Second City ensembles since the 1950s, he wasn't always respected in Toronto.

### Andrew Alexander, Second City CEO and executive producer

I wasn't a great student, so I had quit college. And I was a cabdriver. I also had two speakeasies that were somewhat successful. When I went to Second

City in Chicago, I immediately fell in love with the form. I had an affinity for the work and what they were doing. There was something about it that just immediately spoke to me. It was kind of anarchistic. It was bad-boyism at its best, and I could relate to it a lot.

### Bernard Sahlins

Some weeks after we closed, Andrew and I struck a deal. I would provide the show for ten percent of the gross. So we reopened the show.

### Andrew Alexander

The deal was very simple. He owed some creditors money in Toronto, so I paid those off as we started making money. Over the first few years I fell into arrears on the royalty and would get quite upset for a while, but we eventually worked it out. He was pretty good about that; he could have yanked the rights away if he was so inclined.

### Joe Flaherty

Andrew called me up—I was in Pittsburgh at the time. He had talked to the other cast members, and they said, "You gotta get Joe up here, too." So I went back up again for the reopening at the Old Firehall. It wasn't even a theater. Musical groups played there, and they had a tiny stage. It was really an uphill battle, but we finally got it going, and the audiences started coming in.

### Andrew Alexander

I made a deal with the people who owned the Firehall to put Second City in. I got the ticket sales and they got the booze, basically. At that juncture I wasn't managing the space or the building. There was a bar across the street that was very popular, and they had a lot of lineups. So I'd go grab that audience and put them into this space, just to get an audience. You'd give away tickets just so they would come in. I was barely making payroll with the cast, because that was my responsibility.

### Dave Thomas, cast member

After Bernie bailed, Andrew was unbelievably important in keeping Toronto open. Some nights there were more people onstage than in the audience. And there's an Equity rule where you can go home if there are more people onstage than in the audience. We would come out and say, "You know, it might be more fun if you come another night when there's more people here." It looked like I had the job, but that the job was going to disappear again. And I got really scared. And Andrew, God bless him, is the one who manned the phones. He had a phone room going to keep people coming. And he turned it into dinner theater, and had dinner specials before the theater. There was a whole army of chefs and cooks up there making meals for people.

### Dan Aykroyd

We were saved by Andrew Alexander, who today remains the white knight of Second City. I've got to admire it and say I'm very grateful for his support. And he didn't get enough credit when we were there, because he was our employer, and we were always looking for more of this, more of that. You know—more money, more perks, more time off. But really, if you look at it, there would be no Second City in Toronto and, in fact, maybe even in Chicago, if it weren't for his intervention.

### Andrew Alexander

Any friction came because I had trouble paying bills. They would all rush to the bank to see who could cash their check first. I had a company called Moongold. He who got to the bank first would get the money. And sometimes somebody would be left holding a check that didn't cash. And the space wasn't really built. The space they'd had on Adelaide was a really cool space. You had a nice theater. It was patterned after Chicago's. This was a bar, kind of an L-shaped room with pillars. It was a regression from what they had been at, so they all were thinking, "My God, what have we gotten ourselves into? This is gonna be another disaster."

### Dave Thomas

Andrew's got a good heart. I mean, there were times when we were convinced he was ripping us off, because our checks would bounce. [During] the Second City days, we were getting $145 a week. And when your check for $145 a week bounces, you're pretty much screwed. Things that you wrote checks for to pay bills are gonna bounce now, because your check bounced, and it was just because he was always one step ahead of foreclosure.

We were backstage at the Old Firehall doing the show sometime back in 1975. In the middle of the show an overhead pipe burst and starting leaking down on the backstage area. It was awful foul-smelling leakage that actually smelled like shit. It was coming down onto our costumes back there and into our hair. Andrew came backstage to apologize. I was really pissed off. I told him it smelled like shit. And he replied that was because it *was* shit. It was a sewage pipe that had broken. And I turned to him and said "How can you do this to us? We're making $145 a week. Those measly checks are bouncing. And now we've got shit raining down on our heads!" Andrew just snickered awkwardly—his signature snicker—and said, "One day, you'll look back on these days as the best days of your life." And he was right. Maybe not the best, but they were great days.

John Belushi was an occasional presence in Toronto as well — whether as part of a touring show or on recruiting missions for National Lampoon. At one point, he and Aykroyd fell into a discussion about the blues.

### Dan Aykroyd

John was pretty much confident of his own stardom and magnetism and power. He was as well assured as the ultimate Illinois alpha male. He was a star when he walked into the Firehall in Toronto, no doubt about it. His reputation preceded him. White silk scarf, Lee J. Cobb–style driving hat. We got along right away. It was just relating to everything—motorcycles, cars, music, all of it. We had great parties the weekend he was up. The night we came up with the Blues Brothers, we were at the 505 Club—my key club. Everybody was drinking and having a great time, and I had a blues record on by the Downchild Blues Band, and John said, "What's this?" "Ah, just a local blues band. You're from Chicago. You should know all about that." "No, I'm into heavy metal and crunch. I like crunch guitar." I said, "Well, listen to this." And that night was the seed of the Blues Brothers.

If John Belushi was Mr. Chicago, John Candy was Mr. Toronto. Make that "Johnny Toronto," a nickname bestowed by Joe Flaherty in recognition of Candy's bon vivant ways and penchant for livin' large.

### Sheldon Patinkin

For a long time, when John [Candy] didn't know what to do onstage—he wasn't able to find his place—it was like he wasn't there. He would disappear in front of you. And this would happen during scenes. It took him a long time to get past that. He would just go blank. It was trying to figure out what to do next. That was still periodically a problem. He got his confidence back fully in Toronto.

### Dan Aykroyd

John was an elegant man who was one of the great sartorial examples of Canadian business culture. He was a salesman. He wore suits all his life. Always really well dressed. At Second City, he was the one who was kind of dressed like the grown-up, but looked the youngest of us. And he was very strong physically. It was very exciting to perform with him, because he could pick you up with one hand. And he had a crushing grip. And he had a beautiful sensitivity and heart. We used to call him Aunt Candy because he was just so embracing.

### Dave Thomas

I kind of relied on John's strength. I remember one time I broke my ankle jumping onto a boat down at Toronto harbor front and I had to get a cast on my foot. I was alone at the hospital and I couldn't walk at all. So I called John and told him what had happened. "Aw, you idiot! I'll be right there!" And he drove down to Mount Sinai Hospital and picked me up like a little toy and bundled me into his car, drove me home and set me up on the sofa at my place with some snacks and a blanket before he left. I loved that man. I wish I could sit down and talk to him for a couple of hours.

### Eric Boardman

What I loved about him is that when he did something, he did it a hundred percent. We were up in Canada, and he announced he was going to take up the art of fishing, and he went down to the store, and bought every fishing gimmick, bobble, and device he could. And in those days, we're making a hundred, a hundred ten bucks a week. But yet he spent every cent he had on fishing equipment. He lived large, and I had never met anybody who lived large when they didn't have a dime.

### Jayne Eastwood

John would say, "Come on over. We're gonna have lobster at our place!" and we would all go over to John's and we wouldn't eat till about midnight. And he always had this big easy chair in the middle of his living room—just happy as a pig in shit with everybody there. That's when Joe nicknamed him Johnny Toronto. He was sashaying around town. Everybody knew John, and John knew everybody. He was just this local amazingly popular, colorful figure having the time of his life.

### Sheldon Patinkin

I now weigh about 152 pounds. When I moved from Toronto to Chicago, I weighed 225 pounds, at least 30 of which I gained during the two months that John and Rosie [his wife] and I lived together. When he didn't know what he wanted to eat, we'd order in from three or four different places—and eat it all! Chinese food from here, ribs from there, pizza from there. Our favorite Chinese restaurant didn't deliver, so he would call and say, "It's John Candy," and they would put it in a cab.

### Dan Aykroyd

You'd go to his house and there would always be a snack. He was the greatest host. I remember a meal down in Chicago when we first went down to sniff around there in the summer of '74. Just great food, wine, beer, brats. Johnny Toronto was the ringleader of entertainment. He had become Johnny Chicago.

## Rose Candy, wife of John Candy

John loved to gather friends and family. When we had people over, it was "Enjoy, relax," as we cooked in our kitchen. One Thanksgiving, we invited the cast over from Second City Toronto. A small detail had been overlooked—the turkey was still frozen. Thinking quickly, we put the bird under the shower to thaw, and at around two in the morning we celebrated Thanksgiving.

## Dan Aykroyd

John liked to have a drink now and again, and sometimes he'd go onstage after having a couple, and it would be unpredictable. He picked Dave Thomas and I up and swung us around like beer barrels one night. He picked me up, threw me over one shoulder, picked Dave up and threw him over one shoulder, then twirled us around like a propeller and dropped us.

## Dave Thomas

John was heavy, but he was not a pudge ball. He was *very strong,* and I used to use that onstage with him. Like, I could run at him and jump up and tuck myself into a ball and he would catch me like a football, barely even rocking on his heels. It was hilarious. So that night with Danny, John picked us both up horizontally, like logs, and spun us around. And I can still see Danny's face, wide-eyed and laughing, and the room whirring around behind his head. And I'm sure he has a similar memory of my face.

## Andrea Martin, cast member

I know there was a lot of laughs and a lot of drinking backstage. This was the cast, not me. I never really drank. But, boy, there was a lot of drinking and smoking and coming in late, and oy, my God! The curtain would go up at eight, and key people would get there at ten past eight, and I'd be like, "What the hell is goin' on?" And Joe and John drinking those Irish coffees with whipped cream on top and smoking, and you never knew what you were going to get yourself into.

## Dave Thomas

One of the thrills in the early days on the Second City stage—before we did television and became known ourselves—was when comedy legends would drop by the theater to watch the show and sometimes join us for improvs. Jack Burns and Avery Schreiber dropped by one night; Eli Wallach and his wife, Anne Jackson, caught the show another night. On another night, Peter Cook and Dudley Moore came by. They were very famous back then for their bestselling show *Beyond the Fringe,* and everybody knew their work and admired it. Only this night, the duo was drunk—very drunk. They joined us for the improvs, and I specifically remember Peter Cook backstage with John, going over the beats of something they were going to do, and Cook dropped to his knees in front of John. Then I got distracted by plans for scenes I was going to be in.

When John and Peter's scene came up, I went into the house to watch. The lights came up, and Peter established that he was a priest in the first sentence of the scene, and then dropped to his knees and mimed giving John a blow job. Well, the audience was appalled. There was a collective gasp, and then this awful, endless silence as Cook mimed blowing John. It was really horrible. And John seemed to be taking all the heat for the audience's anger. This happened frequently—where John usually had the audience's affection instantly because of his big, lovable chubby face, he also often became the target of the audience's wrath when things went wrong. This was, in fact, so common that Joe Flaherty used to call him Johnny Lightning Rod. This night was a perfect example of that.

I bolted from the house to backstage to make an entrance and help John out. And when I got to the door and made my entrance, I was shocked to see that Cook was still on his knees in front of John. This was not commitment—hanging in to sell a joke—it was because Cook was so drunk he was unaware of the audience's reaction. Anyway, I don't remember what my entrance line was, but I do remember being surprised that I got a laugh and entrance applause from a line that was pretty mediocre. I guess it was because the audience was so relieved that this horrible moment had ended, they were prepared to laugh at anything. And I'll never forget the look of appreciation on John's face. John was horrified by this incident. He was a little intimidated by Cook because he admired his comedy, and so I think that's why he didn't just run offstage. And I asked him later if he knew that was going to happen, because I had seen them discussing the scene backstage and I had seen Cook get to his knees. And John said "No! He was on his knees as a sinner, begging me—a priest—to forgive him. He changed it when we got out there."

Not long after the Old Firehall opening, in the summer of 1974, the Chicago and Toronto casts swapped stages for several weeks as a publicity stunt to help boost the nascent Toronto troupe's profile. Bill Murray and Dan Aykroyd hit it off from the start.

### Dan Aykroyd

Valri and I went down to Chicago to begin our term there in August, and Bill was the guy they basically sent to be our guide. And so he sort of showed us around. We had heard about him and he had heard about us, Valri and me—that we were the goods, that we were the real thing. We wouldn't be down there doing this if we didn't have talent. Bill has no room in his life for anybody with medium talent. You gotta be a star—as he is himself—to be a friend of Murray's.

### Eugene Levy

The first night we went on and improvised, the Chicago cast was still there doing the show before they left for Toronto. And they introduced us and said we'd be joining them in the improv section. And we started doing some scenes, and there was this odd whistling or something. It wasn't booing. But it was like a whistling sound. And at the end of the night we said to Del Close, "What was that noise? What were they doing? They were whistling." And he said, "They're telling you they're not gonna put up with the kind of crap you were giving them. They want to see some people working at improvising a scene and not just taking the cheap way out." So we went through a bit of a training session, a little workshop section, while we were down there doing our show. We would go through these workshops with Del to try and kick the cheap shit out of our act. And it seemed like it was a good idea, it seemed like we were learning a lot, and then we went back to Toronto and we just kind of went back to our old ways.

I think the basic difference between the two casts was that Toronto to me was always more the revue-type theater in the sense that the Toronto performers brought more in through their characters to get laughs. The scenes and the improvs weren't quite as pure. When we went down to Chicago in '74, maybe a year after having been in the show, the thing I remember about their show was, there were maybe three laughs in the first act and maybe three laughs in the second act. And scenes would play out and they'd be kind of serious in tone and kind of worked out, but not any laughs. In Toronto, if we went twenty-two seconds without a laugh, it felt like dead air.

### Eric Boardman

I don't think our company was as downright funny as the Canadian company. I think the Canadian company of '74 was the single funniest bunch I had ever seen onstage anywhere. And Levy's doing deadpan. No one's doing deadpan. He would come out onstage and with minimal stuff get huge laughs.

### Dan Aykroyd

The Canadian side always had a little bit of an edge. I think that was maybe us trying to get noticed or something, because the Americans were more secure. And so we'd hit the wall harder. We'd hit the floor harder. We'd do stronger falls—anything to sort of say we were ready to die for this.

The Chicago cast's trip north—one of several that took place over the next few years as Toronto struggled to survive—marked what is perhaps Bill Murray's most mythic Second City performance. As the stories go, much of it took place offstage.

### Joe Flaherty *

I wasn't there that night, but Bill was onstage, and there was someone drunk in the audience that just kept heckling him. And he told him to shut up, shut up. And he wouldn't shut up. Murray jumped into the audience, grabbed him, and went to the fire door, which was close by, apparently. Pushed him through the fire door and then beat up on him and broke his arm. I guess he twisted his arm.

### Sheldon Patinkin

I heard about it as soon as I arrived in Toronto. And the heckler did not sue. Bill's the only one I know of who actually jumped out into the audience, grabbed a guy, pulled him out into the alley, and beat the shit out of him. He had been heckling him through the whole show, and Bill finally just lost it.

### Mert Rich

We had a heckler in the audience going off all night. Murray and I, and I think it was either Ann or Betty—someone would sit and take down the notes—we came out for [improv] suggestions. And the guy went off again— or maybe he didn't even go off. All of a sudden Murray says, "Ladies and gentlemen, there's someone who's been interrupting the show all night, but he won't do it any longer!" And he jumped offstage and started beating the shit out of the guy, dragged him out, leaving me alone. I don't remember him breaking an arm. Later on, the guy was so drunk he came back and had no idea—Murray and I were backstage, I think—and was asking us, "I think I left my watch or my wallet" or something. He came back! I was amazed he didn't recognize that Murray was the guy who beat the shit out of him. Bill taught me a valuable lesson in audience management that night!

In the two years he spent at Second City Toronto, from 1973 to 1975, Dan Aykroyd established himself as another formidable force onstage and off.

**Sheldon Patinkin**

I'd never met a Second City person before who loved guns and cops. So Danny was unique to me, and I was unique to him. It depended on the day and what was going on as to whether he was a real sweetheart or just as tough as nails. He could be either, sometimes in the same day. But he was good. He was really good onstage. He was smart, he was fast, and he was in the moment. His choice was to become a Royal Canadian Mounted Police-man or a Second City person. He was still thinking about it.

**Jayne Eastwood**

I've never seen anything like him. Just fast, firing stuff out, unbelievable characters. Really crazed out-of-the-box kind of comedy. He was just a force of nature.

**Joe Flaherty**

His mind was so highly attuned and so brilliant that he could slip in and out of characters. His reference level was absolutely amazing. You could throw him any character and he had the knowledge at that young age.

**Sheldon Patinkin**

At one point something had happened with Catherine O'Hara, whom he was deeply fond of. He threatened to come in with one of his guns and shoot Andrew Alexander and me.

**Andrew Alexander**

He called me up and said, "I'm coming over to kill you and Sheldon." I said, "I'm going out to lunch, but Sheldon's on the first floor rehearsing."

**Dan Aykroyd**

I don't get mad for my own self-aggrandizement, but if I see an injustice, I will get mad. And I've had a few basic, you know, explosions of temper based upon what I perceived were injustices being perpetrated. It must have been about money, because I wouldn't have had it out over a creative thing that passionately. But it must have been a material thing with Catherine. I don't remember, actually. But I remember being mad at Andrew once or twice. For sure.

**Joe Flaherty**

Danny would explode every once in a while, which was a little bit scary. But when you got to know him, that was Danny. I think he was protective of Catherine. I don't know why it was such a problem. Well, Catherine was very attractive. She was a doll. All the guys liked her.

## Andrea Martin

Catherine and I were diametrically opposed. Catherine would go to bed at five o' clock in the morning. That's when I'd be waking up. She had absolutely no training, and I had gone to college and majored in drama and gone off to summer stock. We were just completely opposite in our approach to comedy. And in our lifestyle, frankly. She'd be up all night playing music with her rock 'n' roll friends and I'd be in bed by ten o'clock, worrying about if I could remember my lines. And I think we were fantastic together.

## Dave Thomas

There's Lucille Ball and, like, half a dozen really funny women in the history of comedy. Maybe more than that. I'm lowballing it. But Catherine is one of those women. And when I met her, I was really rigid. Nothing would make me break up onstage. My attitude was, these people paid to come and see the show. Let's just do it straight for them. Let's make the comedy work. I sort of despised *The Carol Burnett Show,* with Harvey Korman and Carol Burnett and Tim Conway breaking up at each other's stuff. It was like, "Oh, come on. You're professionals. Get it together." Catherine made me break up onstage to a point where I was laughing so hard I was crying, and I actually had to leave the stage. Only two people in Second City did that to me: Marty Short and Catherine. We were doing this cop scene one night, where Catherine played this sleazy woman. She was playing this no-teeth character. Her hair was all messed up, and she had stuff stuffed in [her shirt] to make her tits look big and disgusting. And then Sheldon says, "You don't look disgusting enough." This [one] night, she put a belt between the material so she had four tits, and she didn't tell me she was going to do that. I was a cop, and I was supposed to face off with her and argue with her. I look down and see four tits, and I burst out laughing and couldn't stop and had to leave the stage. She was in complete control. She wasn't laughing. She was just looking at me like, "I got ya. I got ya. I got ya good."

## Joe Flaherty

I went backstage one time when I was directing one of the shows, and Catherine had taken off her blouse and was just in her bra, and I walked up behind her and just grabbed both of her boobs and squeezed them. And she was shocked and everybody in the cast was like, "What the hell?" And I said, "Catherine, I've always wanted to do that!" And I think she understood. She didn't get mad. Probably all the guys had the same thought. And it wasn't like I was molesting her. It was a nice squeeze. I wanted to squeeze 'em once. I must have had a couple drinks there, feeling my oats. I was feeling a few things. I just wanted to at some point and it didn't look like we were gonna get together. And I'm glad I did it. She doesn't hold it against me, either. She just went, "Oh, Joseph!"

## Andrew Alexander

The cast had a good working relationship. But most of them were fairly new to the work. Well, John had been doing it for a while in Chicago, and Joe, too. But even people that transitioned in hadn't had a ton of experience. Not like today, where people have years and years of experience. But they were all gifted and terrific performers.

If Alexander drew the cast's occasional ire in his new authority role, Patinkin was more apt to garner mockery or cold shoulders.

## Sheldon Patinkin

It was at a moment when everybody was pissed off about *Saturday Night Live* and they weren't in it. That's part of it. It was "How do I get to America?" It was at a time when it was getting harder and harder for a Canadian to work in America and for an American to work in Canada. And it was a time of not trusting me as a director, because I was fifteen years older than they were. I had a miserable time there. I really did. But I learned a lot—including never to be a director of Second City again. I received a lot of abuse, not all of it undeserved. Because I'm an American. Partly not trusting me because I was older. Partly not believing that I was funny, because I came from a different generation. Various people had various ideas about me.

## Dave Thomas

I can't honestly see how anyone could have liked that job. We were all such a bunch of know-it-alls that the job of directing us must have been terrible. The problem is, I think, that there was an identification system that validated all comments back then. And that is, you had to be funny to be recognized. We all recognized each other's comic sensibility, and there was a common ground that we shared, which was that we could all make each other laugh. And there was a deep mutual respect between us because of that. I mean, there were different comic sensibilities between us; we all had slightly different takes on comedy. But there was enough common comic ground that we all shared, which became the basis of our relationships. We were all from the same generation, exposed to the same television shows and worldview. And we shared common things that we all thought were ridiculous and absurd. So when someone came from the outside who was not from our generation or sensibility or funny in the way that we defined it, we just ignored them or discarded their input. So, where Sheldon could bring knowledge of scene construction, direction, or his experience, it was probably discarded because we didn't think he was funny in the way that we were. Too bad, really. I mean, too bad that it took me thirty years to figure that out.

### P. J. Torokvei, cast member

The cast I got hired into I always called the vipers. They fought a lot more than I was used to. And there was some teasing of Sheldon's personality. "Gimme a hug! C'mere! Gimme a hug!" He was a teacher, and he was knowledgeable, and he knew Paul Sills and all those people. He had Dave Thomas and Catherine O'Hara and Andrea Martin—that cast. And Dave could be very mean. He'd impersonate Sheldon onstage for an audience. Well, he would just make it a funny characteristic and only on the inside would you know it was Sheldon. He'd hold up two fingers like he was holding a cigarette, and then he'd do a take to the side and look at you very sincerely and say, "I know." That was the impersonation of Sheldon. "I know." No matter what you said. Because Sheldon always knew everything. But the thing is, Sheldon *did* know everything. But, really, you've got very badly behaved children in class who kind of have to be encouraged for their badness so they stay funny at night for money.

### Dave Thomas

Everyone in the cast was doing "I know!"

### Andrea Martin

Dave and I did a really funny scene. He was doing a Sheldon Patinkin kind of character, and I was playing his wife. He really nailed it.

### Joe Flaherty

It was called "We Love You," and the scene was this couple that came in to see this other couple and were like, "We love you, we love you," and kept hugging them. And it was based on Sheldon. But Dave went and told Sheldon that it was based on him! I went, "Aw, geez." I don't think Sheldon was too upset. The scene worked.

### Dave Thomas

We were Shelly, Don, Pat, and Ken. Those are the characters. So it couldn't be more obvious that we were doing a thing on Sheldon, but it was like, "Oh, God." I was just mean-spirited, and I shouldn't have done it. Keep in mind that I had tremendous affection for him, but at the same time there was some stuff he did that I thought was bullshit and worthy of parody. I impersonated Bernie. I impersonated Sheldon. I impersonated everybody that I disagreed with. In my sort of warped, egocentric way, I thought, "I have the right to parody this, because I and I alone know what's good and what isn't good."

### Sheldon Patinkin

I liked it. I thought it was funny. It was one of the best characters he ever did. I think Dave thought I was bothered by it, but I wasn't. But Dave thought I was bothered by anything and everything he did.

### Robin Duke, cast member

I loved Sheldon. He was a brilliant teacher. And his focus was on the acting, and the inner wants, and the goals. And he wouldn't let you be up there and lie for a minute. I didn't realize it at the time, just how good he was, but he would not let you get away with a single bit of falseness. He would just push you and push you. Very nurturing. His strength was in the acting, which is comedy for me. It's got to be felt. It's got to be real. It's got to be acted and true before it can be funny. The audience could read you. They can see you in the moment, and you can't fight that, how you're feeling onstage. You have to use it for a scene. And that's what Sheldon taught me, to recognize what I was feeling onstage.

### Andrea Martin

My need for structure was great, and so I really appreciated his approach to directing. It was very formulaic and very structured. Rehearsals began and ended at a certain time, but for most people in Second City, it was really their first time in the theater, so there wasn't that kind of need for discipline. In fact, they probably didn't want any kind of discipline put on them because they were depending on spontaneity and their own personalities to explode. But for me, I needed the structure to be creative.

Since Second City's Toronto branch was established during the reign of Del Close, the master himself jetted up now and then to lead improv workshops and direct shows. As in Chicago, he was a productive and destructive presence.

### Joe Flaherty

The Toronto Second City was much different than the Chicago Second City. Toronto was more comedy-oriented and not so much social issues or psychological character portraits or any of that stuff. They watched TV, they liked show business, they liked the show business tradition. They were show business people as opposed to satiric intellectual people. And then Del came in with these sort of pure forms of improv that they didn't see any value in. And Del would sort of probe, because you have to do that to bring

out yourself more. "We want to see more of you as opposed to this character that you've created." So they weren't comfortable with that at all. When
you go around to all of these people that worship Del, you find this little
pocket of people that just had no use for him at the time. And they didn't
have any tolerance for guys on drugs and stuff like that. It wasn't that sub-
culture. Del had all of these issues—drugs and self-destructive issues—
which they weren't used to. They were all pretty well-adjusted.

### Jayne Eastwood

I understood Del because I understand those kinds of demons. Del liked
the drink, and I could see Joe maybe get a little tight sometimes because
he had dealt with Del, but I think we were all pretty impressed with this
crazy man with the deep voice. He probably enjoyed having fresh new flesh
to devour.

### Robin Duke

I was always a little scared of Del. I could see how brilliant he was, and great,
but he was a character. He was eccentric. I just remember he had hired a big
man named Tiny to keep him from drinking. And one night Del came in to
work drunk, and we were all like, "Well, where's Tiny?" Del had given him
the night off.

### Dan Aykroyd

His influence really didn't come to bear until we came down to Chicago in
August of '74. That's when we really had the day-to-day contact with Del,
and we got to see how much fun it was, and how he basically removed all
fear. All fear of dying. All fear of being bad. All fear of overarching a character. He just basically took all the fear away. And he praised us for what was
good and slagged us for what was bad. And he could be autocratic, discipli-
narian, but also just so much fun. He used to frequently call classes off to go
watch *Star Trek* or go to the Old Town Ale House or say, "We're not gonna
work anymore today," or "Come over to my place." It's not only what he
taught us in terms of the technique that we were already learning from the
Spolin-Sills era, and the era of greats like Nichols and May. It's the frame of
reference this guy had—in music, in art, in science fiction, in technology,
in futurism. You could sit there and bring up any subject and he could give
you a discourse on it. So he was one of the greatest professors ever, because
he was a professor of everything.

### Eugene Levy

In the beginning, he was a very strong personality and very focused. And
then toward the end of my stay at Second City in Toronto, he would come
up every now and then and seemed a bit more scattered, a bit weirder.

**Dave Thomas**

Del's father committed suicide by drinking sulfuric acid. So Del wanted to do a workshop piece in the afternoon on the Second City stage where we would do the scene of him finding out that his father had committed suicide by drinking sulfuric acid. And I was to play the doctor, and Catherine was to play the nurse, and I just looked at him and I said, "You're not serious, are you?" He said, [*deep Del voice*] "Absolutely." I said, "Get the fuck out of here. I'm not doing that." And he said, [*Del voice*] "Theater's not a democracy." I remember him saying that. [*Del voice*] "Theater is not a democracy. You do what the director says." And I said, "I came here to do workshops in comedy, not to do some therapy shit for your fucked-up past. So I can't do it. Sorry. I can't." And he said, [*Del voice*] "Well, then, you're fired." And I said, "All right, goodbye." So I left, and then Andrew called me later that afternoon and he said, "You're coming in tonight, aren't you?" And I said, "Yeah." He said, "Well, good. I thought Del fired you." I said, "He did, but I knew that you have to fire me. And so unless you're firing me, I'm coming in." He said, "No, no, come in." So then that night it was sort of awkward with Del, and I felt really bad because I didn't want to usurp his authority. On the other hand, I didn't want to do bullshit psychotherapy instead of comedy. Because he could teach us comedy, too, if he could get past that other crap. So I went up to him and I said, "Can I give you a ride home tonight?" And he looked at me kind of funny and he said, "Sure." And I said, "All right. Maybe we can have a talk." So we did the show, and then after the show, I gave him a ride home, and he said, [*Del voice*] "You did exactly what I would have done, Dave. Don't ever take any shit from anybody. I have a lot of respect for you and I admire you." And I said, "Well, look, I have a lot of respect for you, too, but I just don't respect that other stuff." And he said, [*Del voice*] "No, no, you did the right thing." It was really weird. I think if I was the way I am now back then, I probably would have done a lot of things differently. But I was a young hothead, and I got mad at just anything. Everything was so important. Second City was my life, and the integrity of the sketches I was in was so important. I didn't have any other stuff to measure it by.

**Joe Flaherty**

Del had just got kicked out of a hotel where Andrew was putting him up because he put kitty litter in a toilet. He came into the theater one day and he was limping. I don't know if his hip was bothering him or something, but he had a glazed look in his eyes. I said, "Hi, Del, how you doing?" and he just walked by me and went backstage. I can't remember the exact sequence, but it was very quotable. He got pissed off at Andrew and went, "You something, you Judas, you cheeser!"

### Steven Kampmann, cast member

Del was challenging. I can remember coming backstage and he and Andrew were out wrestling in the snow, with Del in bare feet. Andrew became aware that he had a real situation because Del was clearly struggling [personally], and yet he had to open a show. And Bernie was aware that performers were saying, "What the hell's going on here?" Because we'd workshop some of Del's personal issues during the day—witches or the death of his father. And meanwhile, a show is meant to open in three weeks. And so I think Andrew tried to bring some kind of order to the situation because it was getting chaotic and it was getting scary and out of hand.

### Andrew Alexander

It was a little tense. Some were dealing with him better than others, because his behavior became pretty erratic to the point that culminated in that day he came down to the theater. I had told him I was taking him off the show. I was going to have to send him back to Chicago. So when I told him in the morning—I can't remember if I told him by phone or in person—he proceeded to block the toilet in his room with kitty litter. And then around ten o'clock, he walked what's probably at least a mile and a half or farther in his stocking feet in January or whenever it was. I know it was cold. And somehow he came in the back door, and I happened to be standing there talking to John Candy. That was when he yelled out, "You Judas, you cheeser!" And then John got in between because [Del] was taking a swipe at me. I wasn't reacting. John just got in the middle of it.

### Sheldon Patinkin

He wanted to kill Andrew. At that point, Andrew asked John Candy and me to take Del back to his apartment in the hotel, to pack him up and get him on the first plane the next morning back to Chicago, which we did—including dumping all the kitty litter that was in one of the drawers in a dresser.

### Andrew Alexander

Customs took one look at him and just waved him through. Didn't even look at his paperwork. And I think he went directly to Cook County [hospital]. It was either rehab or whatever they did back in those days. He used to call us from there with set ideas shortly after he left Toronto. I don't think anyone took it seriously.

### Sheldon Patinkin

Part of the enmity that Del felt for me was [because] I'm the one who picked him up and brought him back to the nuthouse every night. I'm the one who, with John, had to get him back on a plane to Chicago. I'm the one who had to handle him in ways he didn't like being handled.

Close continued his occasional Toronto turns as Second City's Canadian presence grew and more stars were born. Martin Short was already a local luminary when he finally decided to have a go at it on the Old Fire-hall stage in 1977. His Second City stint, which lasted less than two years, saw the birth of a tragically coiffed übergeek he'd soon make nationally famous.

### Martin Short, cast member

Ed Grimley came in that first show. There was a piece called "Sexist," and it was Robin Duke and myself applying for a job. Peter Aykroyd, Danny's brother, was in the company, and he was the employer. And the premise was she was wildly qualified, had MAs, and Ed Grimley was Ed Grimley. And I was kind of doing a little bit of this guy I knew in high school. I was doing a little bit of my brother-in-law. And he was kind of slow-witted. And then one night Peter said to me, "I would grease my hair a little bit to give it a little attitude—in front." And one night before the show, Peter Aykroyd said, "Jesus, Marty, that hair is getting taller every night." And so I put it right up in a point just to make him laugh. And the audience laughed. And I thought, "Well, isn't that what I'm trying to accomplish?" So suddenly it became this abstract painting walking around. I remember after I left Second City, I would just do it around the house with my wife. Like, come out of the shower naked. "Hello, Nancy!" And it would make her laugh.

### P. J. Torokvei

We had a [scene] called "Your Last Chance." It was a television game show to get immigration into Canada. So you'd have these horrible, horrible stereotypes—just awful. Like, one of the contestants was a guy from India who kisses me. I'm the host of the show. And I said, "What did you do that for?" And I think his line was, "I thought there was some food on your face." And it played. It would play for laughs. And then Robin Duke would basically play a retarded person. Huge, huge stereotypes. She worked in fast food. And there was a fecal count joke. Then Ed Grimley came out. I don't know if Marty had invented it someplace else. I had never seen it before. And the character was huge. Even then, even at the very beginning, he was huge, with the "I must say" and all that. And the pants pulled up, and the hair gelled up into a point. And Ed wins, of course. Ed's pretty retarded himself.

### Andrea Martin

I had known Marty, because we had done *Godspell* together. And then I married his wife's brother. So we were very close friends, and then we became family. And so I had seen Ed Grimley many times before I saw him on the Second City stage. I had seen him at parties. I'd seen him at Thanksgiving. That's a character that Marty kind of created in the attic of his home, when he was growing up and so excited about Christmas. I don't know if he called it Ed Grimley, but I certainly saw a version of it.

## P. J. Torokvei

Marty was Mr. Showbiz, same as he is to this day. He proudly carried that actor bag that you take to all the auditions. He was already known well enough in Toronto that there were always people coming up and telling him that they enjoyed his performance somewhere. And he was always laughing, always funny. I think Marty grasped the absurdity of the world better than the rest of us at that time. Maybe we've caught up with him a bit now. He lost his parents [and his oldest brother] when he was fairly young. He could have been a dark, crazy little Irishman, and instead he chose the light.

## Martin Short

I'm one of those few people that actually are laughing on the inside as well as the outside.

## P. J. Torokvei

One night we did an improv scene. I don't know what the suggestion was, or what was going on, but Marty played a guy with no arms. Steven Kampmann and I are two guys in a bar and Marty comes into this bar. And he played the character as such an obnoxious prick that Steven and I started beating him up, and the audience was cheering.

## Steven Kampmann

I don't remember if that got into a show, but we definitely did it in the set. The whole idea was, if someone was obnoxious enough, could we get an audience to laugh at someone who had no arms that we're beating the shit out of? He came in and just started giving people endless amounts of crap, and then we turned it on him. I mean we beat him into a pulp. And I think it got pretty good laughs. To Marty's credit, if you can get an audience to not like you and you have no arms, you're doing something pretty good.

## Sheldon Patinkin

We used to joke that audiences brought their own six-packs on Saturday night. The worst was when Andrew sold out the house to a condom factory. I don't think any of their employees had ever seen a live show before that wasn't a burlesque show of one kind or other. And they had dinner and drinks before the show—a lot of drinks. The fifty-minute first act took over an hour and a half to get through, with people yelling at each other in the audience, standing up on tables, throwing things at the cast to be funny. Everything was to be funny—to be funnier than the actors. The first act of the show closed with a piece called "PTA," where all but one of the actors was in the audience. This was a serious mistake, especially for the two women. I had never ever seen John Candy any angrier as when they threw a glass with a piece of ice in it at him. The cast stayed with it—as much as they could. They did really well. Finally we got through "PTA," and the lights went out, and I went backstage and said, "We are not doing a second act. I don't care whether the management approves or not."

### Andrew Alexander

I told them not to go out for the second act.

### Sheldon Patinkin

The audience didn't know the difference. They were just doing what they were doing. I swear to God, they tried to rape one of the girls, one of the actors, when they were in the house. They had to be fended off. Heavily drunk. I will never forget that night. Never. [The actors] all just tried to get through it. That was their goal—to get out of there.

### Andrew Alexander

We had a restaurant on one floor and the theater was on the first floor. And I really had no background in food, but at the time I thought I did. We had a ground-beef steak on the menu, so I suggested to the chef that we should put an oyster in the middle of it, which we did. It was called the Oyster Moister, and it was on the menu that night. After the audience had left the restaurant and come downstairs for the show, about twenty minutes into it, thirty or forty people got violently ill. In unison. One lady vomited on Dave Thomas's shoes and we had to pull the people out and call ambulances, which were situated right next door at the morgue, just two doors down. So you had this lineup of ambulances and people being shoved into them. The second dinner crowd was standing on the stairs of the Old Firehall, waiting to go upstairs, and seeing throngs of people with puke all over them. I guess red wine and not-great oysters is a lethal combination. Obviously, we took the Oyster Moister off the menu.

### Len Stuart, Second City co-owner

It was a lot of fun. All of us guys were single. In those days we had John Candy and Martin Short and Eugene Levy and Andrea Martin, and they were funny. When I went there, I was just rolling in the aisles. What wasn't good about that? Plus, I obviously knew all about Chicago. At that time, Bernie Sahlins already had some stars, so it was a great thing to get connected to. It wasn't too long before we were making money.

A couple of years earlier, Alexander and Stuart (together with a third partner named Scott Baker, now deceased) had already teamed for another entertainment venture, one that would eventually earn Emmy Awards and influence future kings of comedy. They called it *Second City Television*—later shortened to *SCTV.* Despite ongoing budget woes, production issues, scheduling snags, channel hopping, and the ever looming shadow of *Saturday Night Live,* it ultimately became one of the most revered comedy sketch shows in television history.

# 5

## SCTV: Count Floyd, Johnny LaRue, and a Couple of Hosers, Eh

John Candy
Joe Flaherty
Eugene Levy

Rick Moranis
Dave Thomas

1975–84

**A COUPLE OF YEARS AFTER** Second City Toronto was resurrected, American TV viewers were tuning in to a new NBC late-night sketch comedy program, initially called *Saturday Night.* Half its first-season cast was made up of Second City alums, including Dan Aykroyd, Gilda Radner, and John Belushi. In an effort to harness the talents of their skilled stage actors for a different kind of television venture, Andrew Alexander, Del Close, Bernard Sahlins (who'd already produced TV specials in England and Canada), Joe Flaherty, Sheldon Patinkin, and Harold Ramis joined forces to devise a version of their own. The result, which they called *Second City Television,* was set at a fictional and laughably lame news station in the fictional town of Melonville and began airing in 1976 on Canada's tiny Global Television Network. American syndication on NBC would come years later, along with a large and loyal cult following. The cavalcade of characters included John Candy's swaggering blowhard, Johnny LaRue ("I have more talent in this little finger than in this little finger."); Eugene Levy's moronic news anchor, Earl Camembert; Catherine O'Hara's Vegas vixen, Lola "I want to bear your children!" Heatherton; Andrea Martin's brassy and sassy station manager, Edith Prickley; Joe Flaherty's thoroughly un-scary Count Floyd; and a host of quirky others. In addition to such segments as "SCTV News" with Floyd and Earl (Flaherty and Levy), "Sunrise Semester," and "Farm Report," there were also inspired movie spoofs. A *Ben-Hur* parody starred John

Candy in the lead role as Curly of the Three Stooges. Sheldon Patinkin's loudly adorned legs made an appearance, too.

If the show flopped with viewers, Sahlins told the *Chicago Tribune* in late 1977 (shortly before *SCTV* began airing in the U.S.), "We can always lick our wounds and retreat to our club." More than once, they nearly did.

### Bernard Sahlins

Prior to *SCTV* I did a mock documentary in which Montreal had obtained an atom bomb. There were also some Second City appearances on a CBC magazine show called *This Hour Has Seven Days*. [*SCTV*] grew out of a brainstorming session in Canada where we talked about various kinds of programming. Who specifically came up with the idea, nobody can say. If they say it, they're lying.

### Andrew Alexander

It came more out of a defensive response to *SNL*. I wanted to hold on to my Toronto cast and was deeply concerned that the U.S. networks were going to come calling. Also, Bernie had been asking me to consider doing TV in Canada. He'd had some TV success in England and thought Canada would appreciate the Second City sensibility.

### Eugene Levy

I remember Bernie talking about the fact that *SNL* had scored big and the time is right for this type of comedy and half of *SNL* is Second City and we should actually try and come up with a show ourselves. And it just seemed like a great idea and kind of a natural progression. And it definitely seemed like now is the time, this kind of Second City comedy that had struck me so vividly when I first saw it onstage in 1973 can work on television. So the idea of trying to put something together seemed like a good idea.

### Joe Flaherty

I was directing a show in Toronto at the time. Bernie and Andrew called me in and said, "We have an offer to do a television show from Global TV." And they explained what it was. A half hour on the Global network. Whoopee! But it was television, and it was Bernie trying to compete in this really weird way with *Saturday Night Live*. I thought, "Oh, boy. Yeah, you're really gonna compete with that show." This half hour once-a-month show. So he said, "Are you interested in doing it?" And I said, "Yeah." And he said, "Okay, let's pick out a cast." And so we picked out a cast. I had some input—quite a bit, actually—about who we wanted to use. We picked Eugene Levy and Dave Thomas and Catherine O'Hara and Andrea Martin and John Candy. I wanted to have John on the show because I really liked his work, and as a performer, he was getting better and better. And then I said, "Do you think we can get Harold on the show?" And it just so happened that Harold wasn't doing anything at the time, and he said, "Okay. I'll do it." So we brought Harold in, and that was the first cast.

Then we had to figure out what type of show we were doing. Bernie Sahlins always wanted to do Second City on television. As is. You know, put the camera in the theater and shoot the sketches and present that. And we fought against that. I had had bad experiences with that before with some other projects with Bernie. It's television. You can't go on there with a bare stage and bentwood chairs. It's not gonna work. And I wanted to do television parodies, because I noticed when we did our stage show, any television references we made, the audience always picked up on them right away. And that cut across the board. The smart people and the really hip people— anybody. Everybody watches TV. So I pushed for that. And then Del said, "Why don't we make it a television station? An imaginary television station that puts on TV shows?" And everybody warmed up to that and we said, "Yeah, we kind of like that. Yeah!" So it's a television station that does TV shows, and then Sheldon said, "Why don't we do a programming day? You know, start with the morning—the 'Sunrise Semester' or whatever—and end with the 'Sermonette'?" And we said, "Okay, that sounds good. Let's do that." So that was it.

### Harold Ramis

We had already started on *Animal House* and we were between the treatment stage and the script stage, or maybe we had just submitted our first script. Me and Doug Kenney and Chris Miller. And Bernie said, "We're putting the show together." And so I went up there. No one was so grandiose as to think we were going to compete with *Saturday Night Live*. Because we looked at what they had. We were doing a pilot for a local Toronto production company, Global Television. That's why the *SCTV* concept emerged. We couldn't hope to be a splashy, slick network show. I forget whose idea it was. I think Del takes credit for it. "But why can't we be a really crummy local station?" And I think we all said, "Well, yeah, that would be quite a relief. Let's be really bad. We'll do a lot of bad television and be local personalities." So it wasn't going to be like *SNL* at all, and that was very liberating.

### Andrew Alexander

There were no expectations from an audience or a network or anything like that. There was none of that pressure. It was just another small opportunity.

### Joe Flaherty

All Andrew cared about was "Let's get the show together, let's do the show, and who's good enough for the show." Once we established a cast—he would defer to us a lot of times for new members of the show, although we only brought on a few—he just let us go creatively. He just felt that creatively we were much further along than he was as a producer, and he pretty much let us run the show and produce our little sketches, each one individually. I don't think he gets enough credit for keeping that show together. And that's another story altogether. But the first thing you do is you sign up and lock up your talent with a five-year contract. If you have that talent, they're committed to you. And he was never able to do that because of the way our show was sort of pieced together. We never had long-term contracts with him. So consequently, at the end of every fricking season, he'd have to renegotiate with everyone for the next season. It was very unconnected. There were a lot of seams in it. But Andrew kept it together. He kept it going. Sometimes he had to get extra backers to get some money, and then he'd have to get more backers. And sometimes he'd get too many backers and that would cause him problems, but he was crazy. Because we started off originally with just six shows for the Global Television Network in Toronto. And the Global Television Network was three or four stations in Ontario. And we had a show that was on a half hour, once a month. That was it.

### Andrew Alexander

I was too stupid to give it up. I didn't know. I was flying by the seat of my pants. I loved the show, so I just kept batting away at it.

### Harold Ramis

It was much like the *Lampoon Radio Hour* situation, where somebody gives you a studio and says, "Do whatever you want." And I realized it wasn't much fun while we were doing it, but over the years I came to appreciate the fact that we had no sponsors, no network, and no audience that we knew of. We were on different times in every city. So all we had to do was satisfy ourselves.

### Dave Thomas

When we were doing Second City for a while, after the first season of *SNL*, they were going to replace Chevy Chase. Lorne Michaels was going around, and he went to Chicago, and he came to Toronto. And we all auditioned for him. And Lorne wanted us to audition at Second City, onstage, and he would come to the improvs. Well, that meant Andrew had to agree to have Lorne come to Second City—his theater—and raid his *SCTV* cast for *SNL*. But because he knew how important this was to us, he let us do it. I'll never forget that.

### Andrew Alexander

Here I am trying to keep good relations with the cast, so I said "Okay." At the same time, I was thinking, "What the fuck am I doing? I'm asking a guy to come in, and he's going to maybe take three or four of them? Am I out of my mind?" And he came in, and he didn't take anybody. In fact, he didn't even go backstage to say thanks.

### Dave Thomas

Joe, John Candy, and I were auditioning. And after the audition we went into the Second City audience to Lorne's table—the audience had left—and stood there and talked to him for a few moments. Lorne wasn't exactly warm and so I left right away. Then I heard—from the other guys the next day—that Joe left almost immediately after me, and John stayed for a few more moments, waiting for Lorne to tell him how he did. And Lorne said to John, "Don't give up your day job." Then John left, totally crushed. I remember talking to him about that the next day. And John never really forgave Lorne for that for a long time—like a decade or something. I'm sure he meant it like the old audition joke, but John didn't take it that way.

### Eugene Levy

[*SCTV*] was just a really good job and then you'd go home. But the idea that anybody was watching this show other than Toronto was mind-boggling to us when it started being syndicated. I remember the first review that we got outside of Toronto, and we were kind of like, "Whoa! Whoa! You're kidding!" Even though we knew it was syndicated, we just didn't think anybody was watching. And then we'd start reading reviews from Dallas and wherever else. We at least knew that people were watching and actually were kind of getting the show. We never actually tried to appease an audience. That's one of the magical things about *SCTV*. We never tried to cater to an audience or figure out what does the audience want or who's the audience. We only wrote for ourselves, and that dictated what went into a show and what didn't go into a show, even though our producers would sometimes come in with a script and say, "Do you think anybody's gonna get this reference?" We'd say, "Why does it matter?"

### Harold Ramis

Bernie decided we needed a laugh track, which meant that there would be the worst canned laughter. After whatever you said, there was a huge guffaw from the audience. And the laugh track technician said, "It'll be subtle. I can mix it up pretty good." I remember this session where a line would be delivered, and Bernie would go, "Hit it." He just kept saying "Hit it" on every joke, so everything got the same laugh. And it was embarrassing and it was really ragged, but [the network] liked it and they wanted more. So we did one, and then they wanted six more, and then they wanted six more, and then they wanted thirteen more, and at that point I left.

### Joe Flaherty

Bernie didn't have Lorne Michaels's comedic sensibilities at all. Lorne Michaels did do comedy and he was on a comedy show, and comedy was his business. He performed and did everything. But Bernie didn't. Bernie had his own approach that was sort of intellectual. Well, too intellectual for the cast members. And Bernie loved the parodies we did, like *Moulin Rouge* and *Grapes of Wrath,* and those are the ones he got off on. The rest of the cast weren't quite that high on those kinds of things. So they were building up some resentment to Bernie and Sheldon, and I was sort of stuck in the middle, because I liked doing the show, and I liked working with the cast. I saw their problems, but I didn't think Bernie was interfering with us having a really good show. I thought we did some funny shows those first two seasons with Bernie on board. Mostly it was Harold's influence, too. But I thought we could live with Bernie, even though he meddled more than Andrew did. One person would say it's input, but the other cast members thought it was creative meddling.

On at least one occasion, Dave Thomas was in the latter camp.

### Dave Thomas

I had been on the floor when they were shooting one of Eugene's scenes, and I saw him cutting it together. I came in and I looked at it and I said, "No, no, there's a better take of that." And Bernie said, [*nasal Bernie voice*] "No, there isn't. This is the best take." And I said, "No, it isn't! I remember there's a better take." And I said, "Bernie, did you look at the takes?" He said, [*Bernie voice*] "Yeah, I looked at all of them." And then Roseanne Ironstone, who was the PA, said, "No, you didn't." And then I went berserk, because it was like, he lied to me. He's editing these things, and he's not even looking at all the takes? This is our lives. How dare he do that! And I started screaming at him, and he left. He got mad at me and he said, "I don't need to put up with this shit. I'm rich." That actually made me laugh, 'cause it was really a funny thing to say when somebody's yelling at you. But he left, and he forgot his coat. And I saw the coat there, and I knew he'd be coming back for it. So I picked it up, and when he came back in, I just threw it at him. He wanted to fire me after that. Harold later told me that he and Joe stuck up for me. He probably should have. I mean, when I think of how disrespectful and terrible what I did to him was, I'm shocked that I did it. And I'm shocked that I didn't get fired.

### Bernard Sahlins

Dave admitted in his book [*SCTV: Behind the Scenes*] that he acted like a bit of a shit.

### Joe Flaherty

I feel bad that Bernie was constantly confronted and disparaged over his creative abilities. It became painful to watch, because I really like him. I wanted things to work out with Bernie and the *SCTV* cast sans conflict, but that just never happened. After he left, it was pretty much the lunatics running the asylum. But it seemed that lunacy sometimes bred fascinating results. And bruised egos.

Sheldon Patinkin, a television greenhorn who stayed behind to edit when Sahlins left, was also the subject of scorn and criticism.

### Andrew Alexander

Sheldon was involved in the editing, and so he would go in and edit the pieces, and the cast would have disagreement on the end product. Eventually, they took over that role. So Sheldon was at a very important creative juncture in the process, and I think that's primarily where that conflict arose. And at the time, it was fairly significant, because they were just really upset by the end product—some more than others. Dave Thomas and Eugene probably had a harder time with it.

### Sheldon Patinkin

I was in charge of editing and mixing the first season of twenty-six half hour episodes twice, once for Canada and a few minutes shorter for American syndication. The actor/writers almost never came into the editing room to see what was happening before it was too late, largely because they were too busy writing and shooting, not because they weren't interested. They weren't always pleased with my choices, and one or two of them were occasionally quite angry with me because it was too late to do anything about it. Nobody's fault. It was a very difficult year and a half, as far as I was concerned. I called myself the Mel Cooley of the group, the Richard Deacon character on the old *Dick Van Dyke Show*. John never got competitive. Joe eventually was able to laugh things off. Harold was the calm that kept on making things okay again, but he wasn't around much the second thirteen episodes because of *Animal House*. The women, Andrea especially, didn't do much writing and needed more material than they got. We were all finding out who we were, not so much as an ensemble but as individuals. That, of course, made for a lot of problems.

## Eugene Levy

We were all doing a television show with no experience. Bernie was doing the editing, Sheldon was doing the postproduction. You'd have a scene where somebody punches somebody, and you'd hear like a cowbell sound when they're punching. *Ding-a-ling!* "What are you doing?" "Well, I thought it was funny." "No, no, we just need a good slap sound. That's all we need here." So it was people trying to do their best at something that they had no experience doing, and that's really how we got off the ground. It's shocking that there was a future to the show after the first season. But I think the material itself was funny in spite of the production. And I think that's what kind of initially caught on. The material was standing up, and it may have looked like we were actually having fun doing it.

We were always embarrassed about the production values. We started at a studio that had never really done anything like this before. They only did news programs and lunch-hour chat programs. And we were using their people—their makeup people and everything else. So we'd be doing a scene and we'd run into the makeup room saying, "I need a mustache, quick!" And the makeup guy would just go berserk, screaming, "We don't do instant choreography here!" So it was kind of tough. And we'd walk into a living room set to do a scene and see purple walls, and we'd say, "What? Why is this purple?" And the set designer says, "Well, I just thought it might add to the comedy." So there was a lot of stuff we had to work out in the very beginning. And we were literally working on a shoestring budget [around five thousand dollars per show]. We really had no money. But it's not something that added to the charm. It was always a bit of an embarrassment, because the lighting was bad, the directing wasn't good, the guy didn't know how to shoot comedy. So we actually had to start trying to correct the problem.

## Harold Ramis

At one point Bernie and Andrew decided we needed some guest celebrities. So Bernie said, "Sir John Gielgud and Sir Ralph Richardson are in town doing a Pinter play. And we got them for the show. Write some stuff for them." And we wrote a lot of funny stuff, we thought. They didn't like it. So we ended up performing the stuff we wrote for them. They did one long piece which was very dull and not funny at all. There's a famous picture of the whole cast with Gielgud and Richardson and I'm not in it. I didn't even want to be there. It was so embarrassing.

## Dave Thomas

We wrote some pieces for them and then took them down to see the two lords, backstage at a play that they were doing in Toronto. Andrew got them to agree to be on the show for $1,500 each. And then he mistakenly paid them twice, and they never gave him the money back. They were thieves as well as stuffy Englishmen. It was completely inappropriate to what we were doing. I had done a degree in English lit, and actually stayed on for the master's portion. I just didn't do the thesis. And so I said, "Well, let's do, 'Now here's Sir John Gielgud with the weather.' " [*Sir John:*] "Blow, winds, blow, blow . . ." You know, the King Lear speech. And at that point London Bridge had been disassembled and sold as a tourist attraction in the United States. So Harold came up with this idea that Stonehenge was disassembled, shipped to America, and made into condos in Arizona. Kind of a funny idea, I thought. Gielgud would be the pitchman. So we wrote a few things like that and took it to them to see what they thought. And it was like, "No, no, no, no, no. We want you to do a scene that takes place backstage of our play *No Man's Land,* and it should feature Sir John's hobby, which is crossword puzzles, and Sir Ralph's hobby, which is motorbike riding." And it was just like, "You're fucking kidding me." We go away with that assignment, and we went back to John Candy's place, or it was Sheldon's place—same house. 1063 Avenue Road. And we're all sitting there trying to write this stupid sketch, and we couldn't write it. And we ended up leaving, and Harold wrote it by himself. That's why Harold was pissed off, because he got stuck with it. It was a turd, and they were absolutely horrible in the scene. It was unwriteable by virtue of their directives, and it was badly performed. They both stink in it.

### Andrew Alexander

The cast was definitely influenced by Monty Python and *Saturday Night Live. SNL* had only been on for a year, but the seismic shift that it created had enormous impact on the comedy of the day. Since we were a postproduced show, and because of the way the show was syndicated, to do political satire didn't make much sense. Canada had a rich history of sketch comedy—most notably Wayne and Shuster, which I think had some subtle influence on the Canadians in the cast as well.

### Bernard Sahlins

I think [*SCTV*] was like Monty Python—a little too bright for the majority audience. Remember, you have to get ten or twelve million households in one night. And so you have to flatten out the work to appeal to twelve million households. And we never did.

### Len Stuart

The viewers we did have were really cult believers.

### Andrew Alexander

Bernie and I took the very first episode of *Second City TV* to ABC. We met with Bob Shanks, who was head of late-night TV at the time. He loved the show. He said he could almost guarantee that he would put our show on the network schedule. He just had to check in with the wunderkind Fred Silverman, who ran ABC. Bernie and I left the office euphoric. This was easy: you just did a show, took a meeting, and you were on the network— a very big deal in those days for a kid from Brampton. Two weeks go by, and we finally get a call from Bob Shanks. "Fred thinks the show is too intelligent."

It had another problem, too, though one that was more acute internally. Like Second City, *SCTV* was far from gender-equal.

### Andrea Martin

There were more men at *SCTV*, and I guess Catherine felt it more than I did. For me, if I had two or three good pieces, it was enough for me. So I was never one of those women in the boys' club.

### Paul Flaherty, writer

Andrea and Catherine wanted some women writers. And we got some women writers. But I think the writers that we got just weren't working out. It wasn't that we didn't want them to. Our tendency with Andrea was to always give her these outsize characters. She played one named Big Mama, who was this real tough Polynesian woman. We had her in a big fat suit, with this huge muumuu. And I think she was getting tired of that. She wanted somebody on there who was going to write her some stuff that came from the woman's viewpoint.

### Andrea Martin

I had favorites: Edith Prickley, Pirini, Libby Wolfson, Yolanda, Dutch, Mother Teresa. I enjoyed watching them grow and become more fully realized. I enjoyed creating situations for each of them that were unpredictable. I loved how they interacted with other characters on the show. And then eventually they became my extended family, those characters, and as the characters got a following, the inspiration to create new scenes increased. It was fabulous.

When Sahlins left the show after thirty episodes, he took the Second City moniker with him. Hence the inconvenient but necessary name switch to *SCTV* from *Second City Television*. And while Ramis agreed to keep a hand in the writing process, he was ensconced in Los Angeles and could no longer commute to Canada. So instead the cast went to him. Many of them bunked together during the summer of 1977 at a house Alexander rented in Bel Air. It was their first true taste of Hollywood—and they liked it. A lot.

### Harold Ramis

Twenty-six shows had been done, and Andrew said, "We're going to do twenty-six more. Would you come back?" And I said, "I can't do that. I'm working in L.A. now and this is my life." He said, "Well, what if I brought the cast to you?" I said, "Yeah, I'll do that." So I found a five-bedroom house on the fringes of Bel Air, and several people moved into the house. I think Candy lived in the big bedroom, the master suite, and Catherine O'Hara lived in the house. Eugene lived elsewhere. Dave Thomas might have lived in the house. But we had a pool table and we had a swimming pool. And every day I'd go over there and we'd sit around the big table and just hang out, swim, shoot pool. I think in seven weeks we wrote sixteen shows. It was very productive, because no one had anything else to do. It was fun. And I was still able to pursue the movies.

### Andrew Alexander

It was kind of a suburban tract house. They loved it. They were writing all day. And there were parties at night. I think they all had a great time. And then John [Candy] organized a Hollywood party. That was quite an event. It was back in the days when everybody was kind of starting out. Steven Spielberg was there, and Chevy Chase. John walked around the party for an hour and a half with Chevy in a headlock.

### Joe Flaherty

It became a star party. For us it was like, "Oh, boy, this is great!" We could see stars. That was the closest we got to the epicenter, was that party. And that was highly charged. Some of us drank a little bit too much that night and probably don't even remember a lot of it. But then we were back to that second season, which we had to do without Harold. It was a tough season, and it was our last one for a while.

At the end of season two in 1979, the struggling *SCTV* was kaput, vacating airwaves for lack of sponsors and funding.

### Joe Flaherty

All they knew was Andrew couldn't keep it on the air, and everybody was kind of ticked. I still remember that meeting—Andrew came in with Lenny [Stuart], one of the other backers, and they said, "We don't have enough money. We don't have enough stations." And he said, "Look, we'll even give you a piece of the show if you want. If you guys want to have a piece of the profits, to keep this going, you just have to accept a smaller salary than you made before." And everybody said, "No, no way! Nobody wants a piece of that show. Nope, that's it." And I wasn't real happy. I just didn't want to see that show go. In fact, I had just had a daughter and I thought, "Aw, geez! The one year my daughter's born, the show's off the air." And so we were gone. It was gone. It was finished for a whole year.

Alexander and Stuart, meanwhile, scrambled to revive the show—and eventually did just that. Following a one-year hiatus, *SCTV* was relocated to studios of the Canadian Broadcasting Corporation in far-flung Edmonton, Alberta. The crack cast, gathered with much cajoling and at greater cost, included Robin Duke, Joe Flaherty, Eugene Levy, Andrea Martin, Rick Moranis, Tony Rosato, and Dave Thomas.

### Joe Flaherty

And then, thank God, [surgeon and broadcasting entrepreneur] Dr. [Charles] Allard from Edmonton got in touch with Andrew, or one of his people. And they said, "If you shoot this show in Edmonton, we'll deficit finance it. We'll pick up the tab." And so Andrew had to go around to everybody and say, "We can do the show again, but we have to shoot it in Edmonton." And everybody went, "Aww, geez, are you kidding me? Couldn't be Vancouver? Couldn't be Montreal?" Nope. We had to go up to Edmonton. Gene signed on for a certain number of shows. Andrea said she'd do a certain number. We picked up Rick Moranis and a couple other people, and so we were able to survive that third season pretty well. And then when NBC came on board, it was another big negotiation thing. It was every year, and it drove me crazy.

### Andrew Alexander

It was really just getting from one season to the next season. And as the stakes got higher, the criticism got stronger. The cast really was getting very upset, because the show moved to Edmonton and there were relocation issues and they had trouble with that, which I understood. But that was the way it was. That was the only way to keep the show alive.

### Eugene Levy

People didn't want to move to Edmonton because it was Edmonton. You're spending a lot of time there, months and months at a time. And so you don't want to be stuck in kind of a hayseed town. [Edmonton] thought they were becoming a big city. There was a big oil boom, and tall buildings were going up in that town. But it was still kind of, "What do you do on a Friday night?" Get in the pickup and drive down the main drag. The reason the shows were that good in Edmonton is that we didn't do that much. On our off days we would get together and end up writing. We would just go to somebody's hotel room or somebody's apartment for a visit and you end up writing because there's no place to go, really. There were no distractions in Edmonton, so the work was very, very focused, and ultimately the best work we did on the series came during that time.

I was so blown away by the amazing production values they had in that studio. The direction was great and crisp, and the sets were amazing and the lighting was amazing and I just fell over. I said, "Wow, this looks fantastic." Night and day. Better than anything we had had even when we left Toronto.

### Paul Flaherty, writer

When we were up in Edmonton, you might as well be in the Sahara. But the polar opposite. It's the coldest place in the world. But we had nothing to do but work on that show. There was no place to go, and nothing else to do. We were up there working on these shows, with our blinders on. Tunnel vision. Because you had to have tunnel vision. The workload was so tremendous. And then somebody came in with a *Time* magazine one day, and [the critic] saw *SCTV,* and they said that they thought it was the best show on television—maybe the best show in the history of comedy. And I thought, "Wait a second." You had to shake your head for a second, because you were right in the middle of it, and then it just seems like nuts and bolts and "Is this any good at all?" And then you start reading this stuff. It was strangely disorienting, because I realized that I didn't have any objectivity about it. I didn't know that we were doing anything that people were considering that good. Certainly not in *Time* magazine. It was bolstering, and it helped us, and it made us work harder. But as soon as that stuff started, then the bars were raised on all of the material. Then we started realizing, "Whoa, we've got to live up to something."

### Joe Flaherty

We knew that we were never going to be as popular as *Saturday Night Live.* We knew that. And so, in essence, it didn't wear us out at all. We did our show. We got good critical acclaim. And even while we were doing it, people were saying we were more creative than *Saturday Night Live.* Funnier. What was really satisfying was I eventually got to meet a lot of the *Saturday Night Live* people, after that original cast. And they all respected *SCTV.* They were all saying, "Oh, I wish I could have done *SCTV!*" Everybody that worked on it. They said we set the standard. It was Phil Hartman, Dana Carvey, Mike Myers. Late eighties, early nineties.

### Andrea Martin

I can certainly tell you I was not thinking of how we were going to beat *SNL*. My involvement with Second City and *SCTV* was always about how do we create the work, how do we make each other laugh, how do we fill the ninety minutes, or how do we fill the hour? We were in Edmonton, Canada. We were writing and shooting seventeen hours a day. There was very little time to be thinking, "Hmm, what is the percentage of people that watched *Saturday Night Live?*"

### Joe Flaherty

[*Saturday Night Live*] did come on first. They did pave the way, and they were people that I'd worked with. So I didn't resent them at all for it, their success. And I just knew that we were working at such a disadvantage. I mean, we were shooting out of Toronto at first, and then we were in Edmonton. Not exactly Rockefeller Center, you know? I resented the fact that the media just seemed to really adore them. They got a lot of good media, and we got very little. But that always sort of spurred us, the underdogs.

### Paul Flaherty

I remember when Belushi came and did a little guest [appearance] on the show, telling us how much he loved *SCTV,* that he thought it was so much better than *Saturday Night Live.* He liked it better. I think he said he thought the writing was better. He liked the fact that it was basically a postproduced show instead of a live one, because we could do so much more. That was also the drawback of the show. At one point, there was discussion of taking the entire *SCTV* cast and putting them on *Saturday Night Live.* But you know what? It would not have been as good. Because one of the strengths of this show was the postproduction element of it. The fact that we could craft all of those scenes from beginning to end, and there wasn't that haphazard handicap that the *Saturday Night Live* people had to live with, and that's doing it live. If something's not working, you can't pull back and do take two. So you could do more ambitious things. You could do subtler things. And because of that, I think we were able to do a lot more higher-quality stuff.

### Eugene Levy

It's a different animal. I don't know whether we could have done an *SNL*. I don't know whether we could have done a ninety-minute live show every week just by the nature of what that is. You're talking about bringing tension into the building because the pressures are absolutely amazing, and I think that's where the every-man-for-himself thing kind of comes in. Everybody's trying to save their own ass and get their pieces in, and there's no time. All I know is this was a much better way to work for us, where you do all of your writing and then you get to take the piece and you get to supervise the postproduction and you get your pieces the way you envisioned them and you've got the time to do it. So it's a much easier way to work. Ultimately you're putting in a lot more hours than doing a weekly live show. You've just got more time to hone.

### Paul Flaherty

We did what we thought was funny, what we thought was interesting. And oftentimes, that might involve a reference level that just doesn't go over well with the public. Because it certainly wasn't because it wasn't funny. Within the industry, it had a great reputation. There was one year where we got all five nominations for the Emmys in the category. And it took us a few minutes to realize, "Wait a second, we've won the Emmy!"

I remember coming back to Toronto when I got my first Emmy, and I had no place to put it. I was carrying it on the plane. So I was returning my tux—my rented tux—and I walked in and I was still carrying the Emmy. And the guy behind the counter said, "Aw, geez, where'd you get that?" I said, "Well, I just won this." "Oh, you won an Emmy? What'd you win it for?" And I said, "*SCTV.*" "Oh, yeah, yeah, *SCTV.* I've seen that. But it's a little silly, isn't it?" I said, "What?" "It's kind of silly, I think." "Um, at times, maybe . . ." So you had to deal with that. You could say the same thing about Monty Python. I always thought that our stuff was smart silly. We tried to be silly with a reason, and always put it in a context, so that the silliness was part of something smarter.

### Mert Rich, writer

One of my favorite movies of all time was *Raging Bull.* I think this was the first piece I wrote. It was Jake La Motta doing a commercial for Jake La Motta's Raging Bull-B-Que. But it was a movie. Rick Moranis was Joe Pesci and we did the whole thing. And I remember somebody saying that Marty Scorsese saw it and loved it. Cut to ten years later. I picked up a writing partner for a while and we had a development deal and we were courting Gregory Hines. He was doing *Jelly's Last Jam* in New York. So Warner Brothers flew us out to New York and we were supposed to meet with him after the show. We bought him a hugely expensive cigar. He blew us off and we're walking back to our hotel and who do I see? Marty Scorsese, talking to some people. And I just went, "Excuse me, Mr. Scorsese, my name's Mert Rich. I'm on *SCTV,* and I wrote—" And he finished it, "Raging Bull-B-Que. I loved that. What are you doing here?" I was so stunned. I was standing on a street in New York talking to Marty Scorsese. I didn't have the presence of mind to say, "We're headed back to our hotel. Would you come have a drink?" And off he went.

One of *SCTV*'s breakout stars, John Candy was fast becoming a Hollywood player. Though he was famously gregarious and generous to a fault, his skin could be thin and his grudges were held hard.

### Sheldon Patinkin

John was too easily taken advantage of. He trusted everybody. And he got hurt a lot—I won't go into by whom—by agreeing to do things, and not getting the kind of recompense that was promised. Loaning money and never getting it back. He would do favors for people and not get favors back in turn. He would be nice to people who would be shitty to him. Not all the time, but it was clearly easy to take advantage of him, and therefore a lot of friends just didn't. They respected that. He got angry too many times, and then it got better.

### Harold Ramis

He had a little temper sometimes, but Flaherty was always very protective of John's comfort, and maybe we all were. Make sure John had a comfortable seat. Give John the big chair. Belushi seemed indestructible. He'd walk through a wall. But Candy always had kind of a fragile quality, and you could see in characters John played there was a timid weakling inside that he could reach for comedically. So there was something very vulnerable about him that came through in a lot of his characters. And he could be hurt. John was sensitive. He always joked about his own weight in the material, but he could be hurt if someone actually insulted him.

### Joe Flaherty

I know everybody had an issue with Andrew. John did for the longest time. He had really strong issues. It turned out that at one point Andrew was paying him less than the rest of us because they didn't feel John was writing enough. [Andrew] wasn't around for our writing sessions. He was relying on the word of someone, a cast member. When John found out that he was getting a little bit less, he just freaked out. He freaked out. And this was early on, before he had any kind of a name or anything like that. And he just didn't think it was fair, and it was true. You can't go on favored nations [pay] and then have one guy not making as much. I just know he was furious, and Andrew quickly fixed that. But John never forgave him for that. From that point on, he was John's punching boy. Anything that went wrong with his life or the show was Andrew's fault. And with John, I think it was another thing, too—he had a hard time confronting individuals. If he was having a problem with the cast, he didn't want to get angry at any of the cast members, so he would just take that anger and foist it on Andrew. That went on for years and years, after the show was over. When John became quite popular as a movie actor, he was always saying bad things about

Andrew. And then finally, thank goodness, just a few years before he died, those two got together again, and John relented on his anger. And they sort of became business partners. So that was good. I always like those happy endings. I didn't feel comfortable with that kind of antipathy going on. It was all from John. Andrew was always saying, "What's wrong? What did I do? What did I do?"

### Rose Candy

I remember when their *SCTV* contracts were being renegotiated and it was believed that everyone was getting equal pay. John found out differently. It wasn't good. It threw suspicion into everything from then on. It was difficult for John to shake that. He was upset—so upset that it was many years before he would talk to Andrew.

### Andrew Alexander

John was a very generous guy. But he had a dark side, too, which I was the brunt of a lot. He'd get angry and felt that he wasn't being treated properly, and he had a really good memory for that. You treated him badly and he remembered it for ten years. And there were early issues. In the very beginning, John hadn't been contracted as a writer. Just as a performer. That was a big bone of contention. And then John went into the filing cabinet somehow and found the contract and saw that he wasn't [on the payroll] like Joe and Eugene and Dave were, as writers. Well, I paid dearly for that for many years. Eventually it changed, but John really felt slighted by that. Once we started renegotiating contracts down the line, he had management and agencies, so he was able to express his displeasure.

While Edith Prickley and Bobby Bittman, Count Floyd and Johnny LaRue, and Earl Camembert and Lola Heatherton were certainly beloved among *SCTV*'s characters, their popularity paled in comparison with that of two beer-swilling hosers named Bob and Doug "Take off, eh?" McKenzie. Played by Dave Thomas and Rick Moranis, the decidedly undynamic duo became a smash sensation north and south of the border, with a parade in their honor down Toronto's busy Yonge Street, and even a feature film called *Strange Brew.* Their sudden superstardom brought more attention to the show, but caused a certain degree of discord within the cast.

### Paul Flaherty

When that took off and people started identifying *SCTV* as the "Bob and Doug Show," it was like, "Wait, whoa, whoa, wait a second. That's only one small tiny part of this show." That caused some friction. It was hard when they had their own single out there that was doing well, and they were causing a ripple. I mean, it would be insane not to take advantage of that.

## Dave Thomas

We went to a record signing in New York City at Rockefeller Center. Ben Stiller was there, as a little kid, with his mom, Anne Meara. And he remembers that to this day, getting lined up in the cold to get our autograph for his album. And to have that many fans in New York City. We were in Chicago, we were in L.A.—we were all over the place. Just lines and lines and lines of people. I think Canada embraced it more because they really felt ownership of it, but oh, God, it was unbelievable. It actually made me uncomfortable. The fans of *SCTV* were sort of smarter. They were kind of intellectual. And the fans of Bob and Doug crossed over into heavy metal, so instead of people coming up to you and going, "I love your work. That Bob Hope impersonation is dead-on," the people who were fans of Bob and Doug would just go, "Hey! Uuuuuuuuuuuuuh! Uuuuuuuuuuuuh!" and raise their fists in the air or give you the horns, and it was like, "Oh, no! What have I done?" Rick and I were at morning radio show events in L.A. and on Long Island, and there were, like, five hundred or six hundred kids there, in this little place, drunk. And all they wanted us to do was chug beer. They didn't care what we said; they just wanted us to chug beer. It was an ordeal just getting through it. So it's strange. The thing you do that becomes the most popular is not necessarily the thing that you love the most. I liked doing those characters with Rick, but the context that we did them in was like happy hour. The rest of the cast would go away. They would leave for the day, and then the two of us would stay behind, with the floor director and a cameraman and the switcher, and we would do ten, fifteen, twenty Bob and Dougs—however many we could do. And we never prepared. We improvised them all. So they would just give us a count-in, and they all had to be exactly two minutes long, because there was a programming length difference between Canada and the United States. We created a monster, and the context of it was when we did Bob and Doug, we enjoyed it, and it was fun, because it was just the two of us, having a beer, cooking some back bacon and just making up shit and improvising, in a really pure sense. And then when it became sort of property of the public, it became a different thing, and it was perceived differently, and they had different expectations.

There was a point where I think Joe Flaherty and John Candy thought somehow I was using my head writer status to engineer Bob and Doug's success. I think now Joe's aware that that wasn't the way it was, but back in the emotion of the moment, it was not like that. And I think it's absolutely impossible to be totally objective when you have the media calling the shots. I remember there was a thing on the cover of *Rolling Stone:* "*SCTV*'s Best Joke: Bob and Doug McKenzie." It wasn't *SCTV*'s best joke, but it was written up that way by a really important magazine, so, Christ. The fallout from it with the rest of the cast was something that I didn't enjoy. And I felt that it was unfair, and it was really hard to get a perspective on it back then. Because on one hand you're really excited about doing well, and getting notoriety. On the other hand, you're feeling awkward about it because you know that it's like a kick in the teeth to some of your friends.

### Joe Flaherty

We all felt Bob and Doug were achieving fame, and we were genuinely puzzled—and bugged—by that. But I can honestly say that none of us felt that Dave and Rick wanted to turn *SCTV* into the Bob and Doug Show. In fact, they seemed to be a bit embarrassed by their sudden success. Our fears, the rest of the cast, were that Andrew or NBC would want to make it the Bob and Doug Show. I didn't have a problem with Dave being head writer; he did a really good job at it. But, there were certain issues about one of us wielding power that made the cast—not Rick—uncomfortable. Our egalitarian philosophy was always being stretched to the limit.

### Andrew Alexander

NBC originally had given me grief over the Bob and Doug segments, but we continued to put them in the show. They became huge; they were *SCTV*'s Blues Brothers. Around this time I was getting flooded with book and movie requests. I had one meeting with two really nice Canadian chaps that wanted *SCTV* to endorse a board game and in return get some shares in the company. I knew nothing about board games, so I passed. The next year Trivial Pursuit went on to become one of the biggest board games in the world.

### Andrea Martin

I remember thinking that the [Bob and Doug] characters were from a world I knew nothing about. I was appreciative of the fact that two or three minutes of our show each week was easily improvised by Rick and Dave, and that the characters had a following. I did not begrudge their success, nor did I feel competitive. I thought of Bob and Doug in their own universe. I felt there was definitely a place for all our world and comedy views, and consequently the material in our show was very diverse.

### Andrew Alexander

Len and I were negotiating with NBC, and Rick and Dave were at the height of their popularity. They had met with Joel Silver, a very famous action-adventure producer, and they had somehow convinced him that we were ready to give up the show and that we would sell it to him for almost nothing or very cheaply. All we had to do was have a meeting with him. So he called up me and Len, and we went over to meet with him. And if you've ever seen caricatures of Joel Silver, he's this bombastic, flamboyant producer. And he was saying, "I talked to Dave and Rick. I'm ready to take the show over." And we were kind of looking somewhat dumbfounded at what he was talking about. It was a very odd conversation. He was waving his arms and saying, "I'm gonna take over this show." We said, "Well, that's not going to happen." We left, and I guess he called Dave and Rick up and just reamed them out.

## Dave Thomas

Joel was working for Larry Gordon when we first met him, and they had an office at Paramount. And Larry Gordon was one of these old-time showbiz guys. He came out of AIP, American International Pictures. Larry described Joel as a mongoose in a power dive, and they wanted deals so bad that he would just fly in at full fury. And Joel liked *SCTV,* and Joel wanted to produce *SCTV,* and he wanted Rick and I to help him take it away from Andrew and Len. Well, we didn't have the power to do that. We didn't own *SCTV.* We couldn't take it away from Andrew and Len. I forget the details of all the stuff that went on. All I know is, the worst thing that could have happened for us would have been for Joel to produce the show, because Joel would have destroyed it. Andrew's very smart. And he really gave us a lot of latitude and allowed us to do what we did. And I respect him tremendously for that. Not too many producers would do that. And he put himself in financial jeopardy to keep the thing going. I would do anything for Andrew. I've told him, "All you have to do is tell me where, when, and what to wear."

Although it shifted stations, time slots, and formats—going from a half hour on ITV and CBC in Canada to ninety minutes on NBC (mostly following *Saturday Night Live* at 1 A.M. EST) and ultimately Cinemax—in the United States, *SCTV* garnered millions of fans and plenty of lofty plaudits during its bumpy six-season run. Among the show's most rabid devotees were professional (and soon-to-be professional) funny folks, many of whom consider the series a major milestone in television comedy and a profound influence on their careers. *Tonight Show* host Conan O'Brien is one of them.

## Conan O'Brien

My family used to stay near the state beach in southern Rhode Island, at my grandfather's house. This was sometime in the mid- to late seventies. I went to bed, and in the morning my brother said, "You should have stayed up." They were getting some very fuzzy reception off an antenna that my brother Neal had jerry-rigged. It wasn't a great picture, but they had watched some show, and all they could tell me is it was really funny and different and that it had an Indian-head logo. My brothers saw that, and so they got me to watch it the next time it was on, and you could tell right away that this was a show that wasn't trying to appeal to everybody. It was a show that [said], "You have to pay attention, and you have to come to us." And that's what appealed to me right away. I did, in moments, feel like, "This show is for me. They're making this for me. Whoever these guys are, they are communicating directly with me, and talking to me." And that really resonated. They were smaller. It wasn't really broad. It wasn't a lot of drug humor. It wasn't a lot of the stuff that a lot of people in the culture were trying—to capitalize on the success of *Saturday Night Live,* and do it badly. This seemed like a very different specific sensibility, and I liked that not everybody knew about it. Now, in the era that we live in, there's 650 niche television shows, and everybody can have their own little favorite that they watch on their iPhone. This was like a precursor to that kind of show. This was existing in the days of network television, and there just wasn't anything on like it. I could never understand, "Why isn't everybody talking about this show?"

There's that saying that God is in the details, and I always thought that that really describes the comedy of *SCTV.* They would put these little jokes in there that were so specific, and so small, and you just had to be paying attention. And I've cited this before, but in their "Towering Inferno" parody, at one point John Candy's talking to a group of people, and he's saying, "You do this, you do that. Prickley, you go here, and Prickley's double, you come with me." Because they had had to double up. They just had someone dressed like Edith Prickley with her back turned to the camera. It was said very quickly, and I thought, "There was no attempt to sell me that joke." It's just there. It's this tiny little gem. And here it is, thirty years later, and I'm still talking about it. And I still think about it.

Do you remember? John Candy. He's this cowardly cavalry officer. And then Catherine O'Hara and this little girl say, "Who is that, Mommy?" "That's Yellowbelly." And then they start to walk away, and he turns and shoots them in the back. That was just—he shot a little girl, and that's it. It was an electric moment for me. And their newscasts. Earl Camembert. I mean, the quiet awkwardness that Eugene Levy and Joe Flaherty would play. People who are just uncomfortable with each other. And now it's everywhere. Now it's everywhere, and it's mass marketed, and you can't watch a movie these days without seeing that, or watch a television show without seeing it. But I really thought that was one of the first places that I saw people take their time and really stretch out that kind of awkward energy of guys who aren't in sync. It's not going well. They're quietly muttering to each other, "What . . . What are you . . . What are you talking about?" And I was blown away by that.

Later on, I remember, there was some effort to bring [*SCTV*] to American television in prime time—I would have been starting college or something—and there was some part of me that maybe thought, "Yeah, I don't think this can happen." I remember feeling skeptical about that, like, "This is too good for our country." And maybe that's a snobby thing to say. Maybe I was being proprietary, like, "This show is for me. Not for everybody." I may have helped destroy it.

I think it was just one of those shows that you had to come to, you had to find. It's a dense show. It's a show that probably required you to sit down and pay attention. And it wasn't a show riddled with catchphrases, the McKenzie brothers aside. It wasn't a show that was trying to grab you and put its arms around you. And to me that was a lot of the appeal, that it had this incredible comedic integrity and you had to pay attention, and that doesn't always fly in a big country like America. It's why I've started giving away cars like Oprah. Actually, we give one car and everyone has to share it. It's an old Skylark.

People increasingly want comedy to mean something, and they want it to be relevant to what's happening in the world, and I've always believed the opposite, which is it should be irrelevant. It shouldn't mean anything. You shouldn't look for meaning in comedy. That's my religious conviction, and I'm orthodox about that. And I love that *SCTV* was just relentlessly silly, and it was not lecturing to me in any way. I didn't feel like I was instructed on a point of view. I didn't think that the show existed to topple the powerful, or enlighten me. And so much of it is beside the point. Like, there's no reason for any of it, which is what I love. And you could tell that these were craftsmen, that these were people who put a ton of effort into it. And I know things are supposed to always appear effortless, but you could tell with that show that some really smart, talented people have really polished this. These people are making a Swiss watch. And you wouldn't see any of the cast of *SCTV* hang out at Studio 54. They probably wouldn't get in. They wouldn't have unclipped the velvet rope for Joe Flaherty. And I thought that was really, somehow, part of its appeal.

I got to spend a day with John Candy. I was such an *SCTV* fan that when I was in college, I made sure the [Harvard] *Lampoon* invited him to come get an award. We made up some award—Man of the Year or something. Bought a bowling trophy and put his name on it. But I went and picked him up at Logan airport. And what I remember most is, I had been told by his agent, or whoever, "Now, listen, he's on the Pritikin diet, and here's specifically what he needs to eat." You know, "Make sure he has boiled fish and no oil and no carbs." It was this long list. And I diligently took it all down, and I prepared everything at the Lampoon Castle so we would have exactly what he needed. And I picked him up at the airport, and the first thing we did when we got to Cambridge is got out of the car, and he said, "Come here, kid. Let's walk around." And he was exactly who I wanted him to be. He was Johnny LaRue, and he took me right into this pastry store and started buying éclairs and putting them in a box. And then his eye caught my eye, 'cause I was just staring at him, and he said, "Don't worry, kid. They're Pritikin éclairs," and, like, gave me that John Candy laugh, and nudged me in the ribs. And then the rest of the day he was just larger-than-life—he was Falstaff. It was just one of the great days of my life, hanging out with him. He was everybody I wanted him to be, and I still think about this when I meet young people who seem happy to meet me. I never want to let them down. I want them to walk away feeling as happy as I was when I met John Candy.

So many things are a product of their time, and you see that in music all the time. A group isn't just a bunch of guys singing and playing. [They're] also part of that time they came out of. And that was so much of what was exciting to me about *SCTV,* is you weren't seeing people do comedy like that anywhere else. If there was a show like that now, there's a million outlets for it. And I think one of the things that is so hard for sketch comedy these days is there's so much product out there. It's hard to get people's attention. And *SCTV* was literally coming out of left field. It was coming out of Canada, and it was coming out at a time when there was a lot of sameness on television. With the exception of *Saturday Night Live,* a lot of it was *Donny & Marie* and this same old song and dance bullshit. And then this show came out of nowhere. It's hard to describe to young people today how unusual—and how revolutionary—that show was. Because today all we have is revolutionary comedy. It's everywhere. All I ever hear is "edgy." And you can download the entire season onto your iPhone. I'm always being told, "Have you seen . . . ?" I can't keep up with it all. It's diluted. It's spiraling all around you. What was so compelling about *SCTV,* which you can't create anymore, is that these guys invented something that was perfect out of whole cloth. These men and women invented this thing that literally came from the north and came to us complete. It made me believe that God is in the details, that it's the *Field of Dreams* idea. "If you build it, they will come." They created this show that had no reason to exist, and nobody was particularly looking for it, and it arrived. I know it had a profound effect on me, and I'm sure a lot of people in my generation. It would be hard to do that again.

# 6

## Saturday Night Live, the Brothers Belushi, and a Mom Away from Mom

Jim Belushi
Tim Kazurinsky
Shelley Long
George Wendt

WHILE SECOND CITY REMAINED a tight-knit, albeit dysfunctional, family, its internal dynamic slowly began to shift as external forces exerted more pull. Chief among them early on, of course, was *Saturday Night Live,* which premiered in October 1975. Bill Murray joined the second season, and others followed from Toronto and Chicago. As with *SCTV* in Canada, Second City Chicago actors now began to see what thrilling possibilities lay outside their Wells Street crucible. While *SNL*'s popularity exploded over the next couple of years, audiences, too, started to view Second City as more than just a local comedy theater. It was a bona fide funny farm—one where poachers stalked easy prey. As Bernard Sahlins has put it, "The best of times, the worst of times."

### Eric Boardman

We weren't selling out every night. You could walk in. Maybe Saturday nights it would be tough to get a ticket. But it was just a Chicago theater for Chicago folks. If there was a birthday, on Sunday night they brought in pizza and Joyce would walk around and we'd hug and kiss everybody. It was very, very ma-and-pa. We spent Thanksgiving dinners together. The whole family would gather for dinner at the theater because we were all going to work that night. So Joyce would bring in her baked zucchini. And we knew all of Joyce's cousins, because the cousins and aunts came through.

### Bernard Sahlins

It is true that business got better. In the seventies it really started to take off. That happened seriously when *Saturday Night Live* took off. We were struggling for fifteen years and then we were okay. Up to then, we could keep our ambitions off to the margins and pay closer attention to the work. Once *Saturday Night Live* started, the work became a stepping-stone for something else. Not totally, but a little bit. Attitudes changed, and I realized this when I passed by a member of the touring company on the telephone and she said, "It's my agent."

### Sheldon Patinkin

But it was at least a year before it became clear that most of those people [on *SNL*] came from Second City. It was part of the publicity. It was also part of the publicity of *Animal House,* which was co-written by Harold Ramis and had John Belushi in it. And although *SCTV* was a connoisseur's show, and only in syndication, it produced an awareness of people like John Candy and Marty Short. And business has basically been quite good since 1980. Sooner, really, when people started coming to see the next John Belushi and Bill Murray and Gilda Radner.

### Will Aldis, cast member

Chicago at that point was going through a huge star thing. John [Belushi]'s from there, and there's Bill Murray, and they're on *Saturday Night Live,* and they're Second City, and we own 'em! And if you weren't a star, sometimes you'd feel a little invisible.

### Mary Gross, cast member

There was a point where John Belushi had requested that I come out to New York to audition for a movie called *Neighbors.* He wanted me to audition for the part of his wife. I was working at Second City at the time, and I went to Bernie and said, "Bernie, can I have a day or two off to fly to New York to audition for this movie and then I'll come right back?" And he didn't just say "No." He said, "No. No! No! No! No!" And I said, "What is the problem?" I was very upset at his reaction. And I realized later that here he was nurturing us, and then we'd be taken away just when he'd get a good show together. So he was fearful that I would get this movie and then I'd be gone and then I'd go off and do other movies. I forget how I did this, but I flew to New York, auditioned, and flew back within a day so I could do a show at Second City. I don't remember if I told him. I don't think I did it in a sneaky way, because I was raised Catholic. But I don't think at that point I felt I needed his permission. I just knew that I had to be back in time for the show.

### Joyce Sloane

Lorne Michaels was coming. Bernie said, "Don't let him in." I said, "How can I not let him in?" He didn't want to lose anybody.

### Bernard Sahlins

I wasn't worried about their poaching. I was worried about the people who stayed. Every actor dreams of making it, but up to then our actors were able to subdue that in favor of what they were doing. But once *SNL* started raiding, everybody had a little different orientation toward the work. And that's what I had to fight. I was worried about the psychological effects on the remaining actors. They suddenly had their career at the forefront of their minds.

### Mert Rich

*Saturday Night Live* went on and it was like, "I'm gonna be a star." It hit the air and it was funny and it was pretty big almost right away. And they started making a big deal about Danny and John and Gilda and Second City. It kind of crept in your head, "Hey, there might be a life after this."

### Tim Kazurinsky, cast member

George Wendt had been selling insurance for his father's company, Mary Gross had worked for the American Dental Association, Danny Breen was selling tickets at a racetrack, Bruce Jarchow was a city planner, and I was an ad man. We didn't have eight by tens when we walked in the door. It wasn't our goal to be on a sitcom. That came later. Now kids come in with that clear intent.

### Shelley Long, cast member

It's not like we were really performing for producers. We were performing for Chicago. We were still really very committed to doing things that our audience in Chicago would connect with. We were more fascinated by *Saturday Night Live*. Actually, sometimes we were frustrated by it. Because we'd do a scene, and then somebody would see the scene on *Saturday Night Live,* and it was like "Oh, man! They're stealing our scenes!" But they weren't, I don't think. I think we figured out fairly quickly that those scenes were kind of hanging in the air, and that we both were pulling from the same source. I didn't know any of the people on the show, but there were other people that knew them, or knew of them. But when you're at Second City, at least in my experience, you don't have time to really think about the future or the past. It's all you can do to keep up with what's going on, because it demands so much of you in the performance, especially if you're rehearsing a show during the day and performing at night. It really is some of the most demanding work I've ever done.

### Bernadette Birkett, cast member and wife of George Wendt

I got hired in December of '75, and Second City was getting hot. And people were coming by. Like, John Belushi would drop by occasionally, and Chevy Chase. And so it was getting noticed, and people like Bernie Brillstein and the management behind John were sort of scouting Chicago a little for the next person. I got hired out of Chicago in '79, because people were taking Chicago seriously as a place to find new comic talent.

### Lance Kinsey, cast member

You would know when someone was in the audience. There would be a buzz going around. And it would either be Lorne Michaels or Brandon Tartikoff or somebody, and the energy of the show would change because there was the opportunity that night for something. I remember we used to watch *Saturday Night Live* in the greenroom on Saturday night between shows. They were doing what we did and they were our heroes. There was John and Danny up there, and all those guys had been at Second City. It was really an opportunity to see what could happen, what this improvisation animal could do. It was just a very exciting and electric time.

Despite the increasingly real possibility of getting plucked from obscurity, actors at Second City had little time to fixate on hypothetical fame. They lived, breathed, ate, and often ate *at* Second City. During rare downtime, many of them hung out together as well. A popular gathering spot for several years running was a lethargy-rife dilapidated dwelling on North Orleans Street called the Energy Center — "the E.C." for short.

### Danny Breen, cast member

When I moved to Chicago, I moved into a brownstone in Old Town that George Wendt was already in with some other Second City people. Joyce Sloane gave it the name the "Energy Center," which was ironic. Nobody would get up before three or four in the afternoon. We'd be up all night doing God knows what. It was more of a boys' place. A lot of women wouldn't go in there because it was so filthy. But it was sort of legendary in its day. There used to be a Thanksgiving party every year that was connected to Second City, and somehow we got that honor of hosting it. So each time we had to do that, we cleaned the place. But that was once a year. We actually found a couch we didn't know we had, that had been buried under papers. And the centerpiece was, the ceiling started to chip away, and instead of informing the landlord that he had a problem with the plaster, we decided it looked like Wisconsin, and painted in all the city names. So we had the map of Wisconsin on the ceiling. One day we were late with the rent, and the fellow that managed the building came in and literally ran from one end to the other and started to cry, because it was so destroyed.

### Miriam Flynn, cast member

Oh. My. God. It was the place where all the bachelors lived, and it was truly one of the most horrifying places that you've ever seen in your life. Filth beyond belief. Bags, newspapers piled, pizza boxes. It was the typical bachelor pad gone awry.

### Eric Boardman

Miriam and I open the door and walk in, and there are bags of garbage in the kitchen, and there's two stray dogs going through the garbage. In the other room, the guys are sleeping and oblivious to this. We're just horrified that there are stray dogs going through garbage, and it doesn't bother the residents. It was the worst living conditions of anybody I had met at that point. I had not spent time in the ghetto, so I don't know what life was like there, but I had never seen anybody living like this.

Before, during, and after his Energy Center residency, George Wendt was unusually fond of meat—grilled meat in particular. Neither snow nor sleet nor dark of night kept him from his self-appointed duties.

### Bruce Jarchow, cast member

We'd go out to bars after the show, or we'd go over to George's. George was always barbecuing something at midnight. There'd be ten feet of snow and he'd carve out a little area for his barbecue and we'd go over to his house and he'd have this insane meal.

### Eric Boardman

George and I roomed together in Toronto for the six weeks of our show there. I spent my days roaming through the Toronto bookstores and record stores, looking for things I couldn't find down in the States. George would come back to our room at night with sausages he had found in Cabbagetown. That was his passion. George has loved meat from day one. After the big snow of '79, his choices were to shovel out the car or the pathway to the grill. He did the pathway to the grill. And the neighbors couldn't understand what was going on.

### Bernadette Birkett

Once, I was in the Carnival market near our apartment and someone came up to me and said, "Hi, I'm your neighbor on Armitage. So you burn things at night?" I said, "My husband likes to barbeque." She went, "In February? At 2 o'clock in the morning?" They really thought we were some kind of cult or coven.

### Jim Belushi, cast member

It was two in the morning after a show. I got in a fight with my girlfriend I was living with, who later became my wife. It was the middle of winter, and it was just kind of a dark time. Maybe the sets weren't going good for me. I was real low. Got so pissed I grabbed the mail that had to be mailed and left the apartment. Walked down Dickens, turned right on Larrabee, walked out to where the fire station is on Armitage, mailed the letter, looked over to where George's apartment was, and there was this fucking glow in the back courtyard, at two-thirty in the morning. And there was so much snow that the snow went all the way up the fence, and so I crawled up the snow and looked over, and there's George in a parka barbecuing ribs. I said, "George." He goes, "Hey! Jimmy! Come on in!" I went over there, and we had a feast! Ribs and coleslaw, and his wife was making stuff, and it was just the three of us. And the greatest thing about it was he would never let me use a napkin. Until we were done eating. So he and I had these big rosy cheeks with barbecue sauce all over our faces. I'll never forget that night. It was the sweetest night ever.

Having briefly starred on the Wells Street mainstage in 1975, Wendt had been demoted to Second City's suburban outpost—a cheesy resort called Chateau Louise—for failing to meet satiric standards. He stayed there for a couple of years, during which time he met his future (and still) wife, Bernadette Birkett, who was also in the touring company.

### Bernard Sahlins

We sent him down for a while, as I remember it, and then brought him back. Chastened and subdued.

### George Wendt, cast member

I sucked. I think it was the best thing that ever happened to me. I'd been in the resident company for about a year, and I did all right. I wasn't really embarrassing myself, but I wasn't really bringing what they were used to—a little more of a defined comic voice, a little smarter approach. Just more maturity and sophistication. They said I was playing it too safe, and they didn't actually want me to go away completely. They wanted me to go back in the touring company, and they sort of sold it to me because the touring company was really starting to get a lot of work. Oh, God, I was crushed. I was crushed. And that's probably something that should happen to everybody. Because it had been a pretty smooth ride through the workshops, and the children's theater, and then getting cast in the touring company, and getting my Equity card, and all of a sudden invited into the resident company. So it was my first huge bump in the road. And it really kind of made me sort of take stock in myself and my approach. Just for expedience and the fact that maybe I could redeem myself, I wound up going back in the touring company. Slightly humiliating.

## Bernadette Birkett

He really felt like he needed more time and he wasn't ready to move on, and I think he took it as a challenge. He wasn't terribly morose. He seemed really kind of upbeat. It was more of an ego thing.

## Tim Kazurinsky

Wednesdays were always pretty sad. We looked out and there were two people in the audience. So we took up a collection. We sent George out because he drew the short straw. "George, you go tell 'em we're buying them lunch, we're not doing a show today, and they can come back for this evening's show. We're not doing a show for two fuckin' people." So George goes out, he talks to them, he comes back and they're still sitting there. He says, "It's their twenty-fifth wedding anniversary, they drove down from Wisconsin, they've got a sitter, they have to be back at seven tonight. I couldn't say no." So in this five-hundred-seat theater we had an audience of two. And we had so much fun. It was one of the best shows we ever did.

Toward the end of Wendt's touring company exile, Jim Belushi was wowing crowds on the mainstage. But he wasn't always adored by his cast mates. When Belushi took a sabbatical in the latter half of 1978 to shoot a sitcom out west and then star in a hometown staging of David Mamet's play *Sexual Perversity in Chicago,* Wendt stepped in and stalked the mainstage once more. Belushi reentered the Second City fray in 1980 and performed in two more revues before leaving late the following year.

## Will Aldis

Sometimes it was good. Sometimes it was not so good. Sometimes [Jim] was an asshole. Sometimes we were all assholes. I could be an asshole, too. But when I'm being an asshole, it's Will being an asshole. When Jim's being an asshole, it's Jim Belushi being an asshole, and then somehow he's a bigger asshole because he's a bigger name. Magnified.

## Danny Breen

[Jim] could be pretty volatile. He and I got along really well, actually. We would have a lot of fun onstage. But he would have temper tantrums and stuff like that, which is sort of the polar opposite of the kind of person I am.

I'm very nonconfrontational. But Jim, he would hold his own. If he had a differing opinion, he would be more than willing to share it.

### John Kapelos, cast member

When I first went in there, it was a game of Whac-a-Mole. I instantly locked horns with a guy like Jim Belushi who didn't take a shine to me. It was my first gig and I was arrogant and young and balls-out. I wanted it. I think there's a certain aggression in comedy, in Second City. And there are few spots to fill and people are competitive. And it's funny how that gets loosed in your body. Even though you're in your early twenties, it's like guppies in the pond. Joyce would say, "This is a really good place, you're all going to make friends here, you're going to be working with them for years in Los Angeles." But what they didn't tell us was, it was a shark pond—you're going to run into people in Los Angeles, but they're going to take their dorsal fin and wipe you out. You're forging alliances on one hand, but it's also a bunch of baby sharks.

### Jim Belushi

I wasn't the easiest guy to work with, being a middle child—never getting enough. You do act one, act two, and then you do the improvs. They do it different now, but back then we'd ask for suggestions, go backstage for twenty minutes, try to get scenes, and they'd put them up on the board. And I would go, "I'm light! I'm light!" And the stage manager used to get so pissed at me. He'd go, "You're in one, two, three, four, five scenes! What do you mean, you're light?" I said, "I'm light!" He goes, "Belushi, you're light in life!" I'll never forget that, because no matter how much I got, I always felt like I was light. Because I was light at home. I never got anything. And Joyce filled that for me. And so did the theater. It was family.

I think satirists and comedians are kind of based in anger. Is the anger there now? I don't know. I can't say. It drove my aggression and it drove my desire and it was my friend. Anger was always there to protect me, guide me through scenes. Had great results. Had great shows. I didn't necessarily have great friendships in the cast. I think they liked me fine, but I never really hung out with anybody, except for maybe Danny Breen. And I hung out at the Energy Center. As an adult now, I have to kind of chill out, but back then I was just kind of an angry guy.

### Mary Gross

He *was* an angry guy, and I think part of it had to do with his brother's success. Jim was trying to carve out his own career, and there was this huge personality who was on the cover of *Newsweek* who happened to be his brother. There were times I wanted to kill Jim, but I also, in retrospect, have a great deal of affection for him. I think what kept us from really getting mad at Jim when he was having a bad day was his charm. He could be a very endearing person and still is. I remember having nights when I wanted nothing to do with him. But then a few nights later we would be improvising a scene together and he could be very boyish and very sweet.

On one particularly volcanic evening, Belushi quite literally blew his lid.

### Danny Breen

We had had a table full of people right in front of us who were drunk and being pretty obnoxious. And we were doing some scene where you die and you're out of the scene. Jim and I ended up dying right in front of this table. And they were giving us grief as we're lying on the stage. Jim had this big leather cowboy hat, and he goes, "Watch this." So when the lights go out, I just hear this *Whooomph!* And then we scampered off the stage, laughing. That was the end of the show. And then our stage manager came back and went, "Jim, did you hit somebody in the head with a hat?" We just played dumb.

### Jim Belushi

I didn't smack nobody. I didn't hit nobody. There were these drunk kids in the front row, like six of them. And they had eighty-six dollars worth of kamikazes. Eighty-six dollars in 1980, okay? That's a lot of alcohol. They were drunk and talking through the show, and Rob Riley was playing the pope and I was playing Clint Eastwood and we were having an existential gunfight. And we both end up shooting each other and dying, but only halfway through the scene. And I'm lying on the ground. My head is right by their table, and they're talking to me, saying stupid silly stuff. The lights went out. We disappeared. The lights came up, and I don't know, somebody must have hit the kid on the head with a hat or something. If there was anyone who got hit in the head, which I don't think happened, it was the guy. And there was a girl on the other side of the table that claimed the injuries.

### Lance Kinsey

I believe there might have even been litigation involved. We were all going, "Well, it's about time somebody popped him." Everybody had their role in the company. Jim was our enforcer. I always had the feeling I could walk up to him, even if he wasn't in the scene, and go, "Jim, that guy . . ." And he'd go, "Where?" and he'd take care of it.

### Joyce Sloane

Bernie and I had a big fight only one time—over Jim Belushi. He wasn't at Second City; his understudy was in the show. So Bernie said, "Where is he?" I said, "He's off. He'll be back in a couple of days." "Where did he go?" Well,

I can't lie. So I said, "He's in Los Angeles. He's auditioning for a sitcom." Then, because I put a slip in the safe, Bernie said, "And you gave him the money to go?" I said, "Yeah." "You gave him the money to go? He'll never step foot on our stage again!" Screaming and yelling at me and calling me and hanging up and calling me and hanging up. He was furious. Then Jim called me. He said, "I got the job but I've got to stay because they want to shoot right away." That was his first television show. So I said, "Okay." Then he came back and he wanted to do the set that night when he was here. And I said, "Bernie, Jim wants to do the set tonight." You know what Bernie said to me? "I don't see why not." It blows over.

Especially in those early formative years, Jim lived (not always uncomfortably) in his brother John's shadow—never more so than when John became an internationally known movie star following the release of *Animal House.* A couple of years later the Chicago-centric *Blues Brothers,* which co-starred Dan Aykroyd, launched him into the comedy exosphere. As Jim became even more acutely aware, he wasn't John. Nor did he try to be.

### Fred Kaz

With a presence like John in the house growing up, Jimmy learned how to be very cute on a moment's notice. In order to gain favor. You had a competition there. I don't think I can fill in more than that for you, except that professionally, the few times that I saw them on our stage together, each of them was more aware of quote-unquote rules. You see what I'm saying? Because they wouldn't want to make mistakes in each other's presence.

### Tim Kazurinsky

When I first met Jim, I heard him in the lobby. Somebody said, "Hey, aren't you John Belushi's brother?" And he just whipped around and was like, "No, man! He's *my* brother!" And I saw him do this a couple of times and thought, "I see there's a little bit of tension here." So when I actually met him, I said, "Hey, isn't John Belushi your brother?" And he said, "No, man! I'm *his* . . ." And he just smiled.

### Jim Belushi

John was just a unique creature. He was it. There was no competition, and to me, there was no comparison. And when people say, "I was a big fan of your brother," I will always say, "Me too!" I never felt connected to him that way, because he was never around. I never knew him that well. He was a famous guy. He was a talented actor in my mind. I mean, he never gave me advice. It wasn't like he was taking care of me. He actually tried to talk me out of Second City. He said, "You're a better dramatic actor. You should go over to the Goodman." And I said, "No, I'm here, man. I dig it here." "You're sure you don't want to do drama?" So if there was any competition anyone was worried about, John was worried. I wasn't. I was like, "This guy's brilliant." It's like me and Robert De Niro. I don't feel competitive with Robert De Niro. They exist in the world—great men, great actors—and I just kind of went my own way within the way that was proven accessible.

Together with Will Aldis (then called Will Porter), Jim Belushi performed a scene that's long been a Second City classic. Dubbed "White Horse Tavern," it was a highlight of his 1978 mainstage debut (the David Mamet–inspired revue *Sexual Perversity Among the Buffalo*) and born of a conversation with John at the actual White Horse Tavern in New York's West Village.

### Jim Belushi

I went to see John in a play called *Lemmings* at the Village Gate down in the Village. I was in college at the time, and I was a speech major. In oral interp class you had to pick an author to read, and I picked Dylan Thomas, because he's musical. His rhythms were really cool. So when I went to New York, John said, "What are you doing in school?" I said, "Dylan Thomas." And he goes, "Let's go here." And we went to the White Horse, and me and Judy and him were sitting there and basically romanticizing suicide. He basically said, "You see that bar right there? Dylan Thomas died right there." And I'm like, "Really!" He goes, "Yeah, right there." And I'm like, "Wow." And so I told that story backstage one night to Will, and he goes, "That's a scene." And I said, "Oh, okay." So me and Shelley Long and him went out and improvised two brothers in a bar with a sister-in-law. Will and I had a really good rapport, and Shelley kind of felt left out, so she just kind of bowed out of the scene, and we developed it from there. That's a great scene. It got me all my work, and my company's called White Horse Productions.

### Will Aldis

My fondest Second City memory was doing that scene at the University of Chicago. They went wild. They went nuts. There was applause and people standing up and going batshit. It was great. How much Virginia Woolf had I read? None. They didn't know that.

### Excerpt from "White Horse Tavern," from *Sexual Perversity Among the Buffalo,* 1978

**Will:** Ernest Hemingway!

**Jim:** Ernest Hemingway. He knew how to go, man! He knew how to go!

**Will:** Shotgun in the mouth!

**Jim:** Pull the trigger!

**Both:** Brains against the wall! Sheet over the head! Dead, gone, dead!

**Jim:** Boy, that guy knew how to go, man.

**Will:** Virginia Woolf!

**Jim:** Virginia Woolf, man!

**Will:** Walk in the ocean!

**Jim:** Water in the lungs!

**Both:** Glub, glub, glub! Sheet over the head! Dead, gone, dead!

**Will:** Lady had balls!

**Jim:** She had balls! She had balls, man! I know, man. I know she did. Ah, Sylvia Plath, man. Sylvia Plath. Head in the oven.

**Will:** Turn on the gas.

**Jim:** Like a chocolate chip cookie. Trust modern appliances, man.

**Will:** No way. Jesus Christ.

**Jim:** Jesus Christ, man!

**Both:** Jesus Christ! Hands against the cross! Into the cave! Easter! Move stone! Walk around a little bit! Up into heaven! Sheet over the head! Dead, gone, dead!

## Lance Kinsey

Jim and I were doing "White Horse" [later on] and we didn't know John and Danny Aykroyd were in town. I guess they had just come in. And so we're downstage looking out at the audience as if we're looking over the bar, and all of a sudden we felt a huge rush of energy come up from the audience. Whaoooooooooah! We didn't know what had happened. We knew we were good, but we didn't know we were *that* good. And what had happened was John had entered through the door behind us and we didn't see him. And Jim didn't know he was in town. And he just walked into the scene. Jim turned around and he was totally speechless. Could not talk. And the audience was just up for grabs and screaming, cheering. And after it finally died down, again, Jim was speechless and John was just standing here, he'd just taken over, taken the stage. And finally I think I babbled something like, "Hey, there's another bar down the street, you wanna go?" And off we went. We got out of the scene, but it was one of those moments that was absolutely overwhelming. That's the kind of power John had. He would walk into a room and the room changed.

## Tim Kazurinsky

Nobody ever got the reaction that John got. It was like warp two. There was one night I actually convinced him to do the improv set with us. We'd had Robin Williams come by and do a set; we'd had Albert Brooks. We had a lot of famous people that would come through. And of course the audience would always go wild when somebody famous came up. But the time that I told the audience we had a special guest who was going to be joining us for the set and John walked out onto the stage, I can't even describe the reaction. They went insane. It was like a Roman Coliseum audience when the lions and Christians were in there. It was like somebody put jumper cables on them. People leapt out of their seats. Drinks and tables were knocked over. They just stood up and there was this huge roar like "Whoooaahhhh-hhh!" It freaked me out. I got goose bumps. It scared the shit out of me. I had never seen that kind of reaction. I've never seen 350 people stand up in unison with all the air screaming from their lungs. It was atavistic.

### Jim Belushi

I had to pull John out of Del's apartment. What's he doing in Del's apartment? Bernie told me to go get him, so I went and got him. I said, "Come on, you're coming home with me." And he didn't want to go.

"Come on. I'm having a good time."

And I took him in a cab and we went to Clark Street. There was a little alley back to my place. And he didn't want to go. He wanted to go out and party.

I go, "No, you're coming in the house."

And he goes, "I'll tell you what. I'll fight you. I'm gonna fight you, and if I win, we go out. If you win, I'll go to your house."

I said, "John, I have been waiting so long for this." This is my shot! I'm gonna kick his ass! I'm bigger than him, right? And we lined up on the sidewalk on Clark Street and he looked like a drunken pirate, with his eyebrow going.

And then he goes, "This is like *East of Eden.*" The brothers fighting on the step. I had to go see the movie again to get the reference.

And I barely tag him on the lip and he goes [*sound of surprise*] "I'm an actor. You don't hit an actor in the face."

And I go, "Come on. You're nothing, buddy. Come on, you son of a bitch."

And he says, "Uh-uh. You win."

"No, no, no, no, I'm not done!"

"No, you win, you *win*. You beat me up. You beat me up!"

So we go home and we pass my Jeep. He says, "Come on, let's go," and we jump in the Jeep. There was a Polaroid in the Jeep, and I went out with him that night and I had the best night I ever had with him. He was leaning out of the car taking Polaroids and we had a blast. Went to the Blues Bar and sang. I miss that those kinds of moments couldn't have happened in these twenty years.

## Tim Kazurinsky

John had no idea that I knew Jim, but John would come to see the show at Second City and come up and be in the sets, and he somehow took a shine to me. I'm not sure why. Somebody told me that Marlon Brando and Wally Cox were pals. I don't know. But John would say, "We're gonna hang tonight." And I'd go, "What do you mean?" "We're just gonna party." And I'm like, "Why does John Belushi want to hang with me?" He's in doing *The Blues Brothers*. And people would act insane around him. They would act out and do crazy shit because he was John. People would try and hit him, people would try and buy him drinks. One time I was with him, some woman pulled out her left tit and said, "Can I have your autograph?" It was at the Old Town Ale House. I said, "My friends at the Ale House, they're down-to-earth people. They won't go crazy just because it's you." And I took him in there and of course everybody went fucking crazy. Nobody acted normal around John.

So as to socialize in semi-privacy, John and his pal Dan Aykroyd opened a private saloon across the street from Second City while they were in Chicago filming *The Blues Brothers* during the summer of 1979. It remained a favorite Second City haunt for years afterward.

## Lance Kinsey

Danny Aykroyd always had a bar in any town he was working in. He would kind of open a private bar for him and his friends. And they had what we called the Blues Bar right across the street behind the Earl of Old Town, which isn't there anymore. And they would open that, and it was really like a private club for their group and for the Second City troupe. We would go over after the shows and kind of hang out, so that was a heady time and very exciting. They had bouncers at the door. We were kids and we'd go running over there and go, "Second City," praying they'd recognize us, and they would, and they'd usher us in and we just felt like the kings in there. And we got to kind of hang out and be little puppy dogs in the corner. We'd go in after the show, so it'd be like one in the morning, and we'd stumble out and the sun is coming up and you'd go, "What happened?" It was just an opportunity to hang with the big boys.

## Dan Aykroyd

We had a spectacular jukebox. We had drums, guitars, amps, and a keyboard. It was the first private club we ever had, really. Second City, film crew, visiting musicians, notables. It was our artists' place to have fun and hang out. Inner circle only. It was directly across from Second City. It used to be called the Sneak Joint. So we just reopened the Sneak Joint for our crew, and, of course, everybody from Second City, that summer. That's one of the greatest summers of my life, because it went back to the Second City roots. We had the *SNL* experience behind us, we were making a film that celebrated everything we loved, and we were making the city of Chicago a star.

### Danny Breen

To me, at the time, it seemed normal, but it was pretty insane. It was an all-night party, four or five nights a week, walking outside of a place and seeing daylight coming up and going, "Oh, no!" And then you'd sleep all day. Studio 54 was like, men in lipstick and stuff like that. This was Chicago guys doing their version of that kind of thing. But it was an all-night booze-and-drug-fest every night. There was no fear of police coming in. They were aware of it, but I don't think they cared. We had this great relationship with cops back then. There were two beat cops who were around most of the time I was there. During the winter they would hang out backstage, and God knows what they saw.

### Tim Kazurinsky

Everybody rhapsodized about the famous Blues Bar. Basically it was, like, four pinball machines, a pool table, and a bar. And people would kill to get in. They would pay a fortune to try and get smuggled in there. It was really a big bunch of nothin'. It was just the people that were hanging there. But it became this legendary place. John came over and got me one night and he said, "You gotta come over to the Blues Bar." And I said, "No, I'm busy now." He said, "You gotta come over. You gotta come over." So he dragged me over there, and the place was crowded. I really didn't recognize anybody. And I said, "Who are all these people?" And he said—and this was his little lesson to me—"All right, the Blues Brothers are gonna jam with the Eagles. Here's the Eagles. Those guys there are our PR people. Those guys there are their PR people. These are our assistants; these are their assistants. These guys are all reporters from *Rolling Stone* and *Time*." And he went around the entire packed Blues Bar explaining to me who everybody was, and everybody had a corporate tag, a reason to be there. That place was jammed. And he said, "You are gonna read about this wonderful event in *Rolling Stone, Time, Newsweek,* and what a great party it was and how the crowd really enjoyed it. But you know something? You are the only audience member. We need one person who's not a journalist or an assistant or an aide or a PR person." It was his way of saying, "This is the way the business works. This is a completely planned and controlled event."

When it came to all things musical, Second City musical director Fred Kaz ruled the roost. His "pianistic accompaniment marries mood to movement as expertly as always," wrote *Chicago Daily News* critic Sydney Harris in early 1974. At his stage-side piano (setting the tone, rigging the tempo) since 1964, Kaz was more of a driving force than ever as the theater morphed from local gem to national treasure starting in the mid-seventies. "There was a time when David Mamet used to sit at my elbow at the Second City keyboard," Kaz told the *Chicago Tribune* in 1982. "He was hungry to learn how we do it, and he just hung around long enough till he got it. To this day, we consider him part of the Second City family." And Kaz's opinion mattered greatly—as much as, if not more than, that of Sahlins or Close. If they made Fred laugh, actors recall, all was right with the world.

### Steven Kampmann

Fred made clay figurines of some role you were playing in the current show. He would give it to you on opening night. I don't think he'd give it to you right away when you first joined. He had to kind of buy your act. And Fred was someone whose respect you wanted. I wanted his respect, and I think any performer did, because he'd done it for a long time and he came out of the beat generation. When he gave you one of those figurines, you knew he brought you into the club.

### Nonie Newton-Breen, cast member

The one thing about Fred that freaked out a lot of young people [was] he wasn't a bullshitter. He'd totally tell you what he thought. But as you got to know him, you had such respect for him because he wasn't a bullshitter. His honesty was refreshing and really helpful.

### John Kapelos

Fred's a soulful, incredibly talented guy who's got a long-suffering old soul. When I first met him, he was like Old Captain Fred. I looked upon him as an avuncular type—he's the Zig-Zag guy, that guy on the [rolling papers] package. But make no mistake, he wasn't your uncle. He wasn't warm and cuddly. With an eye or with the cock of his head or with some sort of movement of his hand, he could dismiss you more than anybody ever could by giving you shit. If Fred looked away when you were doing a scene and sort of put his head down, you knew you'd fucked up. That was worse than getting hit in the head with a baseball bat by Barry Bonds. Fred could show his disapproval with a sigh and a slouch.

### David Rasche

I made Fred my friend. He didn't want to be at all, and I just hung around because this guy played jazz piano. As a matter of fact, as a result of him I went and learned how to play jazz piano. I would sit on the bench with him and I just didn't give up, and he became a very, very close friend of mine. Whatever else failed, Fred was classy. Really, really, really classy. He played the most sensational jazz piano you could imagine. So when you had that underneath you and this guy starts playing the piano, people would go, "Well, this should be good." And he was the sixth or seventh or eighth or ninth [cast member]—and even sometimes the director, because he'd play you out. If the scene wasn't going well, he'd nod at the booth and sometimes take the scenes out. He was wild. This guy was wild. And absolutely brilliant. Every show there would be some kind of musical number Fred would do. Two days, three days before he absolutely had to have it, Fred would be gone and no one would see him and he would go into his studio and he would lock the door. And three days later he would come out with something that was absolutely unbelievable, show after show after show. Every single show had a Fred piece, and the Fred piece was always the show-stopper.

### Fred Kaz

I was under everything, or absent when it was the best thing to do. Usually absent from the action. But sometimes, if they got into a funk, or I knew it was going to take a long time to work out, I'd go out for a cigarette and scare the shit out of them. 'Cause who else is gonna take the lights out? I pretty much did that.

### Jim Belushi

He'd get up and walk out. He'd go smoke his Camels. I was like, "Freeeeed!" He got it. Improvising. He's the guru. He was the leader. He maintained that show.

### Rob Riley, cast member

I don't mean to put down Bernie or Del, but I got hip pretty quick that Fred was really the artistic director of the company. He was the one who was always there. He was the one who would underscore scenes and also let you know when the scene was over by playing the-scene-is-over music, because the guy who was running the lights at that time didn't understand that sort of thing. Fred's a jazz guy, and he understood that what we were doing onstage was very much like what he had always done on the piano, as a jazzman. And you wanted to please him, because you knew that he was for real, and he would never bullshit you, and he knew what was good. I don't want to speak for everybody else, but in my company we felt that *we* were getting it together. Not that we didn't need a director, but Del's not there, and then Bernie's there, and Bernie contradicts everything Del said the week before. And so we had to figure out what worked and what didn't. And you had

Fred to tell you—an anchor. You could really rely on him. I'm sure he told me when something was wrong, but he would never raise his voice or show anger, or even really be sarcastic. It would be much more subtle than that with Fred.

### Danny Breen

If Fred was angry with Jim, Jim was devastated. And he would then go around and apologize or whatever he thought he needed to do.

### Jim Belushi

Friday night, second show was the show that we kind of got a little loose in. We'd drink a little bit. We'd have a little fun. We'd fuck with each other on-stage—especially in the second act. Especially if it was a bad audience. Because Friday night, by the second show, these people had worked all week, they've had a drink, and they get tired. And so they don't laugh. So we'd entertain each other. Fred kind of turned his head the other way and let the kids have their fun. Well, I got a little cocky and I started in the first act of the first show on Friday night, and he got pissed. And the way he showed his anger was, every time I was onstage, he pulled his hands off the piano. And I got a third of my laughs. A third! Two thirds of my laughs were generated by the rhythms that Fred created with the piano. And I went on my knees and begged him to forgive me, and he didn't forgive me until Sunday. Stewed another two nights without the piano. Me trying to squeeze these laughs without his help. When he would play, he would play the Second City rhythms. And then naturally, not even knowing it, you'd fall into that rhythm, and you learned those rhythms. And so when he pulled the piano out, I wasn't so funny. I learned my lesson. It was like, "We fuck off second act, second show, Friday night, that's it!"

### Lance Kinsey

Fred Kaz was the heart and soul of Second City. He drove the scenes. We could be out there and have no idea where it was going or how to get out of it and Fred would come to our rescue regularly. He was our hero.

### Danny Breen

He had seen everybody that had come and gone before us, so we weren't doing anything that was blowing him away. And he also knew what it took to keep the show going and what was important. Which we could lose sight of. And so he was the one that had the strongest influence. He had total control over all of us. Fred said something, and we did it. We wouldn't argue with him. He was there every night. He was like the only adult. He was our alpha male.

Kaz was the undisputed maestro of Second City at his keyboard, but Joyce Sloane orchestrated the theater's day-to-day business. She began filling that role on an increasingly time-consuming basis in the late sixties, and it continued for decades. Whether hitting the road with touring companies, doling out paycheck advances to her starving artists, producing revues, tossing birthday bashes, calling ambulances, garnering press coverage, or smoothing Sahlins's ruffled feathers when something (or someone) went awry, Sloane was, for many, Second City's driving force. Ensconced to this day in a photo-and-memorabilia-packed corner office (the theater's largest), she remains a bridge between the past and the present.

### Jim Belushi

It was like the family I always wanted. It was like Joyce was my mother. She mothered me. Truly mothered me. Loved me, threw a shower for my baby when he was first born. She rented me a car to drive down to get my degree at Southern Illinois University. I was burglarized and my rent money was in my book, and they found the money in my book, and I had no rent, and she gave me the money. And I'll never forget—she took me to the dentist. I had four wisdom teeth pulled, and I had Sodium Pentothal, which is truth serum. And I come out and there's Joyce sitting next to me, looking at me, about three feet away from my face. And she said, "Jimmy, the doctor said everything went very well and that you are going to be okay." "Oh, great, Joyce." "Now, how many of the waitresses are you sleeping with?" She wanted to know what was going on in that family.

### John Kapelos

She was instantly maternal. A theater is the people, it really is. She's my mom. She's extraordinary. She had a big heart. She has a lot of pain and life and experience and she has a lot of love. She was manipulative and she was political and she could be bitchy and hard and say the worst things about people. And you'd just pray to God she wouldn't say them about you. But she is also honest. She's an important part of the theater, and she will be looked upon in terms of the overall arc of the place as the connecting spirit.

### Cheryl Sloane, Training Center co-founder, former general manager, producer, and director, and Joyce Sloane's daughter

For a lot of people, Second City is the first time their families validate their career choice. So for a lot of those actors, my mom was an integral part of their family dynamic.

### Aaron Freeman, cast member

Joyce put up with me. I'm not an easy guy to work with. I'm not always an easy guy to hang around with. She forgave me for much, for many stupid things I said, many stupid things I did. We had romances going on in the company—I certainly didn't invent that—but romances that would spill out into the work, that you shouldn't even put up with. But she did, and she forgave me and let me work—let me stay there long enough to learn a bunch of stuff. Not long enough to actually be good at that work, but I learned a lot of other great stuff about comedy and theater and performance. She tolerated me like no one in any professional situation that I'd ever been in. I had my feuds with people, but I wouldn't characterize my relationship as stormy with my fellow Second Citizens. I certainly had sex with a number of them, but actually not nearly as many as I had hoped for. Not nearly as many as I tried to. But I had a lot of passions. And also, I really had a lot of pride. So I would not suck up to management. And I really should have, because everybody sucked up to Joyce. Only a stupid person like me wouldn't suck up to Joyce. She's a nice lady. There's no reason not to. Bring her candies. Bring her stuff. Get her her tea. Do all that stuff, 'cause that's business. And I didn't and wouldn't do it.

### David Rasche

Joyce was always a great champion of mine, and I have never forgotten it. And she made everybody feel really special, including me. "That's my David," she'd say, and I liked that. And if you were in a show, she went to see it. If you had a child, she wrote him a card. She called. "How's your son? I hope you're being nice to him." She would fool around with you. "Are you still married? You should be, because you'll never find another one like that." She was one of the people who promised and came through. And she never let you down. It's not like she was without her faults. She was just deeply generous and deeply caring. And I don't even remember her getting mad. She didn't get mad. She was as important a person at that theater as anyone. She made it go. Whenever Bernie wasn't feeling particularly generous—and frankly, there were times when he wasn't feeling particularly generous—she would say, "Don't worry. I'll talk to Bernie. Don't worry." Bernie doesn't always have the greatest social skills, but she does, and he would have been sunk without her. She made it all work. She greased the wheels. And if Bernie was rude, she would say, "Well, that's just Bernie." Not that he always was. I don't mean that at all. But whatever failings he had, she understood him and tried to make you understand him and said, "Don't worry, it'll all work out." Somebody gets pregnant, somebody doesn't have money, somebody's committing suicide—whatever. It was Joyce, Joyce, Joyce.

### Mike Hagerty, cast member

Joyce was the nuts and bolts of the theater. Bernie had interests and was probably concentrating on the mainstage, but there was a whole big business to run and she was the one who did it from day to day. She was the one you went to and talked to. She and Bernie shared an office. Her aunt Nettie was the accountant. Particularly in the touring company, if you needed any kind of advance, you'd have to go through Nettie to get it.

### Danny Breen

She sort of adopted me as one of her thousands of orphans. She just looked out for you and knew that you were hand to mouth, so if she heard of something, she'd throw it your way. Or if she thought there was something that would be good for you to do, she'd let you know about it.

### Lance Kinsey

The inmates ran the asylum, but you have to remember that Del was the head lunatic. When he was around, there was no bigger lunatic in town and he definitely set a tone. But Joyce was very lenient. However, she wasn't there when the lunatics were out of control. She would be looking the other way. She certainly would not be party to that. She would just happen to not be there. All her kids could really do no wrong. It was kind of an unconditional love.

### Jim Belushi

She said something to me one time, when I got divorced, and I was so low. I was so depressed. She said something about my wife, which I won't quote, but she said to me, "You know, Jimmy, even when you're wrong, you're right." And it relieved all kinds of pressure. It was just love, you know? It was just pure love. She was always there. I could always count on her. She was the net. She liked her bad boys. I was kind of a bad boy.

### Michael Gellman

When I was in the touring company, my parents came to see the show. It's the only time they ever came to see me work. And my mother and Joyce go out for fifteen minutes and they come back, and my mother says to me, "I am your mother and I will always be your mother, but when you're in Chicago, this woman is your mother. You listen to what she says and you do what she tells you to do." And Joyce is still my mom.

# 7

## Mummy Opium, Death of a Hero, and the End of an Era

**Dan Castellaneta**
**Mary Gross**
**Richard Kind**

1975–85

AS SECOND CITY'S PROFILE ROSE, so did its collective intake of drugs and alcohol. From ubiquitous grass and alcohol to hardcore narcotics, abuse was rampant in the 1970s. As the free-flowing, hard-partying decade ended, that culture was more accepted (and even expected) than ever—not least of all by improv sage and eccentric Second City director Del Close. John Belushi, too, had been unabashed in his pursuit of chemically induced mind expansion. His seemingly iron constitution finally failed him in 1982, when he died of a drug overdose in Los Angeles. But even then—even after this internationally beloved icon became yet another statistic, not everyone paid heed. It would be more than a decade, in fact, before Second City made concerted efforts to clean up its act.

### Danny Breen

Rob Riley and I had pot brownies at my house. It was a Friday night. We had a little cookout. It was one of those things where I had never done that. And it was, "Gee, I don't feel anything. Let's eat another one." So I think I had three brownies. And we were driving to Second City and I remember going, "Ohhh, myyy Gaawd." And we did the show, and it was the longest night of my life. It was like, "What's my next line? What's my next line?" For two hours. We got through the night, and we were high-fiving one another, and I'm like, "Oh, my God, what a nightmare that was." And there was a waitress there, Janine, and she comes cruising back and she's giving us this look.

And she goes, "All right, I want to know. What the hell are you two on?" And we were like, "What are you talking about? What?" And she said, "All I know is, any time one of you two had a line tonight, there'd be a ten-second pause." And she goes, "It was the weirdest show I've ever seen at Second City." And we had thought we had pulled it off brilliantly.

### Rob Riley

The waitresses are hipper than anybody about when somebody's having a good show or not. "You guys were terrible! What was with all those pauses?"

### Nonie Newton-Breen

We would drink kamikazes and stuff between shows on Friday, so second show Friday it was "Yee-hah!" But you know what? Nobody was ever falling-down drunk. We were lubricated, and we were pretty lubricated for the set on Saturday nights, too. And actually, sometimes you came up with great stuff, because you were absolutely fearless.

### Danny Breen

Del would never say anything. Bernie didn't like it. I think even though he tolerated it, he'd always just be kind of horrified when he'd come back during a show and there'd either be a live joint going, or we'd all be sitting there with a couple of drinks and stuff. A lot of it was looking the other way. We weren't the first cast to do it, God knows. And so we were sort of doing what everybody else had done.

### Aaron Freeman

When I was at [Second City's suburban outpost] Chateau Louise, we experimented to see whether or not we could do a show without smoking dope. And we found that it was possible. We were pleased to hear that. When I was there was also when they were shooting *The Blues Brothers*. Lots of drugs going around. Lots of people running around with cocaine and pot. The drug culture was there big-time.

### Danny Breen

[Second City] women didn't really party like the guys did. And Del would look down on them for that. It was like, "Come on! That's what we do here." That enabling really cost them down the line. And now that doesn't exist anymore, which is probably really good.

### Mary Gross

I tried to avoid mayhem. Even in the greenroom when there was the occasional use of drugs, I would always say, "I'm gonna go home and have a nice cup of tea and read a good book." I just could not get into the drug culture. I think there was a lot of grass and I think there was a certain degree of co- caine. I would say for the most part it was not used while people were work- ing. It was probably an after-work sort of thing. We could have as many drinks as we wanted. The bar was right back there, close to the greenroom. You really could get away with drinking as much as you wanted, but it wouldn't behoove you to do that because then you couldn't perform. So you tried to control that as much as you could.

### Danny Breen

Saturday nights we would really misbehave. There were two shows and an improv set, and that was usually a pretty wild set. And there was a very pop- ular pastime of sucking the gas out of whipped cream cans. For about a minute, you're just on your ass. They literally had to put a padlock on this cooler where they kept the whipped cream, because their Irish coffee was one of their top sellers. Between the staff and the cast, everybody was doing this. So Jim Belushi and I took our whipped cream cans out onstage and told the audience we were going to conduct a scientific experiment. And we go, "We understand that the test will have an effect on you." And there's a game called "First line, last line," where you get the first line of the scene and the last line, and go from there. So we got that information and then we sucked the gas out of the whipped cream can. And all we could do then was giggle at one another. And after a while our stage manager, Larry Perkins, very slowly brought down the lights on us to boos and hisses. But we used to love that kind of stuff, when you would infuriate the audience. We'd scamper off the stage giggling, like, "How hilarious!"

Despite the impact of Fred Kaz, Joyce Sloane, and Del Close, Bernie Sahlins was the big boss, the money man, the cigar-puffing patriarch who'd been there since forever and held fast to his theatrical principles— even if those principles sometimes puzzled and/or miffed colleagues and casts. Throughout the seventies and into the eighties, he scouted for talent and signed the checks and sometimes delighted in needling his hires. "Five of you," he'd say following a six-person show, "were ter- rific."

### Aaron Freeman

Bernie is just a great human being. And he is the heart and soul and spirit of the whole thing. The whole place is infested with him. Arguably, the most important thing I ever learned about comedy was to always work at the top of your intelligence. And that's Bernie. He's the only person in comedy who I ever heard say that. Ever. Nobody thinks that, but Bernie does. That's anti–show business. That's not how anybody is.

### Shelley Long

I turned to Bernie when I was struggling. I was in the company and I was not happy. He said, "Let's go out to dinner, and we'll talk." And I sat down with him, and he made some suggestions of what I could do personally, and I did. I talked to somebody he recommended, and I stayed at the Second City a little bit longer as a result of that. Which is good, because I was ready to leave. I thought, "This is not working, and this is not helpful." I was seeing somebody in the company, and that went sour. So these are good reasons not to see somebody in the company. And I thought, "Uck!" So the dissolution of that relationship was affecting the work, because I was working with that person. So it was hard. The two were affecting each other, and that's why I felt like I needed to leave. But in the course of the conversation, Bernie was very compassionate and understood what I was saying and suggested someone for me to talk to, and I did.

### Danny Breen

Quite often, Bernie didn't care how much they laughed. He just wanted the material to be a certain type of material. And he would often put a scene in that didn't work as well as something we had conjured up. But it was more in keeping with the tone of the show he wanted. And it would fit his running order, too. He had this very scientific [method]. You can't do the silly stuff till later in the show when you've earned the audience's respect. You had to make them respect your intelligence before you could do a fart joke. He would realize that you had to have a few of those things, and that's what a lot of the people in the audience came to see. I remember Rick Thomas and John Kapelos did a scat singing type of thing, but it was totally scatological. They really were good at it. And they worked at it, but Bernie hadn't seen it. Maybe the third or fourth time they did it, it brought down the house. And Bernie went flying backstage. He said, "I never want that done on my stage!" I've never seen him angrier. He was literally red in the face. It was crazy.

### John Kapelos

I think part of Bernie hated the success aspect [of Second City]. That's not a revelation, but I think what is a revelation is that people criticize Bernie for the wrong reasons. They look at him as being someone who's trying to hold up old elements of Second City, whereas what I think he was trying to do was make sure people were in touch with what Second City was about, but yet to evolve it. Bernie's a very evolutionary type of guy. You can tell I like the guy. And believe you me, he wasn't my biggest fan, either. Joyce was my biggest fan. If it was up to Bernie, I don't think I would have gotten into the resident company. I don't think I was his type of actor.

## Tim Kazurinsky

Bernie never raised his voice, he never yelled, he never screamed. He was a very modulated guy. He would just be disdainful. He would imply that it wasn't worthy of the place. He's really, really smart. He's smarter than everybody else put together. And he and Del did this odd little dance around every show. Del would create these scenes that were really brilliant. Bernie was not so good at that. When Del couldn't really put the show together—he would get drunk, OD, spin out of control, leave in a huff, whatever—Bernie would come in like the United States Cavalry, put all the pieces together, do a little editing, and come up with a running order that was brilliant. And I don't think either of them realized that they needed each other in this symbiotic relationship to get the shows. They worked as a team, but neither one would ever give the other one the time of day or the credit.

## Miriam Flynn

Second City wasn't quite as commercially oriented in those days and we did a lot of political stuff. You had to be up on politics because you would get suggestions at night and you'd better know what was going on politically. Bernie was always after us to work at the top of our intellect and to not pander. He always wanted political pieces in the show.

## Bruce Jarchow

We always said, "All we have to do is add Henry Kissinger to a scene and Bernie'd love it." It would get on our nerves a little bit, but not that much. We'd do what we wanted anyway. We knew he was right, in a way.

## Lance Kinsey

There were times when all of us could go cheap and be rewarded, and for that moment think, "Well, that felt okay." But in the long haul, I think most of us understood that Second City was much more than that. And Jim [Belushi] certainly could get away with it. We actually had a scene that was probably in reaction to Bernie's lectures. I think it was called "Fuck," and we went out and basically just said the f-word over and over and over. It was two guys bumping into each other in the street, "Hey, how the fuck are ya!" "I'm fuckin' great! How the fuck are you?" "How're the fuckin' kids?" "Fuckin' kids—great!" "How's the fuckin' wife?" "Fuckin' wonderful!" And on and on and on. And the audience would be screaming. It was our little wink at Bernie.

## Richard Kind, cast member

With all my heart and soul, I love Bernie and Joyce and Fred. They made me who I am as an interesting individual. Or I hope to be an interesting individual. My parents were great, they taught me manners, they taught me morals and everything like that. These guys made me who I am. And Second City did that, too—some good and some bad.

While Sahlins produced, occasionally directed, and kept an eagle eye on the bottom line, Del Close continued his tumultuous tenure as Second City's artistic director. Close was even hired at one point by *Saturday Night Live,* where he spent a season as acting coach and had himself billed in the closing credits as "house metaphysician." "Other men have lived lives of quiet desperation. I have lived a life of wild desperation," Close told the *Chicago Tribune* in late 1978. He'd spent the start of that year undergoing alcohol-aversion therapy at the Schick Shadell Hospital in Texas.

### Michael Gellman

Donny DePollo and I would go over to Del's house after notes. We'd say, "Let's go to Del's house and get real notes."

Nasty-ass place. I'd have to get high just to deal with the smell. The cats shit for months and he wouldn't clean it up. A sushi joint was next door. He'd let 'em out, they'd have supper with the used fish, and come home and crap in the house. It was nasty. And he'd wear the same clothes for three weeks at a time. It just smelled bad. But if you smoked a couple of joints of really good shit, you never noticed.

### Bernard Sahlins

I never went in there. But I hear it was the worst—hygienically removed from cleanliness.

### Joyce Sloane

Del was insane always. He made several suicide attempts at his apartment right across the street. He would call me first to say, "I've tried it again." Then the ambulance would come and I would get hysterical and he'd be getting in the ambulance and he'd say, "My respiration should stop any moment again."

### Michael Gellman

I'm sitting in Del's apartment and I'd never met John Brent, but I knew he did the *How to Speak Hip* album with Del. So there's a knock on the door and Del's got, like, five locks in his lair.

He says, [*deep Del voice*] "Who is it?"

[*Stoner/hippie voice*] "It's John, man. Let me in."

"John's in New York."

"No, Del, man, it's me, John. It's Brent, man! Let me in."

"All right, very well."

He opens the locks but he still has two of them on. "I better let you in. What are you doing here?"

And John's like, "Oh, Del, I was in the Metropolitan Museum of Art this morning."

"And you had to fly back to Chicago? That doesn't make any fucking sense. You were in the Metropolitan Museum of Art and you had to come and see me?"

"Yeah! Oh, right, dig. They were cleaning the mummy cases, man."

"They were cleaning the mummy cases and you had to fly here? John, you're not making any fucking sense at all, man. What are you doing here?"

"Oh, right, dig, Del."

Here he reaches into his jacket and pulls out an opium pipe, and Del goes, "John, that appears to be an Egyptian opium pipe."

"Yeah, man!"

"You stole an Egyptian opium pipe from the Metropolitan Museum of Art?"

"Yeah!"

And Del says, "John, there appears to still be some shit in the pipe."

"Yeah!"

"John, you stole an Egyptian opium pipe with opium in it and brought it here to me? You are a true friend!"

And he turns to me and says, "Gellman, you don't do needles, do you?"

I went, "No, man."

He went, "You better split."

So the next day, Del comes in. He's like two and a half hours late for rehearsal. And there was a little restaurant on Wells called the Stagecoach, but we called it the Roach Coach. He goes, "I don't know what's wrong. Sorry I'm late. It's either the ham and cheese sandwich I had at the Roach Coach or the two-thousand-year-old opium I shot up last night."

Well, at this point, Mert Rich and Betty Thomas are beside themselves. And I'm going, "Del, you can't direct like this." He goes, "Gellman's right, Gellman's right! I can't direct, I can't direct! I don't know what the fuck I'm doing! I'm done! I'm through!"

And he goes racing down the front stairs and locks himself in his apartment. And we're all sitting around going, "Well, I guess we're not having rehearsal today. What the hell?"

Then Del calls up Joyce Sloane and says, "I've just drunk half a bottle of vodka and taken all the pills in my apartment. Goodbye, Joyce, goodbye!" And Joyce comes up to Donny DePollo and me and goes, "You better go over to Del's apartment. I think he's trying to kill himself again."

So we're banging on his door, going, "Del, come on, man. Let us in! Del, man!" Finally the fire trucks pull up and the firemen come in and he won't let us in. And they've got an ax. I actually saw this. And just as the ax is about to hit the door, Del opens the door and goes, "Uh, I'm better now. Let's go and rehearse."

That was kind of a typical day in the life of ol' Del.

## Tim Kazurinsky

Del was a wizard. He was brilliant and he was horrible. I did three shows: one when he was an alcoholic, one when he was a junkie, and one when he was straight. You didn't know which Del you were going to get. He would literally try to get women to disrobe onstage. He would savage people who didn't follow the rules of improvisation. But you took all of this craziness, because when he was on, there was nobody like him. He'd be drunk for two or three classes, and then you would come in and he would say things that were so astonishing and brilliant, and he'd get you to do work where you couldn't believe you were coming up with the stuff you were coming up with. The best stuff that I probably ever did was in the workshops with Del. There are actors who will tell you that they hated Del, because he was devoid of social graces back then. A lot of people know the old Del from the nineties, when he was this mellow pussycat—this guru. We didn't know that Del. The Del in the seventies and eighties was a different Del. But it was exciting.

I remember Robin Williams once showed up and he wanted to meet Del. He'd always heard about Del. So somebody went over to Del's apartment across the street and had him come over. And Del was so hammered that when he walked down into the greenroom, he missed a step and just crumpled down and totally collapsed, drunk and stoned, and we were like, "There's your genius."

## Lance Kinsey

One of the very first workshops I was in—we were all new—Del's standing up right at the very edge of the stage, and we're all sitting at the little tables in front. We've heard this guy's a genius and we're all scared of him, and who knows what he's going to say. A pearl is going to fall out and diamonds are going to glitter. And he's pushing his glasses up his nose, and he goes, "All right, everybody, I'm going to count to three." And he proceeds: "One, two, three." And all of a sudden he plunges straight forward and crashes off the stage onto the tables where we're sitting. And we were all stunned and shocked. We go, "Holy crap!" And we picked him up, and he's practically knocked silly, and he gets up and goes, "I thought you were going to catch me." Well, we didn't know that was a trust exercise. No one had told us, "Oh, you've got to catch the guy." And that was our introduction to Del.

### Jim Belushi

Del was drinking quite a bit. And typical addicts, they try to push everyone in their life away from them, especially people who care for them. So he was going through that process. He was pissing off Joyce and Bernie and Miriam Flynn, particularly. She was kind of the conscience of the cast. They'd want to ban him from the theater and they couldn't take him anymore. I was in the theater, right by the entrance, and he was walking up as I was walking in. And I said, "Hey, Del, I know what you're doing, and I know everybody's hating you right now, but I love you, man, and I trust you." "Oh, you trust me, do ya?" "Yeah, Del, I trust ya." And he wound up and kicked me in the nuts! I mean, a full kick in the nuts. Nothing soft. Committed. And I bowled right over.

### Bruce Jarchow

We were always worried about him. We were up having a meeting with Bernie and, ostensibly, Del about the running order of our new show and throwing back some ideas of what to develop and what not to develop, and Del didn't show up for the longest time. Since he lived right across the street, they sent Larry Coven to go out and get him. So Larry goes out and he comes back about five minutes later, and he's ashen and goes, [*high, worried voice*] "Del's door was open. I could hear the shower running. I think he's dead. I think he's dead. He's finally done it! He's dead!" So Tim Kazurinsky, Rob Riley, and I went over to Del's apartment, and the door was unlocked and the water was running, and we go into the bathroom and there's Del, sitting in the shower in a little baby bassinet tub kind of thing, and he's out. And I thought, "Well, he's dead." So I poked him, and he goes, "I must have fallen asleep in the shower." And he eventually came to the meeting. But we were always on a semi suicide watch for Del.

### Nancy McCabe-Kelly, cast member

I got along with Del. I don't know why. In our era, he didn't seem to have a problem with the women in the cast. Del had sort of mellowed a bit. He was caustic, but we took it with a grain of salt. We said, "Del is Del. He's a character." He did crazy things. And at that point we were sort of watching out for him to make sure he stayed on the straight and narrow. He didn't scare us. He could say things.

### Mary Gross

I once met a young girl on the street. She introduced herself to me and said that she was taking a workshop with Del and she was afraid that she was not doing very well in the class. And she proceeded to tell me that he had asked the students to take off their clothes so they could learn how not to be inhibited onstage. And I said, "Del asked you in front of a class to take your clothes off?" She said yes, that he had asked everyone to take their clothes off. And she said, "I just couldn't do it." And I said, "That's okay. Now, what was Del doing while people were taking their clothes off?" She said, "Well, he was in the back of the class with a camera." And at that point I felt like saying, "Run! Run! Run for your life!" Because I thought, "What in the hell is he doing?" And this girl was saying to me, "Gosh, do you think I'm in trouble? I feel like I'm failing this class because I could not take my clothes off." He was having some fun at their expense. They were trusting him the way altar boys trust priests. They thought they were in safe hands, but from that story I did not feel they were, on that day. He didn't do anyone serious harm, but I still thought it was out of line. The thing about Del is, in spite of the presentation he gave us, it wouldn't have been Second City without him.

On March 5, 1982, John Belushi died of a cocaine and heroin overdose at the Chateau Marmont in Los Angeles. He was thirty-three. Family, friends, and fans mourned the loss while also taking stock of their own mortality. His Second City siblings were no exception.

Del Close—his mentor, fellow addict, and sometime enabler—was especially shaken and became deeply depressed. Not long thereafter, upon reading an advance copy of Bob Woodward's often unflattering Belushi biography, *Wired,* Close grew despondent. According to a 2003 account in *Chicago* magazine, an acquaintance of Close's "found him sitting alone in his darkened kitchen staring at a gun and a copy of *Wired* on the table." After reading aloud a portion about "the first time he had gotten Belushi high," Close asked the acquaintance, "Why should I keep on living?" But he did, for another seventeen years—partly by quitting hard drugs in Belushi's memory.

### Will Aldis

John died, and that was it. It really did stop. Like, on a dime. On a dime. It was like, one day it was going on, and then the next morning it wasn't. And in that sense, he did not die in vain. I'm sure his death saved a bunch of people. You go, "Jesus Christ, that guy was a bull. And he's *dead*? Fuck it. Fuck. It." And everybody stopped. Cold turkey. Good night. That's it. No more. I mean, people still smoked dope. But cocaine? No. Over. Over and out.

### Nonie Newton-Breen

When I first heard it, I wasn't sure who had died. I just heard "Belushi." I didn't know if it was Jim or if it was John. It was really sad. Our cast went to New York for the funeral, and the weather was shitty, and the plane got delayed in Boston. And by the time we showed up with Joyce and Bernie and Fred and all of us, they were packing up. The last camera crew was leaving the cathedral, and we were trying to find out where everybody went. And finally we got Father Guido Sarducci to tell us it was Peter Aykroyd's apartment, so we all went and got sloshed. I knew John and Judy when I was pregnant. I went out with them and took them to a jazz club on Rush Street and called ahead and made sure nobody bothered John, because at the time people just wanted to eat him, he was so popular. We had a great night out. When my son was born, they sent him stuffed animals, and I always remember John putting his ear to my stomach and just sort of winking at Judy. I often thought, "God, if he had only lived, maybe they would have had a kid, and who knows what?" But it was a terrible time. It was a terrible, sad time.

### John Kapelos

I worked that Friday night and then they flew us to New York and we went to the funeral. Because of the proliferation of drug humor in our show and cocaine jokes and this and that, because of how Belushi died, we had cops out in the audience watching our company because Second City got to be known as some sort of haven for that sort of behavior. I didn't actually see anybody in the audience sitting there like John Candy at the end of *The Blues Brothers,* with their glasses on—obviously not part of the audience. But I believe that we probably had some plainclothes people coming in and watching the show. Bernie pulled a cocaine blackout that Lance Kinsey and I did. Immediately, it was just out of the show that day, and drug references were curtailed.

### Bernard Sahlins

When John died, there was a service on Martha's Vineyard and then we flew to New York for another service at Saint John the Divine. Jim and my wife, Jane, and I shared a taxi. And Jim asked me to stop at the White Horse Tavern. We got out, drank a toast to John, and got back in. It was homage to his brother.

### Will Aldis

It got very macabre. Because the line [in the "White Horse Tavern" scene] was "Sheet over the head! Dead, gone, dead!" And it's all about these guys who die and it's about Jim Belushi and his brother. And then the next thing you know, there's John being pulled out of the Chateau Marmont with a sheet over his head. It's so fucking prophetic. That's the weird thing. We did the scene four years before John died, and it was about him. Jim played John. That was a chiller.

I was actually in Chicago when it happened. I was visiting because Jim was doing *Pirates of Penzance.* We were out just hanging around, drinking, fucking around. And then I got up in the morning and there it was on TV. And my relationship with Jim has never been the same. It was too weird. Too weird. We did that scene, and the scene was about the destructiveness of artistic geniuses, and there it was. And it was his brother. I stayed and watched the performance that night. I was in his dressing room, and he went on. I couldn't believe he went on, but he did. And he was great.

### Jim Belushi

When something like that happens, you go into denial and shock. I'd been doing the show for so long that you just kind of go on memory, instinct. I found out about five o'clock, and then I did the show that night. But I do remember one moment. After the show there was a press conference, and I walked out into the lobby, and it was just filled with press and cameras. And I stood out there ready to get barraged. And it was silent. I sat there, you know, waiting for a question. And nothing. Nobody said a word. "Anybody have a question?" And [movie critic] Roger Ebert walked up and said, "I don't have a question, but I just want to say how terrible we feel about the loss of your brother." And that was the nicest press thing I've ever heard. I'll never forget Roger for that.

While mainstage performers garnered most of the spotlight, other Second City companies performed greatest hits shows at Chateau Louise and on the road. In the early eighties, one such group made a plea to perform original material instead. With the surreptitious assistance of Joyce Sloane, who aided the ambitious ensemble while Sahlins was out of town, they staged their first revue, *Cows on Ice,* at a small and run-down theater one floor above the mainstage space. That was in the autumn of 1982. Twenty-seven years later—having showcased the likes of Dan Castellaneta (the voice of Homer Simpson), *SNL's* Horatio Sanz, movie and TV star Steve Carell, and Emmy-winning cable bloviator Stephen Colbert, among many others—the so-called e.t.c. company is a bigger draw than ever.

### Joyce Sloane

The Practical Theater Company had started there, and *Saturday Night Live* came and there was no Practical Theater; they all went to New York. Julia Louis-Dreyfus, Brad Hall, all of them. That place had been built for Paul Sills originally. He did *Story Theatre* back there. So we were bringing acts in. We'd bring Judy Tenuta, Emo Philips—all those people were working back there. So Jeff Michalski came to me and said, "Why can't we work back there?" I said, "No reason at all." Bernie never thought it was a good idea because he

Bernard Sahlins in front of Playwrights at The Second City (which became the second Second City), 1961. *(Morton Shapiro)*

Alan Arkin, Paul Sills, and Anthony Holland confer in 1961. *(Morton Shapiro)*

The Second City cast, 1961. Clockwise from top: Anthony Holland, Bill Alton, Joan Rivers, Hamilton Camp, and Avery Schreiber. *(Courtesy of* Chicago Sun-Times*)*

The Second City cast, 1962. Avery Schreiber, Bill Alton, Del Close, Mina Kolb, and Dick Schaal get flu shots from Dr. Meyer Pedott of the Chicago Board of Health. *(Courtesy of Chicago Sun-Times)*

Sheldon Patinkin, 1966.
*(Morton Shapiro)*

Judy Graubart and David Steinberg, 1966. *(Morton Shapiro)*

Fred Willard, Mina Kolb, and Robert Klein, late 1960s. *(Courtesy of* Chicago Sun-Times*)*

John Belushi and Joe Flaherty in the scene "Brest Litovsk" from *Cum Grano Salis*, 1971. *(Dick Klein)*

Judy Morgan, Eugenie Ross-Leming, Jim Fisher, Joe Flaherty, and John Belushi in the scene "Young Totalitarians" from the revue *43rd Parallel, or, McCabre and Mrs. Miller,* 1972. *(Dick Klein)*

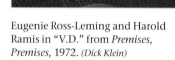

Eugenie Ross-Leming and Harold Ramis in "V.D." from *Premises, Premises,* 1972. *(Dick Klein)*

Betty Thomas, Jim Staahl, and John Candy in "Traffic Bust" from *Phase 46, or, Watergate Tomorrow, Comedy Tonight!,* 1973. *(Dick Klein)*

Bill Murray and Jim Staahl in a blackout scene from *Phase 46, or, Watergate Tomorrow, Comedy Tonight!*, 1973. *(Dick Klein)*

Bill Murray, Betty Thomas, Tino Insana, Cassandra Danz, Raul Moncada, and Del Close, 1974. *(Courtesy of The Second City)*

A promo shot for *Alterations While You Wait*, Toronto, 1975. Clockwise from bottom left: Andrea Martin, Eugene Levy, Dan Aykroyd, Catherine O'Hara, and John Candy. *(Hugh Wesley Photo)*

Dan Aykroyd and Eugene Levy in "Cadets" from *Alterations While You Wait,* Toronto, 1975. *(Hugh Wesley Photo)*

Bernard Sahlins, Joyce Sloane, and Fred Kaz pose onstage with The Second City's now-famous bentwood chairs, 1977. *(Courtesy of* Chicago Sun-Times*)*

Will Aldis and Jim Belushi in *Sexual Perversity Among the Buffalo*, 1978. *(Jay King)*

George Wendt as
George S. Cardinal
Cody, from the 1979
revue *I Remember
Dada*. *(Jay King)*

Martin Short as Ed Grimley with Catherine O'Hara at a Toronto cast reunion, 1980.
*(Hugh Wesley Photo)*

*SCTV* crew Martin Short, John Candy, Rick Moranis, Dave Thomas, and Eugene Levy at a United Way Benefit, Toronto, 1982. *(Hugh Wesley Photo)*

Martin Short and John Candy at a United Way benefit, Toronto, 1982.
*(Hugh Wesley Photo)*

Andrew Alexander outside the
Old Firehall in Toronto, 1985.
*(Hugh Wesley Photo)*

Bonnie Hunt, The
Second City Train-
ing Center Polaroid,
1985. *(Courtesy of The
Second City)*

Dan Castellaneta as Hitler in *How Green Were My Values*, 1986.
*(JenniferGirard.com)*

Richard Kind, Dan Castellaneta, and Isabella Hoffman in *How Green Were My Values,* 1986. *(JenniferGirard.com)*

Mike Myers and Deborah Theaker in "Wayne and Nancy" from *Not Based on Anything by Stephen King,* Toronto, 1986. *(Rick Alexander)*

Steve Carell, The Second City
Training Center Polaroid, 1986.
*(Courtesy of The Second City)*

Stephen Colbert,
The Second City
Training Center
Polaroid, 1987.
*(Courtesy of The
Second City)*

Amy Sedaris, The Second
City Training Center
Polaroid, 1987. *(Courtesy
of The Second City)*

Bonnie Hunt, Mike Myers, and Barbara Wallace in *Kuwait Until Dark, or, Bright Lights, Night Baseball*, 1988. *(Rick Alexander)*

Chris Farley, The Second City Training Center Polaroid, 1987. *(Courtesy of The Second City)*

Chris Farley, Jill Talley, Bob Odenkirk, Holly Wortell, and Tim Meadows in "Motivation" from *Flag Smoking Permitted in Lobby Only, or, Censorama*, 1990. *(JenniferGirard.com)*

Stephen Colbert
and Nia Vardalos
in a Second City
Northwest produc-
tion of *Destiny and
How to Avoid It*,
1992.
*(JenniferGirard.com)*

Amy Sedaris and Steve
Carell in "High Rise"
from *Truth, Justice, or
the American Way*, 1992.
*(JenniferGirard.com)*

Steve Carell, Paul
Dinello, Stephen
Colbert, and David
Razowsky sing
"The Obvious
Song" from *Take
Me Out to the
Balkans*, 1993.
*(JenniferGirard.com)*

Scott Adsit, Jon Glaser, Adam McKay, Jenna Jolovitz, and Rachel Dratch in "Fifties Scene" from *Piñata Full of Bees*, 1995. *(JenniferGirard.com)*

Scott Adsit and Tina Fey in "Stripper" from *Paradigm Lost*, 1997. *(JenniferGirard.com)*

The Second City co-owners Andrew Alexander and Len Stuart outside the mainstage theater at 1616 North Wells Street, 2009. *(Courtesy of The Second City/Bob Knuth)*

After a special performance of *Between Barack and a Hard Place,* 2007. (Back row) Craig Taylor, Robin Hammond, Andrew Alexander, Barack Obama, Amber Ruffin, Brian Gallivan, Alison Riley; (middle row) Joyce Sloane, Ruby Streak, Brad Morris; (front row) Molly Erdman, Ithamar Enriquez, Kelly Leonard, Joe Canale, Kirk Hanley, Monica Wilson. *(Courtesy of The Second City/Bob Knuth)*

didn't want us to compete with ourselves. We weren't going to tell Bernie about it. He was out of town.

### Jane Morris, cast member

When Joyce hired me, she said, "You'll be in the touring company. I can't promise you'll ever be in mainstage. It's just a leg up and that's how you have to look at it." And the truth is, there was only the touring company and mainstage. So you were literally waiting for somebody to die or something. There were a bunch of us at that point like Bill Applebaum and Jim Fay and Jeff Michalski. During the summer, you were completely out of work, and so we're like, "What's the deal?" And Joyce thought that was a pretty decent idea and let us do one night a week [in the small theater]. But we were supposed to do our tour co. show, which is old Second City scenes. Well, what we had been doing on the road is writing stuff, and we would take it out on the road.

### Bill Applebaum, cast member

It was pretty haphazard. It was pretty slipshod. The booth was barely functional. It was this old movie theater projection booth. The lights worked. You could sort of hear things. The stage was sort of configured like the mainstage, where there was a window and a revolving door and a side door. Or a couple of windows and doors, and a left and a right wing. The stage itself was small. The backstage was almost nonexistent. It was cramped, but we didn't care.

### Dan Castellaneta, cast member

We were on an outpost, I guess, and we were able to do a lot different stuff than your traditional Second City show. As a matter of fact, that company kind of directed themselves. Don DePollo was kind of the director, but Donny was one of the crazy free and easy guys, you know? He loved anarchy. And so it was sort of up to us to pull it together.

### Jane Morris

We were doing our pieces elsewhere, and then we started doing them back in that space and we just kept taking out more old Second City material and were putting in more of our new material, and then we wanted to open the show. And Bernie said no. He thought he'd be competing with himself. And we're like, "No, you'd just have more of what you have." He just didn't want us to do it, and he told us in no uncertain terms that we were not allowed to do that. But we ignored him and—this is the hilarious part—Joyce became like Sergeant Schultz. "I see nothing, I see nothing." And she would tell us when Bernie was out of town, because Bernie would go on these archeological digs. So she would tell us what to do. Like, "You need to have a listing in the paper by x date." And, "You need to send a press release out by this date." And she would tell one person that, or somebody in the office. And then we would go do it. So she clandestinely, quietly helped us. Like, "I didn't tell you this. Don't tell where you found this out." And so we opened the show, *Cows on Ice,* when Bernie was out of town. And he was livid, but the show was a hit.

### Jeff Michalski, cast member

I don't know Bernie that well, but I got the idea that we were upstaging what was happening up front. He was directing the shows up front, primarily. But I'm just telling you that we had full houses, we got great reviews, and it was smart material. It was zany. It definitely had a bizarre twist to it because Jane's a bit bizarre, I'm a bit bizarre, Jimmy Fay was a bit bizarre. And Bill Applebaum. The scenes had all of Bernie's criteria except that maybe our characters were eccentric. But we were eccentric.

### Bill Applebaum

As I recall it, nobody was pleased. I don't think mainstage liked the fact that we were doing this. Bernie was certainly not pleased. Joyce was great. She was very supportive of us, and I think she believed in us quite a bit. And we opened and got extraordinary reviews. Stunningly wonderful reviews.

### Jane Morris

We just had nothing to lose. If we all get fired or we never leave the e.t.c., we will have work that we wrote that we put up. We will leave with characters we've developed, scenes we've developed. We'll have a body of work to show for it at least, which is not something we'll have in the touring company. So we just went for it.

An especially glowing review, by the *Chicago Tribune*'s Larry Kart, was headlined: "Brilliant 'Cows on Ice' a Must for Laugh Lovers." And Kart didn't waste time getting to the plaudits. " 'Cows on Ice,' the Second City National Touring Company's first original show, is absolutely superb—as funny and pointed as any improvisational comedy revue I've ever seen," it began. "At least two scenes from the show, 'War Games' and 'Toxic Waste,' are as good as anything that has been on the Second City mainstage in recent years . . ."

### Joyce Sloane

Bernie got into a limo at the airport to come into town, picked up a newspaper, and the review was in there. He was going to let them all go, but of course he didn't. I let Bernie yell. It was such a ma-and-pa thing that we never had a fight. I let him yell, and the next day he forgot about it.

### Cheryl Sloane

They had an interesting working relationship. My mom knew how to get what she needed from Bernie to keep the theater going. But she never really knew what was going on completely. I mean, Bernie sat with the checkbook on his desk and he handled all that. And they were kind of like good cop, bad cop. The actors went to my mom when they needed something, then she'd go to Bernie—she knew how to work things out. Like, if Bernie didn't want to put somebody in the resident company who my mom thought should be there, she'd be like, "Just hold on, sit tight, sit tight." And eventually she'd get her way.

### Jeff Michalski

Bernie didn't even see the first e.t.c. show. He saw maybe a couple scenes in the second act in previews. And that show was a great show. It really was. There are still people who say they came to Second City to be in the company because they saw that show.

### Bernard Sahlins

Terrible show. It was just pandering to the audience, as I remember. But they loved it, so what the hell.

### Cheryl Sloane

That was so exciting. It was what Second City was about. And it was such a good show. The staff loved it. We'd be back there all the time.

### Bill Applebaum

We started to fill the house every night. And we didn't even have a contract back then. Somebody said, "You can split the house. Whatever you bring in, that's fine," not expecting us to do anything. And as I recall, we were filling the house so much we were making more than the mainstage, and that really ticked people off.

### Jane Morris

Bernie actually did come in and look at a rehearsal of our show at one point. And several points thereafter, too, in subsequent shows. But early on, the thing I really remember about Bernie is that he would come in and look at a scene and he would tell you what was wrong with it. And he would be right about what was wrong with that scene, what it was lacking. He had a great eye for that. But he was always wrong—and I want to say one hundred percent always wrong—about how to fix it. It was really stuff that would kill the scene flat.

### Richard Kind

Bernie knew where there was a problem. He didn't know how to fix it all the time, but he always knew where there was a problem. He's a man of great taste and smart taste and he didn't care about pleasing the audience. He cared about doing a good job, and that really was first and foremost. But he wasn't that good. He would just say, "This is not good," or "This doesn't work," or "Something's wrong." He was like a Geiger counter. It's like, you see that there's gold, but somebody else has to start digging for it.

### Dan Castellaneta

Bernie had it fixed in his head what was funny. "This is the way things work. There's a formula, and a way, and it goes this way." And we were always of the mind of, "Let's throw whatever we can up there and see what sticks on the wall." If we ever tried to tell him what it was, he would pooh-pooh the idea. So we just did it. And then Bernie would go, "Okay. I see what you're doing. But you've got to not do this, because the audience doesn't understand. You've got to add this piece of information." He would refine or reject. He was a great editor.

### Jeff Michalski

At the time, they weren't doing such great shows on the mainstage; it was a transition period for them. Belushi and those guys had left, they'd lost Del, they'd brought in a director who didn't know what the fuck he was doing. And they just couldn't get a good show up for a while there.

Eventually, Del Close's artistic brilliance failed to compensate for his bad behavior, and at the end of 1982 he was once again asked to vacate the premises. This exile, however, would be shorter than the first.

### Nonie Newton-Breen

There was a time when Del wasn't well, and we were in rehearsals for something, and I had a deal with Bernie and Joyce that I could bring my son Spencer to rehearsals. It was bad enough we were paying babysitters at night. That was sucking up my entire salary. So we brought him to rehearsal. And Del, who hated women and babies, said, "What is *that*?" I said, "Excuse me?" And he said, "What is *that*?" I said, "*That* is my child." And he said, "Well, you don't bring a dog to rehearsal. What's *that* doing here?" I was like, "All right, that's it." So we went and talked to Bernie and said, "Look. We're going to make it easy on you. We know you have a long history with Del. We're giving our two-week notice. We just can't afford to hire sitters and be in rehearsals and leave our kid alone at night. We can't leave him night and day." He was a little boy.

### Danny Breen

We gave two-week notices that night, to the show, and Bernie was out of town. But he called and said, "Listen, what would it take to get you two to stay in the show?" And we said, "Well, Del would have to go," thinking, "That'll never happen." And Bernie just went, "Consider it done," and hung up. And I stared at the phone, going, "Oh, no! What have I done?" Four of us from the cast—Lance, Noni, Meagen Fay, and I—were very happy. And John Kapelos and Rick Thomas, who were also in the cast, were very unhappy, because they wanted to work with Del. And then there were the workshop people. Del was into his witch thing at the time, so he had workshops doing voodoo against the four of us. People were coming up to me after shows, going, "I'm in Del's workshop, and we're putting curses on you." Luckily I didn't take it too seriously, but it was sort of like, "Really? Ugh!" I think he was having fun.

### Bernard Sahlins

I had to make a choice between Nonie and Danny, and Del. And it wasn't a hard choice because he had been acting up in several respects and he never finished a show. So I met him at the Old Town Ale House in the afternoon and said, "Del, we've got to part." And he said, "Fine." He was like a pied piper to a lot of people, though. He indulged the actors in a dual conspiracy against either me or the world or somebody else. And I think he was relieved when I let him go.

Although Sahlins continued to direct mainstage revues, he also began to contemplate a departure from Second City. In January 1985, a couple of weeks after the theater celebrated its twenty-fifth anniversary with a star-studded assemblage of specially flown-in alums, Sahlins phoned Alexander. Having guided Second City for a quarter century, the co-founder and sole owner of Chicago's most venerable theatrical institution felt the time was right to make his exit. At first a bit reluctant to part with a place he'd nurtured from birth, Sahlins ultimately cast aside his doubts and made Alexander and Stuart an offer they couldn't refuse. Sahlins didn't tell Joyce Sloane, however, until after the deal was done.

### Andrew Alexander

Right after the twenty-fifth [anniversary], in January, Bernie called me and said that he wanted to sell. And I said, "Definitely." And we concluded a transaction before March. So it was a fairly painless negotiation. Bernie was good in that he didn't want everything up front. He gave us terms, I think five years. It worked out for both of us. He got the price that he wanted, and we got the ability to spread it out over a bit of time, which was great.

### Len Stuart

There's a lot of politics with actors, a lot of babysitting. And Bernie got tired of it all.

### Bernard Sahlins

I was getting to the point where nothing was new enough. Somebody would come up with an idea, and I thought, "Gee, we did that." So the work was not as interesting for me.

### Sheldon Patinkin

I've never heard Bernie express a single misgiving. Of course it must have been difficult; it's always difficult to say goodbye to something or someone you've been part of. It happens all the time in our business.

### Andrew Alexander

Toronto was doing well. I had just wound up *SCTV* in '84, so we were going into syndication. I think he felt that it was logical and realized that I did a pretty good job in Toronto. And I don't know for sure, but I don't think there were that many people who would have been right for it.

### Cheryl Sloane

It was just different. Actually, a lot of it was good. All of a sudden there was somebody who wanted a management team and wanted people to be aware of monthly statements and numbers and bottom lines and all this stuff that was Bernie's thing before. So it was definitely different from the business end. I don't think from the creative end. It was very immediate. Everybody who was at Second City in those days felt ownership, like it was theirs. It wasn't. It's not theirs. But they felt ownership. You couldn't move the furniture around or put up a picture without everybody commenting on it. So when it was sold and nobody was a part of it, they all kind of felt like, "Hey, what's going on here? This is my home." It's like when you grow up in your house and your parents decide to sell it. But I think that over time everybody's okay. Life goes on.

### Andrew Alexander

We had signed an agreement over at the Ambassador hotel, and then I walked back to the theater, and we walked up to the bar, and Bernie said, "I'm going to talk to Joyce and tell her what I've done." And then, within five minutes, he came back and said, "Okay. I told her." I went in and said,

"Joyce, believe me, you're a very important part of this, so don't worry." And we continued talking.

### Joyce Sloane

I knew what was going on, because everything went through me. But I didn't say anything. I figured, "When Bernie's ready to tell me, he'll tell me." That's why we had such a good relationship. And he came in, and I cried and he cried and he said, "It'll be very good for you."

### Andrew Alexander

I didn't know who he'd talked to. It definitely came as a shock to her.

### Bernard Sahlins

Since it was a confidential matter, I didn't talk to anybody. I think any change of that sort might be upsetting. Joyce is still well treated, and any doubts she had were, I think, allayed.

### Cheryl Sloane

She was really hurt. But she didn't take action on it, which I think is part of what their relationship was. Because it was ma-and-pa and it wasn't a business company relationship, she didn't actually take action on it. She kind of got wind that it was going to happen, and watched it happen. I think her emotions guided her on that. She was hurt that he wouldn't talk to her about it first. It was weird. A lot of people would have been hurt to a point of not being able to have that relationship anymore, but that's not my mom. My mom is just not a grudge holder.

# 8

# Triumphs in Toronto, Shake-ups in Chicago, and a Van Down by the River

**Chris Farley**
**Bonnie Hunt**
**Mike Myers**

1978–91

**NOT LONG AFTER** Second City Chicago began getting more notice as a result of *Saturday Night Live,* a similar phenomenon hit Toronto courtesy of *SCTV.* By the late seventies, due in part to the growing popularity of Count Floyd and Yosh Shmenge and the rest of their Melonville compatriots, the Old Firehall was a top destination for locals and tourists. It remained so throughout the next decade. And while the Chicago influence lingered (visiting directors included Bernard Sahlins, Sheldon Patinkin, Del Close, and Michael Gellman), Toronto became so successful that outposts (now closed) opened in Edmonton, Alberta, and London, Ontario.

**Andrew Alexander**

The feeling was that Second City Toronto was doing better work than Chicago at the time. There was more going on in Toronto than there was in Chicago.

**Sally Cochrane, producer**

By the time I got there as a waitress in '78, it was moving and shaking. At the beginning of the eighties, there was a time when we were sold out every single night of the week for eight shows for three months. Toronto was a big tourist market for Americans at the time, so there were a lot of Americans coming up. We also did a lot of corporate business—groups of people that would come in. Basically it was office parties, but it was a real backbone. We didn't have to rely entirely on single tickets.

### Andrew Alexander

The law in Ontario at the time was that fifty percent of your revenue had to be food, and the other fifty percent could be liquor. The percentages were ridiculous. And I had come from Chicago, where dinner theater was huge back in the early and mid-seventies. So I said, "Okay, let's put a dinner package together." Then I hired this young British kid, David Thompson, who ran a phone room—a boiler room full of people who were out of, like, the bar in *Star Wars*. They were a weird bunch. I'll never forget there was one guy named Bob Sprott who used to come in, and he would bring his bottle of vodka and put it on the table. And he would talk [on the phone] to the CEOs of any big company. He was amazing. He'd put his coat over his head, and have his bottle, and he was eloquent. He was extraordinary. So there were people like that who would sell these dinner theater packages, and that was what kept the place alive.

### John Hemphill, cast member

There were broken tiles on the floor. It smelled like beer and cigarettes. You'd walk in there and you wouldn't be shocked but you'd be like, "Really? There's a show that goes on here?" But it had a real comfort zone and it was great for comedy. If you faced right [onstage], you could see the audience. And if you faced left, you could see the other part of the audience. But right down the middle, it was just sort of the entrance. It was a very odd kind of setup. But that was the charm of the place.

### Bruce Pirrie, cast member/director

I was in the touring company while *SCTV* was on the air, and I was on main-stage during the ninety-minute incarnation. We would run shows for six months at a time, and the houses were full. If you wanted to go on a Friday or Saturday night, you had to book a ticket two or three months in advance. We had to run shows for six months so everybody who wanted to see it could see it. We were selling tickets for shows that we hadn't even started work on. If [audiences] didn't draw a direct connection, the *SCTV* brand was really highly visible. The TV show used to end with a shot of the Firehall theater. So I think the general consciousness about Second City was that people would come down expecting to see John Candy and Catherine O'Hara performing onstage. I'm certain I was a little bit of a letdown. But even when I was in the touring company, we would show up at places and they'd all rush out to see John Candy stepping lightly out of the van with square wheels that we traveled in. And that would be the first disappointment of the evening. "He's not here." "Is the Jewish guy here?" "No, none of them." And then it was, "Well, who are you?" "Well, we're the next wave." "I'll come back when you wash ashore."

It wasn't so bad. It wasn't as if the entire town all of a sudden started looking around for a rope. Just every once in a while people would take Second City to mean the *SCTV* cast. The touring company can nowadays hardly get a gig—and it's no reflection on the people in it—but the branding of Second City preceded us. So we were getting booked into all manner of things—universities, bars that wanted to try and raise the tone of the place because they'd lost their liquor license. One time we pulled up in front of a place that said, "Tuesday mud wrestling, Wednesday Second City." It was a biker bar. The stage manager had to persuade them to unplug the jukebox while we were performing.

### Bob Martin, cast member

The social aspect of it was fabulous. Especially at the Firehall. We had our dressing rooms right off the back of the stage, and it was one communal room. So all the guys and the girls changed together. There were no barriers. Literally no barriers. I remember this sexual harassment memo went around because somebody in the office had been harassed by someone within the staff who was not in the acting company. And so all of these sexual harassment guidelines were posted all over the building, and we looked at them and were just laughing. It didn't apply to us at all. I mean, we're onstage grabbing each other's asses and changing in the same room. Imagine working in the same advertising company and all changing together. So the bonding thing was really unprecedented for me.

### Robin Duke

It never seemed to me that Andrew got involved with that much creatively. And that's really smart on his part. He let everybody run it. He let the cast be creative, and the directors. Occasionally a mandate would come down, like, "We need more of this for the show." I remember one show we were in: "All the characters are too dumb. We've got to make them smarter." So we would make that adjustment. But other than that, he did not have his hand in there fixing it or anything.

### Nia Vardalos, cast member

Mine is one of those insane stories that you hear about in folklore, and it actually happened to be true. I couldn't get in. I had auditioned and auditioned and I couldn't even get a callback. And somebody said, "You know, if you work there, they get to know you, and sometimes they'll give you a shot in one of the touring companies. And you get to take the classes for free. It was like, 'nuff said. I was a starving student and I couldn't really afford much. So I took the job in the box office, and I would just sit there and answer the phones and watch the show for free, which was my favorite part. And I took every class I could.

I have one of those memories where I can hear or see something and sing it back to you. So I'd watched the show for a couple of weeks. It was about seven thirty, and let's say the show started at eight. And the stage manager came running into the box office and she was flipping through the Rolodex looking for the understudy's number. And I said, "What's going on?" And she said, "This actress is sick and we need to find the understudy." And it was before cell phones or anything. So they were calling around, they couldn't find her, they couldn't find the second understudy, and [the stage manager] was freaking out. And she left the box office. And I don't know what came over me, I went backstage and I went, "Um, hi." And she went, "What!" She was on the phone with Chicago and trying to find a producer in Toronto. "Yeah, hi, I'm a member of Actors' Equity and I think I know your show." She said, "Get out." And I went, "Okay."

So I walked back down the hall, thinking, "Well, now I've just lost my job in the box office. Idiot, idiot, idiot." And she came running up behind me and she said, "Let me ask you something: Do you really know the show?" And I said, "I do." And at that point one of the actors was walking in and said, "Who knows the show?" And the stage manager told him the story, what was wrong with the actress—Deb McGrath—who'd been rushed to the hospital with an inner ear imbalance. And he turned to me and said, "Do you know 'Nun'?" which was her opening scene. And I said, "Yes," and he started firing the lines at me and I started firing them back, and they just went, "Okay, you're on." So I went, "Good God, oh, no."

So they threw me backstage. The cast comes in and looks at me like, "What is going on?" They were not exactly friendly about it. They were horrified. "Who *is* this person? And she knows our show?" So the lights go down and I go through the first three short scenes, and I think I was in two of the three of them, and I'm stumbling around. They're taking me by the hand leading me this way and leading me that way. And then suddenly I'm onstage for "Nun," and I did the scene and it goes perfectly and the lights go down. Mark Wilson [a cast member] grabs my hands and goes, "Jesus, kid!" and throws me into the wings, and then the cast was amazing. Now they're throwing costumes at me and going, "Okay, go stage right. You're in this, do this, go here!" It was unbelievably fun and terrifying. And so the next day they hired me.

### Colin Mochrie, cast member

I think each company has their own ways of doing things. But the Chicago company is so much more politically charged, because American politics is so much more interesting than Canada's. Our most interesting prime minister was Trudeau, and that's, like, one in hundreds of years. Even within the city [of Chicago], you have such a vibrant political atmosphere and there's always something going on. You guys have sex scandals. We don't even have that. So I think our stuff tends to be sillier. We certainly could do political satire, but not in comparison to Chicago. I thought their stuff was always more deeply satirical than Toronto's.

I know there were times where every once in a while they would try to push a Chicago scene on to us when we were doing a new show. And we always felt, "We can do this, we can come up with a new show." All of it was pride. But I think there was also this thing where you had a big brother who was an exceptional sports hero and you're starting out at the junior level. It did sometimes feel that way, but I don't think it was put on us from Chicago. I think it was our feeling. There was a bit of a chip. We wanted to prove we could do anything as well as Chicago did, so we would push against taking Chicago material.

### Bob Martin

There were some periods where there definitely was friction. People are so touchy and there can be little incidents that spark. There was definitely a rivalry, but the fact is that for the most part, the Chicago companies had more experience. At least when I was around, you were in the tour co. longer before you got to mainstage in Chicago. Sometimes people were there for years and years and years. It was unusual to be in tour co. for more than a year and a half, two years, in Toronto and not be promoted to mainstage. If you weren't promoted by then, you were usually let go.

### Ryan Stiles, cast member

We wanted to put up better shows than Chicago. They were the older brother and they had been there a lot longer. I remember we sometimes used to have to put Chicago scenes in our shows if we were short, and we didn't want to do that. As the years went by, they started using some of our scenes, which made us feel a lot better. But it's two different things. You'd try to be political and you'd try to be current, but we were dealing with a Canadian-type mentality and they weren't.

### Nia Vardalos

I remember being heckled for the first time in Toronto. I was onstage when I was joining the cast for [improv] sets after I'd just gone on. And I remember that moment of, "Well, I've got the mike." So I just turned it. It hurts, it stings, and I just turned it around. I went right into the audience. What happened is, I was heavier at the time and the guy said, "I just like you, thunder thighs." And so I put the pad down that I was holding—it was when I was taking suggestions—and said, "Let's take a look at your body," and I walked into the audience and made him stand up and was like, "Love handles!" And then the audience turned on him, and it's all great, ha-ha-ha, and then you pat the guy on the back, like, "No hard feelings," and then you go back onstage. But I knew in that moment—it's almost like you have your bat mitzvah. You just grow up and you go, "I'm in control. I can handle this. I am a woman today."

*Not Based on Anything by Stephen King,* which opened in Toronto on November 12, 1986, contained a scene called "Wayne and Nancy." It featured Deborah Theaker and Mike Myers, the latter of whom eventually took his sardonic stoner-slacker character (last name: Campbell) sans girlfriend to *Saturday Night Live* and far beyond.

### Nia Vardalos

Mike Myers was in the cast when I was in the box office, and I remember it being a crazy hot time because Chicago had just come up and scouted him and brought him down there. So there was a lot of excitement and tension in the air. I think that people always felt that improv was about supporting your buddy, and when Mike got into Chicago, I think that everyone felt like, "Yeah, we all did it." And that's definitely the way Second City operated, in that you're only as good as your partners make you look.

### Bruce Pirrie

People say, "Did you know he was going to become what he's become?" I said, "No. If I'd known he was going to become what he's become, I would have become his agent."

I started in the touring company with him. We were a young bunch, but he was even younger. And at some point that can make a vast difference. He was a very funny guy, I knew that right away, and we seemed to hit it off. But even then he seemed young. He was expecting dinner. We were all living in this sitcom situation in this old hotel, and Mike would go, "Well, what's for dinner?" 'Cause his mum made him dinner the week before. But he was ambitious. He was very serious about comedy. I think he had a plan.

### Ryan Stiles

Mike always strived a little bit harder than everybody. I think he wanted to be a star more than anybody else did. And he was comfortable being onstage by himself. We all did that. Some people click and some people don't click. That's just the way it was. He always seemed to work better with the women.

He wasn't a guy that you would go out and have a few drinks with afterward. He's not the kind of guy you're going to sit down and have a lot of laughs with. He was very serious about what he did.

### Colin Mochrie

I was in a touring company when he was on mainstage, so every once in a while I would get to fill in for someone when they got film work. Within ten minutes of talking to Mike you know he's highly intelligent, very well read, and extremely knowledgeable about all forms of comedy. When we would improvise, there'd be Peter Sellers quotes and references to things that I'm sure half the audience didn't understand. When I started directing the touring company, Mike kind of inspired me, because I found a lot of the younger people coming up had no sense of the history of comedy and what had come before. And this is a gross generalization, but they thought there wasn't anything useful in that. So part of my process as a director is every once in a while we watched some old comedy, whether it be an old *Dick Van Dyke Show* or some classic Marx Brothers or even just listening to a Nichols and May routine.

### Patrick McKenna, cast member

It was still a time when it was always Chicago directors coming in to do the show, so there was a certain hierarchy. And there was always an understanding that it was easier for Chicago people to come to Toronto than it was vice versa, because it was far more political in Chicago and we did a lot of social satire in Toronto. So it wasn't as easy to transition to the Chicago style, because the politics is very specific to Chicago and that's something you have to live and breathe. So that was something that had to be nurtured in the Toronto company as well. But Canadians just weren't into political humor as much. So there were different styles that came and went, and I always thought there was a bit of difficulty for Chicago directors because they wouldn't understand that for the first little while. They were always trying to create a Chicago show on the Toronto stage.

### Bob Derkach, musical director

Toward the end of the eighties, there was still this resonance of *SCTV*, and there seemed to be a path that a Second City actor in Toronto could possibly aspire to. But as time wore on, obviously [the show] didn't have the profile anymore. What was really cool in the late eighties and during the early nineties is, a lot of folks were coming to mainstage and wanted to work for Second City Toronto because they just dug what you were doing onstage. And they were there for that specific reason. They didn't have the sense that this was going to be a stepping-stone to an immediate television career.

Back in Chicago, having made a low seven-figure profit on his initial six-thousand-dollar investment, Sahlins relinquished his day-to-day duties within the Second City organization, but stuck around to direct three more Chicago mainstage shows: *How Green Were My Values, Catch-27,* and *Jean-Paul Sartre and Ringo.* Meanwhile, Alexander began jetting west to work on expanding Second City's presence in Hollywood. Despite his extended absences, the mom-and-pop shop on Wells Street slowly started to metamorphose. After a storied quarter-century run, the Bernie and Joyce show was off the air. Its unfamiliar replacement—from a foreign land, no less!—drew intense scrutiny and searing criticism. Still, since Alexander was not yet a permanent fixture at his Chicago property, Sloane remained queen of the comedy castle. Or, as some have implied, warden of the inmate-run asylum.

### Andrew Alexander

Because there was a transition in Chicago, I didn't just want to say, "Okay, from now on, this is the direction we're going in." I don't know if "regret" is the right word to describe it, but I had made a deal out in L.A. with Imagine Films, so I was immediately flying over Chicago rather than living there.

### Debra McGrath, cast member/director

In Toronto, it was fine. I think the mood was a little different in Chicago. I do know from my friendship with Andrew that he had a rough go at the beginning. But I think it was nothing he didn't expect. Does it still hurt, is it still alienating? Yes, but he obviously weathered it, and now these people are his people. But in Toronto, I knew that Andrew was going to make that move. I knew he was going to go to L.A. or somewhere. So it wasn't surprising to us. I think he always wanted to go south of the border. I know when I resisted, he just could not fathom that I would want to stay here. Couldn't fathom it. Because that was his dream, to go there. I know to this day he talks about being shocked that I came home, because he never did and he doesn't understand the concept—because that's what his dream was. I don't think Andrew was ever a rabid Canadian. I don't mean that as a criticism. But we've had that discussion many times of, "Why didn't you stay?" He followed his dream. He's living where he wants to live, doing what he wants to do.

### Andrew Alexander

It was kind of business as usual. I kind of stuck with the structure that Bernie had left for a while. Cheryl [Sloane] was general manager at the theater and Joyce was producer, and I didn't make any dramatic changes. I thought, "There's no need to."

## Tim Kazurinsky

I remember coming into *Saturday Night Live* after John and Danny and Gilda and Bill Murray were there. Nobody wanted to know you. [In the same way,] Andrew Alexander had to come in after Bernie and take over the reins.

[Second City] had more success financially, and Andrew grew the brand and started a corporate division, and there were actually jobs for people that matriculated from Second City. A lot more people getting paychecks, paying mortgages, getting married.

Chicago-born Jeff Garlin, a successful stand-up comic who went on to star in and executive produce the HBO hit *Curb Your Enthusiasm* with Larry David, never quite made the grade. Not that he didn't try.

## Jeff Garlin, box office employee and cast member (sort of)

I couldn't get an audition. I couldn't get hired. All I got was a job in the box office. So it was very frustrating for me to see all these touring companies come and go, and the mainstage and the e.t.c., and not be part of any of it. Second City workshops used to be just Donny DePollo with level one and level two—beginner and advanced. That was it. And I remember really not enjoying that, and not getting a lot out of it. At a meeting of teachers—they were discussing what to do with me—I said, "My taking classes here has nothing to do with me being hired here as an actor, so I'm not taking classes anymore." Because I wasn't learning anything. I was kind of an asshole. I was kind of defiant.

I made a pretty good living doing stand-up, working the road. When I say a pretty good living, back then, I was making thirty-five thousand dollars a year. But when you're young and you're living in a studio apartment, it's fine. The minute I committed to Second City and said, "I'm going to do touring company, I'm gonna do this, I'm gonna do that," my car got repossessed, I went from making thirty-five thousand to maybe five thousand. What happened was, I got hired for the Northwest company [a suburban outpost], and there was a lot of anger, a lot of pressure on me. We were going to Mr. G's hot dog stand, and I remember Mark Beltzman telling me he didn't care if I was Bill Murray, he didn't want me in the company, that other people had earned it. There's a big thing at Second City about earning it.

I never actually put up a show. I remember they were doing one in the e.t.c. that was a takeoff on *Our Town,* and they thought, "Oh, it would be a good thing for Jeff Garlin to play the narrator in our version of *Our Town.*" And I said, "Please just let me be a normal cast member, and don't do this." And it just didn't work out. The director [Nate Herman] called me, and I said, "You're too scared to fire me, aren't you? How's this? I'm gonna quit, but you tell everybody you fired me." And then I went and told the cast, "Look, I'm outta here. But I want to let you know, I'm going off to Holly-wood shortly, and I'm gonna become a big success, and I'll end up hiring all of you." And guess what?

Shortly after Andrew Alexander assumed ownership of Second City, he asked Sheldon Patinkin and improv instructor Martin de Maat to set up a training center similar to the one Patinkin had established at Second City Toronto. Whipped into shape by Cheryl Sloane, it started with a handful of students and today boasts more than twenty-five hundred.

Del Close and de Maat, the nephew of Second City improv instructor Josephine Forsberg, were Chicago's improv gurus. In many ways, though, de Maat was the anti-Close. Not surprisingly, the two were often at odds. After a tense joint appearance on an improv festival panel, au-thor Jeff Griggs writes in *Guru: My Days with Del Close,* de Maat referred to Close as a "deranged crackpot drug abuser that has been falsely ele-vated to a deity status." He also called him an "awful man. Terrible man." Riding home with Griggs, Close referred to de Maat as a "fucking faggot" and "that fairy." He also suggested, mockingly, that the gentle and intro-spective de Maat give himself a hug.

### Anne Libera, former box office manager and current Training Center director

Marty was this odd-looking man, very tall, very thin, with the worst toupee you can possibly imagine. He'd briefly been a stage manager here during the Bill Murray era. Marty was interested in how improvisation is sort of revelatory, how improvisation makes you a better person. He could also be insufferably full of himself. I remember the night Don DePollo died, we were all over at the bar talking about Donny and feeling sad, and there's this lull in the conversation. Marty looks up and says, "You know what? I'm so glad that when David Mamet was my student I told him, 'Go write.' " We'd been talking too much about Donny.

### Tim O'Malley, cast member

Martin de Maat taught me about love and accepting everybody that's in the class, because they're there for a reason. I went into Marty's office my first few years sober, and he's like, "You can't tell somebody they don't belong here. If they're in the class, they belong." And I didn't learn that until Marty dripped love on me. It's like, people are there for whatever reason they're there for. They need something, and so your job is to just facilitate them being together, to help them. You're not to weed out people who are supposed to be in show business or not. This is the beginning of their life.

Ninety percent of these people won't pursue this for a living, but your job is to facilitate this room to be a supportive unit and teach them how to work together kindly and nicely. And I thought it was all bullshit before, because I'd come from this angry, bitter [place].

### Mick Napier, director

He was very inviting. He had a lot of turmoil in his own mind and his own life. I used to introduce him as, "This is my friend, Martin de Maat. He is the best improv teacher in the world." And I had no problem saying that, because I really think he was. He would just change people's lives. He would teach improvisation, but he also had amassed a life philosophy attack that he would thread through all of his teaching. People felt like they were being life-coached while they were in his class.

Training Center aside, changes in Chicago were minimal. For some, that wasn't necessarily a good thing.

### Andrew Alexander

Before I got to Second City, artistically there was no need to make any dramatic changes at all. So that's exactly why I wanted Bernie to continue his role as a director. Because I had relied for many years on Bernie and Sheldon to come up to direct in Toronto, until we got our sea legs.

### Barbara Wallace, cast member

I think Bernie held a bake-off for a spot on the mainstage with the women. I don't think too many people were happy about it. I remember being passively angry and not wearing any makeup for it and wearing the sloppiest clothes I had because I was so mad about having to do it. It was called a bake-off just because it was a competition to win the spot.

Bernie's saying was that the women weren't funny. There were a lot of people who felt like women weren't funny. So you were always working against something. And to be completely frank, I never felt that way with my colleagues onstage. I never felt like the guys onstage treated me like that or thought that the women they worked with weren't funny. On the contrary, they were always great.

The women were forced to compete with each other in a way the men weren't. Bernie would joke that when two women were onstage it was time for him to get a cup of coffee. And he would go get a cup of coffee. He would actually leave the theater. It was not his favorite thing. I think women were pigeonholed under Bernie. He was hard to work for in that way. He had expectations of women that weren't necessarily expectations you had for yourself.

### Kevin Crowley, cast member

He saw them as accouterments. They were the wife and girlfriend in scenes.

### Bernard Sahlins

How could anyone work with Barbara Harris, Gilda Radner, Mina Kolb, Andrea Martin, Catherine O'Hara, Shelley Long, and others and maintain that women aren't funny? Quite the opposite. I wasn't that stupid. It must have been a joke. What is true is that we got in the mind-set that a cast consisted of two women and four men, and we kept that notion for some years. It didn't quite rise to the level of chauvinism, but it was unthinking.

During the same period, a Chicago-born nurse from the city's Northwestern Memorial Hospital applied what she'd learned from caring for cancer patients to her scenes on the Second City stage. Laughter, it turned out, was the best medicine Bonnie Hunt had ever dispensed.

### Bonnie Hunt, cast member

I had been doing shows at Bob's Bar across from Wrigley Field at night and working at the hospital during the day. And I had been doing both for a very long time. Steve Rosen [now director of cancer programs] was my boss at the time and said, "I think you need to let go." Because I was still too attached to my patients. When I was in the touring company, I was calling the hospital every day to say, "How's so-and-so doing?" Steve was like, "Bon, you've got to put both your feet in and try the other thing."

### Dan Castellaneta

Bonnie had no problems. As a matter of fact, she would disarm the toughest cynic. She just had a way. I guess it was the nurse in her, because she had dealt with patients in all kinds of situations. She really knew how to ingratiate herself with all of us. And she did it very quickly. She was the new gal in the group, and generally we would get a little off if a new person came in. They had to really prove themselves, because we were still competitive. But I immediately saw that she was really talented and smart and funny. And so I don't think it was hard for her. She not only was completely accepted, but she became one of the driving forces of the group. I didn't know whether she would be a star, but I knew she was really good right off the bat. Some people get on [the stage]—they have some quality that gets them on—but they don't really have the tools. And then they get better. All of a sudden they get really good. But she had all of that going in. And she had absolute confidence. Nothing tentative about her.

### Bonnie Hunt

I think everybody there kind of knows when somebody's ready. They know the difference between somebody who's politicking and somebody who isn't. I was a cancer nurse during the day, so it wasn't like I was getting into the theater politics. I was just so thrilled to be a part of it and to get an opportunity to be there. And it definitely showed in my performance because I just loved it. I loved the audience, I loved being accepted by the audience, I loved making them laugh. It seemed almost as healing as my job during the day.

It was definitely a release at the end of the day. When you're working in oncology, you see people at their most vulnerable, intimate time. And it's such a gift to share that with a family. It gives you a healthy perspective, and laughter is so important during that process, even for the patient, to find some humor in some things of each day as you're going through healing or struggling through chemotherapy or whatever your challenges might be. And for me, personally, I did connect pretty strongly with my patients. I lost my own father when I was eighteen, so I always felt for each family. My dad died of a heart attack, but I understood the sense of loss to a very deep degree. I felt that same kind of connection with the audience. Like, "I know what you're going through. I know what it's like to get up every morning and go to work and wait for the bus in seventy degrees below zero with the windchill factor." That's what I was doing. There's such a strong connection at Second City between the audience and the actor, because the actor is still struggling. They know, "We're in this together."

### Joe Liss, cast member

Bonnie wanted to get her stuff done. [It was] kind of like, you're on Bonnie's boat, so Bonnie wanted to be the boss. Maybe make things go her way in scenes and inject herself more into the process.

### Rose Abdoo, cast member

She's a very forceful person. I went to Detroit to visit my mother, and I remember my mother being on the phone, going, "Okay. All right, I'll put her on a plane." And she hung up and goes, "Bonnie needs you to fly back to Chicago." My mother is the most strong-willed [person]. No one can tell my mother what to do. Bonnie could get anybody to do whatever she wanted them to. I'm like, "What? That's crazy."

### Kevin Crowley

I remember the night before we opened, Bonnie having a big crying fit because she didn't feel like she was well represented [onstage]. And she was brilliant at manipulating men, particularly Bernie, and so she convinced him that some scene she used to work on with Richard Kind should go in the show. This is the night before we opened. So I went back to her apartment with her, we stayed up all night long and re-created this scene so that it would fit me, and then put it in the show and opened it the next day. And it was a piece of shit. It was not a good scene, and it really didn't belong in the show. Barb [Wallace] was furious that Bernie could be played like that.

### Bernard Sahlins

I don't remember the scene at all. I do remember—though Bonnie was a crowd pleaser—sharing an uneasiness at the ruthlessness of her ambition. As to the scene under discussion, while I don't remember details, I have always thought it necessary that no cast member be "light"—or heavy—in a show. Not out of feelings of equity, but because it hurts the show. This may have been one of those cases. I question any suggestion that I used a scene just to please Bonnie Hunt.

### Dan Castellaneta

She was one of these people where I go, "Okay, I'm not gonna compete with Bonnie. I'm just gonna set her up." It was the same way when I was with Jim Fay. It was like, "This guy's way too funny for me to even match wits with."

Fay was a biting satirist and, as admiring cast mate Jane Morris puts it, "a laser beam of humor." But his Second City stint was a rocky one.

### Jeff Michalski

Jimmy was a unique individual. He was a very powerful improviser. Bernie kind of tried to limit him to playing schoolboys and husbands, and that wasn't his thing. He was a wild man. He was more Severn Darden than he was schoolboy. Insane intelligence. And biting, the way Irish people can be when they're really angry. Just a brilliant guy. But I don't think he was very happy on mainstage.

### Richard Kind

You've seen angry comedians, right? People who just are fed up with what the world is like? That's how it used to be to these people. Rick Thomas was one of those people. Dan Castellaneta is actually one of those people, but because he's such a mild-mannered guy it didn't come out so angry. But Jim Fay was a very angry man. Do you have any friends who, when they're really angry, are the funniest people in the world?

### Cheryl Sloane

I wouldn't compare him to John Belushi, but Jim was quick-witted, and he could outwit anybody onstage. And we sometimes saw him tear somebody apart onstage. Whoo, boy. I'll never forget. Somebody brought this guy in for an audition on the mainstage and he was going to go right onto the mainstage and not go through tour co. Mainstage actors don't like that. And he was supposedly this hot Chicago comic improviser actor that everybody loved. He did the set, and Jim tore this guy apart. It was painful to watch. But Jim could also make you look like a star.

### Jane Morris

Jim had a drinking problem, the likes of which I've never seen. And so it became impossible to have him onstage. He would sometimes be so drunk onstage that they finally fired him from the mainstage in the hopes of making him sober up or go to AA or something. But it was before rehab was a thing. It's like, no, you just drink less.

On April 19, 1987, Fay died at his home in the Chicago suburb of Park Ridge. According to the Cook County medical examiner's office, the cause was "chronic alcoholism." He was thirty-three. In Fay's *Chicago Tribune* obituary, Joyce Sloane called his passing "a terrible loss, on a personal and an artistic level. He had a brilliant comedic mind." Just sixteen days later, on May 5, a Second City waitress, the wife of stage manager Craig Taylor, also died. Natalie Taylor was twenty-five. Ruled accidental, her death stemmed from substance abuse as well—officially, "cocaine intoxication." The narrowly separated deaths made it painfully and acutely obvious that although many claimed otherwise, John Belushi's fate in 1982 had not been the eye-opener it should have been. Five years after Second City's favorite son was carried lifeless from his Hollywood bungalow, the organization remained a bastion of hilarity fueled by drugs and booze. Despite the latest warning signs, it would remain that way—however gradually tempered—until well into the next decade.

### Craig Taylor, stage manager

We had a bad span where Jim Fay passed away on Easter Sunday. He was a pretty heavy drinker. And it was a terrible loss because he was just a terrific guy and funny as hell. And then my wife died. She was a waitress there, and we had a one-year-old daughter, and it was from the bad stuff that was going around in those days. I think the whole lifestyle was a wake-up call. Things change. It was like, "This isn't cool anymore. This isn't what people do, and you've got to take it a little more seriously."

### Barbara Wallace

They were two people that everybody knew and liked and we were all with every day. It was a terrible situation. They were great tragedies. They certainly made things somber. I don't think they did anything to change the atmosphere as far as drugs and alcohol went. That may have happened later.

### Ron West, cast member

I'm pretty sure the after-hours social aspect of the workplace is not unique to Second City. But since many of the performers are single twenty-somethings in the early stages of their drinking careers, perhaps Second City ranks above average on the National Carousing Index. I think the road is wilder, actually, because you're visiting colleges where people think you're a genius and a sex god because you said "asshole" onstage. During the [conclusion] at a college show, I would announce from the stage, "We don't have any per diem left," and then we didn't have to buy any drinks. I was lying, but it worked.

### Richard Kind

[The cast members] were very, very close. Very, very close. You would go out to the Belden Deli. You would go to the Blues Bar. Always drinking. Always drinking. Drugs were prevalent before us. I never did drugs that much. They may have been around, but, man, there was a lot of drinking. Oh, my God! These people were downright alcoholics. There's just no other word for it. They were alcoholics. Every single night. And at the time, liquor was free. They didn't pay us a lot, so we would stay after and drink for half an hour or an hour before going out. You got home at four in the morning. But God almighty, you were working till twelve or one at night. How many people get out of work and go home and go to sleep? But oh, my God, they did love to drink. They loooooved to drink.

### Andrew Alexander

I'm much more knowledgeable about it today than I was back then. There was a lot of it—the booze thing. The beer was free. Then I think we turned it into fifty percent off, and now I'm not even sure if it's that. I think you get a small discount. But today people have more knowledge about that type of enabling than they did back then. I mean, it wasn't frowned upon and it was a culture coming out of the sixties. Addiction or any of those issues weren't even on their radar. Or on mine, either.

I don't think we stood alone in that culture—the eighties was a big co-caine decade. And the knowledge issue was just so limited. Now you have TV shows called *Intervention.* And there's a much bigger awareness of drug addiction and alcohol abuse.

The following year, Second City alum and *Hill Street Blues* star Betty Thomas returned to her comedy college—this time as a director. Second City's seventieth revue and the first in its history to be helmed by a woman, *Kuwait Until Dark, or, Bright Lights, Night Baseball* (an allusion to Wrigley Field's first night game that same summer), premiered in June 1988. The show also marked the Chicago debut of Mike Myers, who had been imported from Second City Toronto. During Myers's short stint on the mainstage, *Chicago Tribune* theater critic Richard Christiansen described him in print as "hyperkinetic" and called the ensemble "a good group, quick-witted and agreeable. The two women, Barbara Wallace and Bonnie Hunt," Christiansen went on, "are among the show's sharpest performers."

### Betty Thomas

Toward the last couple years of *Hill Street Blues* I was trying to be a director, and [writer/producer] Steven Bochco let me observe a million places. And then I couldn't figure out how you go from wanting to be a director to being a director. And I went to Steven first just be clear about it and said, "Steven, I don't want to be a theater director, but if I went and directed this show at Second City, do you think it would do me any good in terms of becoming a director?" And he said, "I definitely do." And I said, "Well, why? How would it translate, exactly?" He said, "Well, you'll learn to say 'no' to actors." I was like, okay, whatever that means. But I did eventually understand what that meant, especially when you have Mike Myers and Bonnie Hunt in the company. It was a truly great experience, and they were really wonderful people.

### Joe Liss

That was a wacky show. That was probably the worst mainstage show. Because it was, like, the battle of the egos. You had Mike Myers and Bonnie Hunt. Well, they were the two big ones.

### Kevin Crowley

They share this trait that I've come to recognize in a lot of people. In their own minds they were big stars, and why was it taking the rest of the world so long to figure that out? And that's not a great personality trait to have in a situation that requires teamwork.

### Barbara Wallace

That was a difficult situation. But Betty, at the time, had some kind of weird health problem that took her away from rehearsals a lot, so I think that probably affected how much she was able to control whatever strong opinions the cast had—through no fault of her own.

It was a terrible show. Second City actors are very strong-willed. I don't think it's unusual for a cast to be as strong-willed as the cast that I worked with. I think that's pretty much the norm. And a director is really there to stop actors from things that they shouldn't be doing and to stop them from putting scenes in that shouldn't be in and to keep the level of material up to a certain degree. The actors need to be saved from themselves many times, and there was no mechanism to save us from ourselves at that point.

### Kevin Crowley

It was not a good show. Betty started the show, then she got very ill and dropped out and we were rudderless. Sheldon would pop in when he had time and kind of clean things up. And they had to open something, so they just threw it up. That's why they included stuff like Mike playing "Wipe Out" with drumsticks on a chair with me [singing through] a megaphone. It wasn't avant-garde theater. It was just lazy or bad.

### Betty Thomas

Bonnie and Mike were a lot to deal with, both of them. In that sense, perhaps, it was a fine learning experience about people who are really, really talented and really smart, and how do you help them be the best that they can be even though they're already great and they're possibly smarter and better than you are?

They both seemed to be so clear about what they wanted to do, and their sense of humor didn't come from the same place. That sort of put them at opposite ends. But essentially they were the same. They were both very strong performers that were intellectually superior to most people in the audience.

### Andrew Alexander

Mike Myers was such a talent and had done a great job in Toronto, so when an opportunity came up on the mainstage, I asked him to move to Chicago. He was smart, inventive, and funny—something I thought the mainstage could use at the time.

### Barbara Wallace

Second City has a long tradition of hiring out of the company below, and Mike got hired out of Canada and it was right after Andrew had bought the place. So I think people had mixed feelings about someone being able to come in and just nab a spot.

### Joel Murray, cast member

Mike was in with a strange group with Aaron Freeman and Steve Assad, and all of a sudden he's doing these heavy political scenes. And here's a kid from Canada. He must have read a lot or something. It was never a scene I wanted to dive into. William F. Buckley scenes and stuff like that. He would go in and hold his own with these guys, but he wasn't a guy that hung out afterward. He didn't close Burton Place [on Wells Street] with us. He was kind of maybe one drink across the street and then go home. He didn't fit in socially as much as a lot of people did, and especially not as much [with us], as our group was so social.

### Kevin Crowley

He was very pompous and he didn't share the stage well.

I almost came to blows with him. We were fighting so loudly in the greenroom that the cast had to come offstage and tell us to shut the fuck up.

### Kelly Leonard, former host and producer, current vice president

Mike was not as tight with the rest of the cast, and they weren't even particularly gracious to him necessarily. You have different casts that are a little more cutthroat. I was a dishwasher, so I don't know what was really going on at the time. But Mike would hang out and we would talk about hockey, because he was a huge hockey fan and I was into hockey at the time. The relationship you have as a staff member with the cast is, you're a little intimidated, so you figure out where you stand with each of them.

### Joe Liss

I wouldn't say Mike was a perfectionist. I would say squeaky wheel. Squeaky wheel gets the most grease. So he would garner more attention from the director. "I need stage time." It's like, "Well, wait a minute, where's my scene? Where's the scene that showcases me?" That's the thing: sometimes when you got on the mainstage, it was a lot of, "Okay, get your elbow pads on." That was my first mainstage show, and I was very much about the process and improv and creating scenes through improvisation. And then I ended up just being the helper guy. I was always dishing it off, and everybody else was getting the shot.

The Second City family was diminished yet again in 1989, when forty-two-year-old Gilda Radner died in her sleep at Cedars-Sinai Medical Center in Los Angeles after battling ovarian cancer for three years. "Gilda had a childlike quality that came through many of her characters and endeared her to everyone who saw her," Sheldon Patinkin wrote several years back in his book *The Second City: Backstage at the World's Greatest Comedy Theater.* "Her passing was a hard blow to the entire Second City family at the end of a decade filled with successes, failures, opportunities, changes and tragedies."

That same year, Del Close darkened Second City's doors once more to direct *The Gods Must Be Lazy.* By then a full-blown guru, he populated his company with several devoted students who'd worked with him at the competing ImprovOlympic (now iO) theater up the street. One of them, Chris Farley, was a deeply charismatic performer who hit the stage like a bull. Like, in fact, his idol John Belushi. Sadly and famously, the similarities didn't end there.

### Pat Finn, cast member

I can picture it like it was yesterday. Chris and me. "What do you wanna do?" "I dunno." Honest to God, it was like three o'clock on a Friday or something and we said, "Let's go down by Second City." And we literally walked in front of the place. We kind of paced, like we were picketers without signs. Our unspoken reality was, we were two basketball players walking around a court with the team going, "Hey, you two guys! Yeah, come on in, play some ball!" And we just kind of walked back and forth. And Chris goes, "Wouldn't it be great if somebody looked out the window and they needed two guys and they saw us?" And I was like, "Yeah, that'd be perfect"—thinking that's how it worked at Second City. "We're down two guys. Look out the blinds, see if there's anybody just walking aimlessly. These guys look pretty funny."

The great part about it was that fate [played] its wonderful hand. Joel Murray came walking down Wells Street, and I had gone to grammar school with Joel. So Joel comes down, and Chris is like, "There's Joel. You know him." And I'm like, "But he was a senior when I was a freshman. I don't know."

"You gotta say something."

"All right."

So Joel walks up and says, "How's it goin'?"

"Joel, hey. Pat Finn, Saint Joe's."

"Oh, yeah. Little Finner. What's goin' on?"

"This is my friend Chris. He's really funny."

"Hey, Chris, how's it going?"

"Uh, good. We want to do comedy here in Chicago."

"Okay, great. Well, go into the Second City and take classes, and there you go. All right. See you guys later."

And we walked inside and we were like, "Ohhhh, the keys to the city!" And then we went across the street to the bar and just sat there and stared at Second City and drank, and took classes the next day.

### Joel Murray

We were in the touring company and I got moved up at the end of the old regime, which was Bonnie Hunt and Steve Assad and Aaron Freeman and Mike Myers and Kevin Crowley and Barb Wallace. And so we started to be understudies, and we were filling in. As that show ended, we came in with a whole group of people—Del's people. We talked Del into coming back and directing a Second City show, so we thought we were truly given the keys to the kingdom at that point and all was going to be incredible. It was all gonna be exciting and new.

### Tim O'Malley

I tell this story because perception is so funky. I'm understudying the main-stage finally and sitting at the bar with Del. And he's like, [*low Del voice*] "These fools will do anything I say. I'm gonna paint this fuckin' stage with spray paint, charge 'em twenty grand. Anything they do, I'll call it a scene. I'm gonna walk out of here with a ten-thousand-dollar check and put the biggest mess I can possibly put up there." And I'd go to hang out with them at night, and they'd be like, "Quit bad-mouthing Del." And I'm like, "He thinks you guys are idiots and you all worship him." Maybe Del would never do that to them personally, but he was taking out his resentments on the theater.

### Kelly Leonard

The cast was great—[David] Pasquesi in particular. One of the best impro-visers I've ever seen onstage. He killed me. And Farley was great, too. Physi-cal comedy wasn't my cup of tea, necessarily, but it was brilliant and you could see that. People actually came [specifically] to see Chris Farley at Sec-ond City, and that was the first time I had ever experienced that phenome-non. That doesn't happen here that often.

### David Pasquesi, cast member

The overwhelming recollection is audiences just fuckin' loved that guy. It was confounding. He had a presence and also this unabashed energy. He'd give it his all. There was no holding back. I think that was a great group that Del put together, all seven of us different, and we complemented one an-other really well.

### Joe Liss

The energy that Chris had just drew everyone to him. And he was funny! So even looking at him, you're thinking, "Oh, he's gonna do something funny." So he always got people's attention. He had that soul when he was onstage. Wild eyes. He was always disheveled. Trying to get him to clean up his act backstage was just a chore: comb his hair or put on a shirt that's not wrinkled. 'Cause he never hung anything up, so he was always just picking it up off the mound.

In the fall of 1989, shortly before its thirtieth anniversary, Second City rolled out a revue directed by mainstage alum Nate Herman called *It Was Thirty Years Ago Today*. The show contained such scenes as "Puttin' on the

Hitlers" (as per the scripted introduction, "America's favorite half-hour of nonstop Nazi nuttiness!"), "Stripper," and "Whale Boy." The latter two prominently featured Farley and enabled him to literally throw his weight around as only he could. Although not the most profound or bitingly satirical part of the show, "Stripper" marked the mainstage debut of a sleazy and soon-to-be-storied exotic boogie Farley would one day perform (alongside super-svelte actor Patrick Swayze) in a Chippendales sketch on *Saturday Night Live*—licentious crotch buffing and all. On the other hand, "Whale Boy"—wherein Farley sports a blowhole and sings forlornly about his odd lot in life (he's the half-whale son of upper-crust Brits)—never left the building.

### David Miner, former host

Watching "Stripper" was particularly memorable. All of us in the house on any given night knew what was about to happen: the prior piece lulled the audience a bit, and they were about to be jolted awake by Chris. Half the time I'd just watch the audience. The bass riff from "Dance, Dance, Dance" would kick in, and seconds later everyone would be dying—spit takes and people choking with laughter.

### Joel Murray

We did a lot of things together back then. A movie was coming out, and we'd all go see the movie together, as a cast. Or we'd all go to Joyce's cottage together and just hang out. And we closed Burton Place every night, as a team. It was a constant bonding kind of thing. We spent just an inordinate amount of time together. So when you were onstage, you clicked. And even though we all knew we weren't as well read as some of the older groups, we did try to keep very well versed in the local news and the national news, and knew what we were talking about on that level. But from Del's training, a lot of the scenes we did were more personal relationship-y kinds of things that you just brought your own reference level to. You didn't try to fake like you were some kind of scholar. That would be kind of lying onstage. Pasquesi was very smart, and Joe Liss was very smart, but the rest of us just kind of played our honesty, and that worked. Chris was insanely physical.

### Joe Liss

Del told us all, "You guys should all go and do shrooms." As a company. As, like, a bonding thing. We took him up on it. We went up to Joyce's summer house in Lakeside, Michigan, and we tripped on some mushrooms. And we came up with a scene, "Whale Boy." Everybody got into a character. We were all inside Joyce's house. And we said, "Oh, we gotta get down to the beach." And this was in, like, January. So we all got out to get some fresh air, and we all had different characters—except Farley. Farley had run off on us.

It was almost like he was the dog. We're all out walking Farley on the beach. I think it was Tim Meadows who said, "I found him! I found him!" And there was Chris. I think he had a jacket on, but it was half-off and the T-shirt was half-undone. I had some British accent, and I was like, "Oh, bring him to the house! Bring him! Who is he? What is it?" He was on the beach and someone said, "It's a whale!" And then somebody said, "It's a boy!" And then somebody said, "It's a whale boy!" And we brought him up to the house. That was a loose shell of it. But Nate Herman was the one who took our wild, drug-addled scene and made sense of it.

### Joel Murray

We were having a lot of fun, and Farley was literally shirtless, diving around on ice floes on Lake Michigan. This is razor-sharp ice, and he's just diving on it, pretending to be a seal or a whale. And we just laughed our butts off that night.

### Joe Liss

We had to figure out some kind of a headdress, because Chris had to have a blowhole. So Craig Taylor got an old football helmet and some flesh-colored adhesive tape and he covered the helmet to make it look like skin. And he got some squirt gun system that you could put in your pocket and ran the hose up through the hole in the football helmet. So when Chris got excited, he just put his hand in his pocket and squeezed the trigger, and water went shooting into the audience. It was just great.

### David Pasquesi

Chris was thrilled [to be at Second City]. He was absolutely thrilled. But he hadn't been on the road long. Ordinarily the custom was, you work in the touring company and then you work on either e.t.c. or, at the time there was the other theater out by the airport, [you] put up a show there before you end up downtown. But he didn't do that. He just went from a very short time on the road to downtown because Del wanted him.

I believe there was [jealousy], through no fault of his. But nonetheless, there he was. We didn't care, but maybe other people did who thought they should have had the job. Not us. Not at all.

### Mark Beltzman, cast member

I was supposed to go to the mainstage. Joel Murray and Dave Pasquesi and I were all kind of being moved up together, and then when those guys got put on mainstage, Del decided he was going to put Farley in my place. And I actually had a conversation with Del about that, on his deathbed. He brought that up and wanted to tell me that he knew Farley had a short fuse, and that he put him up there, and that I was really talented and he respected me and all that, but basically our lives were the story of the tortoise and the hare. And those guys are dead and I'm still alive, so I win. That kind of freaked me out for a couple months.

## Joel Murray

Del would insult Farley. Being a drunken idiot isn't necessarily the way to always go. But he was being funny onstage. Chris was great onstage. Del never followed him out and went to the bars with him, and never saw him get uproariously drunk, so he didn't know what was up on that end. Del used to give little gems of wisdom, like, [*deep Del voice*] "Now remember, anything you do three days in a row, you're addicted to. If you can remember not to do it three days in a row, you're fine." [*Jokingly*] And that has always been a rule in my life. I lived next to Farley, above Las Piñatas [restaurant, on Wells Street]. And I swear that when Farley was looking for apartments, I think Joyce might have put him in that apartment. Jackie Hoffman, who was in the touring company, had lived there, and she was moving out, and I think Joyce might have known that that place was open and that I would be a guy who would look after Chris a little bit. And when we would close Burton Place, people would come over to my house, and then they'd go over to Farley's house, and then I would come and kick them out of Farley's house. "Chris, that guy, right there, he has to leave." "Why, Joel?" "You know why. He has to go. That guy's gotta go. These two girls can stay, but these guys are out." I wasn't religious about it, but I used to come in and point the finger. I would reprimand him and tell him when he was being an idiot and things like that. Throwing up over your shoulder and walking is not a neat ability to have in life. But he was under control. He was never ridiculous.

## Joe Liss

We were all in the pot with him. We were all going out drinking. We were smoking dope, snorting cocaine. He wasn't alone. Oh, my God, no. But unfortunately, he didn't know when to quit. He had no off switch. We had an off switch. Most of us.

## Tim O'Malley

That was a nightmare when Chris met Del. That was gasoline meeting the match. That's the worst possible thing. We were out of control, but this kid was just impossible to control.

## Anne Libera

When I got here, there were free drinks at the front bar after work. And on the level of something like Chris Farley, there was certainly an implied sense of "Well, we want to keep him a little crazy. Because what if that makes him funny?" There's that sense that alcoholism and other things are hand in hand with the creativity.

### Kelly Leonard

I remember going to Farley's apartment above Las Piñatas, and in the refrigerator were two gallon things of vodka, and then the mirror was down and blow was on there. And that was it. Everyone was doing that. We partied a lot. That was the scene.

He did drugs like the rest of us did. He was a bigger guy, so it took a little bit more, but there was nothing unusual about that. The unusual thing was that it was everything in his life. He ate too much. He had obsessive-compulsive disorder. He'd touch stuff. He'd lick the back of the stage. They worked it into the shows.

### Joe Liss

Chris would always touch the walls before he went out onstage. And he'd always lick his belt when he put his clothes on. Before he hitched his belt, he would lick both ends, and then notch it.

### Tim O'Malley

This is just the wrong person to fall into this place at that time. He was saddled with OCD where he's kissing parking meters and licking the floor. And it took him ten minutes to get from there to here every night, touching everything, and everyone's babysitting him, and talking to him, and he's a big sweaty mess. But there *we* are, up doing coke till seven thirty in the morning and then taking downers to go to sleep and walking onstage at 8 o'clock at night in a blue haze.

### John Rubano, cast member

One time I saw Chris doing this stuff, and I'm like, "What the fuck is going on here? Everybody thinks this is okay?" They're acting like nothing is really going on. So I said to him, "Chris, what would happen if you left the greenroom without touching the stairs?" And everybody looked at me like [*gasping sound*], "He's talking to the Great Farley." He just kind of turned around and didn't say a word. He just walked away. So I don't know if that meant he didn't have an answer, or he was shocked that somebody had called him on strange behavior. But I will tell you this: a nicer guy you would never meet. Really an incredible guy. He just happened to have the worst case of self-loathing I have ever witnessed in a human being.

### Tom Gianas, director

I went over [to his apartment] one day, and I went to use the bathroom. When I finished, I yelled out, "Chris, where's the toilet paper?" And he popped his head in and said, "I don't have any." I go, "Well, what do you use?" And he kind of grinned and pointed to a corner of the bathroom, and I looked down and there was a sock with shit on it. And he just kind of giggled like he would. He was a charmer. And then I was resigned that, oh, there isn't any toilet paper here. A few nights later, [the cast] were changing into their more informal attire for the improv set. Chris was changing his shoes, and Holly Wortell noticed something. She said, "Chris, what's that on your sock?" And Chris looked up and looked over at me and he started laughing, because he clearly was wearing the sock that he used to wipe his ass. The shit sock. It was in all its glory. He had that same look again that he would always have, where he knew he was going to get in trouble, and you would love him for it. He would do something wrong, and you'd always love him for it.

### Alison Riley, former house manager and current co-producer

The minute he walked out onstage you couldn't take your eyes off of him. But he was kind of a lost boy at the time he was here. He had a lot of issues. He kind of made you sad, ultimately, at the end of the day. Because you saw how talented he was and you saw where it was going and you didn't feel that you could stop him or rein him in. And he couldn't be sweeter or kinder or more humble if you were to talk to him about it. But still, you weren't getting through to him. I know that people had had conversations with him about trying to get sober, about where he was at. And he had spikes and valleys. Times when he was better, times when he was worse. I think that Chris could never feel and accept all the love that was around him. He just couldn't feel it and he couldn't absorb it in any way, which is just tremendously sad, because people truly cared about him. It wasn't some bullshit because he was Chris Farley.

A John Belushi fan extraordinaire, Farley was deeply enamored with his outsize Second City predecessor.

### Joel Murray

He used to try to pump me for anything I knew about John. Bottom line would be like, "That's all I know, Chris. And nothing more." I knew John when I was twelve and I knew him when I was sixteen, eighteen. I used to go out at the height of *Saturday Night Live* and visit. So any story I could have that had John in it would just make him think he was that much closer to getting the Holy Grail or something. I don't know what he was thinking.

### Tom Gianas

It was no secret that Chris idolized John Belushi. One time I was at Chris's apartment on Wells when he showed me a huge footlocker that was once used by Jake and Elwood in the Blues Brothers movie. He had purchased it at an auction and was giddy with excitement. When Chris was hired by *SNL*, before he moved to New York, he proudly donated the locker to the U.S. Blues Bar, a tavern down the block from Second City that was once owned by Aykroyd and Belushi. Years later the bar closed down. A couple days after that I was walking in the rain in the alley behind the bar, when I noticed the footlocker had been discarded next to a dumpster and was decomposing in a pool of water. Somehow this thing Chris once cherished was ruined. Nothing lasts.

### John Kapelos

I remember meeting Chris, and he wanted to have the same fate as John. And it was horrifically shocking to me that that was actually his career goal. That is how badly the Second City thing had morphed in my opinion. It's one thing for me to come to Second City and want to be like Alan Arkin and Harold Ramis and so-and-so. It's a different thing to literally want to flame out.

During rehearsals for the Tom Gianas–directed mainstage show (his first) *Flag Smoking Permitted in Lobby Only, or, Censorama,* a Chicago-born comedy mutineer named Bob Odenkirk returned from his writing gig at *Saturday Night Live* to briefly appear on Wells Street. Gianas had recently produced a one-man show of Odenkirk's in the e.t.c. theater, and now the decidedly un–Second City–like Odenkirk was suddenly being elevated to the mainstage without putting in time on the road. Naturally, his ascension caused much grumbling. But there were positives, too. During his brief stay Odenkirk devised one of Chris Farley's most memorable characters: an overweight, underachieving motivational speaker who lived "in a van down by the river!"

### Rose Abdoo

You're not just supposed to waltz in as an *SNL* writer and get on mainstage. So there was unrest with that, and anyone who said [there] wasn't would be lying, because there was just a paying of dues that everybody kind of went through that Bob did not. And I'm sure that was very difficult for him, too. He's very talented and innovative, but it was sort of like, "Wait a minute, you're an experienced new kid." That's the worst place to be. Because at least if you're a new kid, you're wide-eyed and you're like, "Teach me!" He knew a lot because he had done so much performing and writing. I think that must have been a very difficult position for him to be in. I didn't care, because it was him and I knew he was good. But it seemed unfair. But that's the first best lesson that we could ever have had in show business. It was like, "Welcome to how it's going to be for the rest of your days."

### Ruby Streak, musical director

Bob was already made. He was cooked. He was out of the oven. He's not here to learn and grow. He's here to do what he does, and no one else was in that kind of shape. They're all forming and formulating and learning and growing and very emotional.

He wasn't getting laughs. His stuff wasn't funny. The audience wasn't ready for Mr. Show. That's what the humor was, and we don't do that at Second City. It was like, "What is this humor?" I can't even think of how to describe it. I loved it. I thought it was great. It was new, it was like nothing else. If you don't have a pigeonhole to put something in, you get scared, you get nervous, you get challenged or threatened.

### Bob Odenkirk, cast member

I was a little torn, because I knew there was a whole sort of Second City club that I wasn't really a part of, but I couldn't say no. I grew up in Chicago. The first live theater I ever saw was Second City. I was inspired to do sketch comedy based on that show partly, but in a big way. That's a strong memory from my childhood. You can't grow up around Chicago and get that kind of offer and not do it. So I said yes, and I ruffled a lot of feathers. And thanks to Joyce Sloane, because I would never have been allowed in. She put her foot down.

### Joyce Sloane

They told me, "You can't just put Odenkirk in the company." Like Bernie always used to say, "It's not the post office." Because I would get angry with him if he hired somebody before somebody else. So it shook everybody up, which was good, and it turned out to be a terrific thing for everybody because Odenkirk has used so many of our people in so many things.

### Bob Odenkirk

I think what Joyce did was right with me. I get why she did it. She said this to me: "You gotta shake this place up once in a while." And I think they should shake it up even more regularly. Not that I should be telling them what to do. I think the system's great and the goals and the structure are great, and then you have to shake it up on a regular basis. You have to absolutely shake the shit out of it. Because it's theater and it should be lively and things should be more uncertain. It's showbiz.

### Tom Gianas

When you bring someone up out of nowhere, it shakes up that whole sense of security. It turns it on its head. And people resented that. I don't think it was so much Bob's success already as a writer on *Saturday Night*

*Live.* I think it was just that, "Wait, I'm supposed to be up next." And also when someone moves up to mainstage, the people on the other stages are counting on moving into their slot, because of the domino effect of it all.

### Bob Odenkirk

They hated me, a lot of them. Farley and Tim Meadows and Jilly Talley, who I'd worked with years before, were on my side. Pasquesi and O'Malley and Holly Wortell, they weren't so into me. Because by me going there, one of their friends didn't go there. Ron West didn't move up, or Mark Beltzman didn't move up. I kept those guys out, and those guys worked years to get there. And all of a sudden I go, "Yeah, I'll come over there and do it," even though I had, in some ways, moved past the place. But I have sympathy now for those guys and I'm not sure I would do it [again].

### Tom Gianas

The motivational speaker was based on a character Chris did. For months and months he was doing that onstage, but there was no place for him. There was no strong scene for it. It was just a guy who played this attitude. It was hilarious. It would crush every night. And we're in rehearsal, and we're starting to get closer and closer to shaping the show, and I talked to Bob, and I said, "We've got to come up with something that houses this character. We can't open a show without it." And that's when Bob came up with the idea of a guy who is a motivational speaker who teaches by example of the disaster of his life. Not what he has accomplished, but what he hasn't. He celebrates his failures to motivate people. And once we had that, the scene just took off. The character existed. Often at Second City, when there's a friend in the audience, they name a character after a friend when they're improvising, so it's sort of an inside joke and they laugh. And their friends are kind of honored that they used their name. Chris's priest, Matt Foley, showed up, so that one happened to stick.

### Rose Abdoo

No one could hike up their pants funnier than Chris Farley. Just the act of hiking his pants up would kill people. And he was a person that, before the show, would make you feel like, "Oh, I really have no idea what this sketch is going to be about." And he would get me so nervous, and then every time he was perfect. I don't think I've ever been onstage with someone who had the audience more in the palm of their hand than Chris Farley. The big sadness for me was that no one ever really got to see him do as much acting as he could have. Everyone got to see the big goofy stuff with all his movies, but I thought he would go on to be an Academy Award–winning kind of actor.

## Bob Odenkirk

I had seen the Matt Foley character. Chris had done versions of that in an improvisation. In a sad way there was a little bit of truth to it. Chris kind of used himself as a negative example. He put himself down all the time. I think he could relate to what was at the core of the character, but the abandon with which he did it was just amazing. I really put the structure around it, and I came up with the catchphrase and the backstory and the catch of the scene, which is that he uses himself as a bad example of what you don't want to happen. But give it up for that performance. Because, holy shit, that's an unbelievable performance. Legendary. And it should be because, oh, my God, you couldn't keep your face straight when Chris was doing that. It was unbelievable. It was the greatest thing ever. To have him in your face doing that character was heaven. It's what comedy exists for, to be that happy.

### "Motivation," from *Flag Smoking Permitted in Lobby Only,* 1990

BOB ODENKIRK AND HOLLY WORTELL ARE STAGE RIGHT. JILL TALLEY SITS STAGE LEFT, AS TIM MEADOWS ENTERS.

**HOLLY:** I think it's a great idea.

**BOB:** Great idea.

**TIM:** Hi, Mom. Dad.

**BOB:** Byron. Your mother Kate and I are so glad that you've decided to join us for this family communication session.

**HOLLY:** The big "C." We're gonna have the whole family communication sort of thing . . . right here, right now.

**TIM:** All right. Well, let's get it started, all right?

**BOB:** All righty. Say, how are those American Express cards working? Huh?

**JILL:** Great.

**BOB:** Great.

**HOLLY:** All right. Well, Amy . . . Byron . . . Your father Jason and I are a little bit concerned. Alva the cleaning lady was in the family room and she found a bag of pot.

**TIM:** She didn't smoke it, did she?

**HOLLY:** No, she didn't smoke it. Now, it's not mine because you know that I quit over a year ago.

**BOB:** And we're not here to say, "Don't smoke pot." I mean, we don't want to cut you kids off from experiencing life in any form. I mean, we're not gonna come out here and say, "Hey, we're the parents. Stop doing illegal drugs."

**HOLLY:** No, no. That's not what we're about.

**BOB:** No . . .

**HOLLY:** We're just concerned that they can lead to other things.

**BOB:** That's right. And when your mother and I were doing drugs heavily, the drugs were just a lot safer.

**HOLLY:** We bought them from our friend Ceri, so we knew what was in our drugs.

**BOB:** You knew what was in the acid. You knew what was hash oil.

**HOLLY:** Today your drugs are so much more violent and dangerous.

**BOB:** Crack! Ice! Boom! Pow!

**HOLLY:** So, I was on the phone just the other day with Jason's lover . . .

**BOB:** Kathy. She's great.

**HOLLY:** She's great.

**TIM:** Yeah. She is great.

**HOLLY:** (*suspicious*) Yes . . . So I was talking to Kathy, and she came up with an idea that I think can set you on the right track—a motivational speaker.

**BOB:** Yeah. One of these guys that speaks to big groups at high schools and churches.

**JILL:** You mean to come here, to the house?

**HOLLY:** Uh-huh . . .

**BOB:** Yeah. Set me back a few bucks.

JILL AND TIM GET UP AND HEAD TOWARD THE DOOR TOGETHER.

**TIM:** Yeah, right . . .

**JILL:** Okay . . .

**BOB:** Come on, you guys. Hold on. I'll bump you up to gold cards.

JILL AND TIM DUTIFULLY RETURN TO THEIR SEATS.

**BOB:** Okay. His name is Matt Foley and he's been down in the basement drinking coffee for about the last four hours. He should be all ready to go. And I'll just call him up.

BOB CROSSES TO DOOR, OPENS IT AND YELLS:

**BOB:** Hey, Matt, we're ready for you. (*To Jill and Tim*) His speech is called "Go for It." Make him feel like there's a crowd. (*Shouting*) Matt? Now, buddy!

JILL AND TIM BEGIN TO CHANT AS IF THEY WERE A CROWD AT A ROCK CONCERT. CHRIS ENTERS AS MATT FOLEY—MOTIVATIONAL SPEAKER.

**CHRIS:** All right. As your father probably told you, my name is Matt Foley, and I am a motivational speaker. Let's get a little better acquainted by letting me give you a little bit of a scenario of what my life is all about. First off, I am thirty-five years old, I am divorced, and I live in a van down by the river. Now, you kids are probably gonna go out there and think, "Hey, I'm gonna get the world by the tail. I'm gonna wrap it around, pull it down, and put it in your pocket." Well, I'm here to tell you that you're probably gonna find out, as you go out there, that you're not gonna amount to JACK SQUAT! (*Turning to Tim*) Now, young man, what would you like to do with your life?

**TIM:** Well, Matt, I'd like to become a writer.

**CHRIS:** Weeellllllll, la-di-freakin-da! So we got ourselves a writer here.

**BOB:** Well, actually, Matt, Kate and I have encouraged Byron in his writing.

**CHRIS:** Dad, I wish you could just shut your big YAPPER! I wonder. . . . From what I've heard, Byron, you're using paper, not for writing, but for rolling doobies. Now, you can do a lot of doobie rolling, when you're living in a van down by the river. (*Turning to Jill*) Well, young lady? What do you want to do with your life?

**JILL:** I'd like to live in a van, down by the river.

**CHRIS:** Well, you'll have plenty of time to live in a van down by the river, when you're living in a van down by the river! Now, you kids are probably asking yourselves, "Matt, how can we get on the right track?" Well, there's only one real solution to that. And that is to move my gear in and I'm gonna bunk with you, buddy. I'm moving in and we're gonna be BUDDIES! We're gonna be PALS! We're gonna WRESTLE! Old Matt's gonna be in your shadow.

CHRIS EXITS TO COLLECT HIS GEAR.

**JILL:** No . . .

**TIM:** No, Matt, you don't have to do that! Look, we'll never smoke pot again.

CHRIS STICKS HIS HEAD BACK IN THE DOOR.

**CHRIS:** I don't give a rat's behind, because I'm moving in. I'm sick and tired of living in a van, down by the river!

THE FAMILY ALL STARE AT ONE ANOTHER IN SHOCK.

**BOB:** Lock the doors!

After a few shows on the mainstage, Farley was off to *Saturday Night Live* and international fame. At Second City, the promotion was cause for elation, envy, and worry.

### David Miner

There was frequent talk that Chris and Tim were going to get *SNL* soon. Then one night when I was hosting, Lorne [Michaels] came to the show. The whole staff was buzzing, and when it was through, he had left a hundred-dollar tip! As I recall, the next day Chris arrived at the theater in a limo. I'm not sure anymore if that was real or just how I had imagined his night went, because everyone instantly knew he would be moving to New York. Seeing that life-changing moment happen really left an impression. I often think of Chris as I watch my own clients get their first high-profile jobs. That moment generally happens once. Few things are as memorable as seeing someone's life suddenly change direction like that. I like to call it "the moment before." It's one of the last pure moments in an artist's life.

### Fran Adams, cast member

How could you be jealous for Farley? He was so sad at that point. You're like, "Dear God, he's gonna derail." It's the enabling hole, that place. There came so many points where it's like, "You guys! Why are you letting him do this? Why is this okay? Why is everybody laughing that he came to work and his clothes are urine-stained?" That's not funny. It's depressing. But train wrecks did well. It makes me sad. I wish I could redo it. I wish I wouldn't have gone to his apartment to parties. But I did. I wish I wouldn't have had fun. I wish I wouldn't have stayed. I wish I didn't know the drug lady. Because you saw what was going to happen.

### Cheryl Sloane

We were sitting across the street one night and [Chris] said, "Cheryl, everybody likes me. Why don't you like me?" And I said, "Chris, I like you. It's not that I don't like you. It's that I don't want to be close to you because you're killing yourself, and I just lost two wonderful people here [actor Jim Fay and waitress Natalie Taylor] and I don't want to be as sad as I was then when you die. Because you're gonna die." He went, "Whoa!" I said, "You asked me. I'm just being honest."

# 9

## Out with the Old, In with the New, and a Sweet Talker in Sweatpants

Steve Carell
Stephen Colbert
Paul Dinello
Amy Sedaris

1988–95

BY THE LATE EIGHTIES Second City was booming, thanks in part to the success of *Saturday Night Live* and *SCTV.* Seeking to expand his brand, Andrew Alexander moved to Los Angeles, formed partnerships with budding movie moguls Ron Howard and Brian Grazer, and opened—with the help of alumni from the Chicago and Toronto stages—an outpost in Santa Monica. It lasted for only a couple of years and marked the end of musical director Fred Kaz's long and colorful Second City career.

In 1991, upon Chris Farley's exit from Second City, a new crop of mainstage performers began graduating from touring companies and gigs in the suburbs. They included Steve Carell, Stephen Colbert, and Amy Sedaris. Around the same time, Alexander shook the place to its core by effectively removing Joyce Sloane from power. A rift formed, and mutinous mutterings abounded.

**Andrew Alexander**

There's really not a strong theater audience in L.A. You're sort of the flavor of the month, and then the audience just doesn't show up. The first year it was really hot. I had a deal with Imagine Films and CBS and we were trying to develop half-hour sitcoms. And I think it conflicted. Here we're asking the cast to be edgy satirists at night, and then during the day they were trying to develop and write half hour sitcoms for CBS. It was just conflicting agendas, so it created a bit of acrimony, ironically. Because it was really about everybody getting more work. That was the reason for coming to L.A. in the first place.

It wasn't just the idea of throwing a theater up in L.A. and seeing what would happen. It was all tied into the philosophy that you've got people leaving Second City from Toronto and Chicago and they come out there and have careers or don't have careers, so it made sense to find ways to work with those people on developing projects. I was using the model of what had happened with *SCTV.* We could use people right off the stage, and it worked.

### Jane Morris

It was just a weird thing to me. He wanted to have a television/film production factory running out of Second City. Like, any scene you did could be a potential sitcom. And so we actually did a lot of pitches and meetings and stuff. It was horrible. People got so frustrated and beat down by it.

### Jeff Michalski, director

We did an excellent show. It was just insanely difficult to put it up. It was one of the first times they tried to put together a cast of all-stars or people that were big in their companies. And that was a mistake, because the way these companies work, there might be one guy. There might be a Jim Belushi in the company who is getting a teeny bit of special treatment. Or a David Steinberg or somebody like that. And when you had a company of people that were the big fish in their companies, it was really hard to put that show up. And we were basically doing a best-of show anyway, so it should have been easy. But it wasn't like that. People were watching [to see] who had more time or what kind of scene they were doing, and they'd be calling Andrew at four in the morning complaining about the scene that another actor was doing, or this or that. And I witnessed some of that at the bar, where people would kind of be betraying each other for really stupid reasons. And I understood it. It was high stakes for some people. There were some people who had gotten really big agents coming out here, and it was more about the individuals in some cases than it was about the show.

### Ryan Stiles

It's Hollywood, and everybody wanted to be on TV, and it wasn't the same work ethic. You didn't find a lot of people coming down in the daytime to work on stuff. There definitely wasn't the same kind of feel that there was in Toronto or Chicago. And there are directors and producers in the crowd, so it's a little different in the way you play the show.

### Andrew Alexander

We eventually got a show on the air for a year. It was kind of an innovative show that got great reviews called *My Talk Show*. And we got picked up, syndicated to almost 80 percent of the country. That and a Comedy Central pilot I did with Steve Carell and Ryan Stiles called *Life as We Know It* ultimately came out of the Imagine–Second City partnership.

### Bonnie Hunt

It was not pure Second City to me. But I understood why they were doing it. It made business sense. I got it.

### Jeff Michalski

It was almost too much of a good thing. And eventually, they hired Andrea Martin to do the second show, but now you've got a giant fish in the pond. And that's not going to be a Second City show, either. No matter how generous she is as far as making sure people get their stuff, it's too big. But the nature of the show was different. It was slicker. We got a great review from the L.A. *Times,* we got a lot of great press, but people were wanting out the door.

Alexander had imported Fred Kaz to guide things on the musical front in L.A. It turned out to be the jazzman's last stand.

### Jeff Michalski

Andrew wanted me to fire Fred, and I refused. I think there were some people in the cast that wanted a more modern flair to the show musically. Fred scores the shows tremendously, [but he] doesn't play rock 'n' roll. Number one, to put it on me to fire a guy who's been at the theater for thirty years is off base. He should go talk to Fred and do it. Why have the director fire Fred? So I refused to do it. I said, "No. If you want to do it, you go do it. But I'm not doing it." So that happened and they gave me a pink slip—first time I ever got a pink slip—but Andrew let me start the workshop program, which I did, and I brought Severn Darden in again and Mina Kolb and all these great people that I really loved.

　　When they did fire Fred, I called Jimmy Belushi. They gave [Fred] nothing at the beginning. They gave him nothing. So I called Jimmy and said, "Jimmy, they're doing this to Fred." So Jim went in and strong-armed them into giving Fred a pension and a boat. I called Jimmy because it was horrible what was happening. I was appalled by that behavior. Andrew was mad at Fred because Fred is outspoken when stuff's going down, and he can be a little pouty and sharp about it, and he obviously had more stature amongst the alumni than Andrew did. And the same thing was true with Joyce and the same thing was true with me.

### Andrew Alexander

Fred had been working in Chicago for twenty-five, twenty-six years, and I think he was getting a little unhappy there, and I suggested he move out to L.A. And I don't think it was going as well as I'd hoped on our side creatively. There was a lot of needle drop going on in the shows at that time. A needle drop is where you'll find a piece of music—it could be a Rolling Stones tune or something—and you'll take ten seconds or fifteen seconds of that piece of music and you'll put it in your synthesizer as the musical director. And Fred was a purist. His technique and his contribution to the art was always underplaying a scene. And he was the best at it. There was nobody ever better than Fred Kaz at underplaying a scene. But then we started moving into more needle drop, and it was sort of an opportunity. So I went to him and said, "Fred, maybe it's time to retire." And he said, "Yeah." I said, "What would make you happy?" He said, "God, if I had a boat I'd just sit on the Pacific Ocean." So Len and I went out and got him a $125,000 boat. And I had said to him, "Fred, I'll keep paying your salary even though you're retired. And if the L.A. operation tanks, we'll have to work something out." And it did tank eventually, and that's when he brought Jimmy in and Jimmy's lawyer. The boat wasn't part of the negotiation. We had already offered that up. We gave him a big going away party and a $125,000 boat.

### Jim Belushi

Bernie never provided any kind of retirement for anybody at Second City. I don't think he felt it was his obligation. And Fred had been there for twenty-five years. So when it went down with Fred, we talked to Andrew. The boat idea was Andrew's idea. He was out [in L.A.], so we just sat down— me, him, Fred, and my attorney—and kind of negotiated a pension. And here's Andrew, who just lost a business in L.A., and then provided a pension for Fred, when the whole time Bernie should have done something before he sold the business. Andrew totally stepped up and has been paying for years.

As Second City's L.A. branch foundered, its Toronto and Chicago theaters continued to pack 'em in. Guided by directors Barb Wallace, Ron West, Nate Herman, Tom Gianas, and Sheldon Patinkin (who became chair of Columbia College's theater department in 1980, but continued to direct occasionally and dispense wisdom in his still vital role as "artistic consultant"), the shows took shots at everything from the Gulf War and beauty products to high school bands and suicide videotapes.

The relocation of Andrew Alexander—who moved to Chicago from L.A. in the early spring of 1992—brought with it both more and less change than staffers had anticipated. Still, many were intensely wary. This wealthy, well-coiffed, aloof-seeming interloper had a lot to prove.

### Andrew Alexander

I'm a Canadian, so you're coming into Chicago, which is a city that really takes care of its own. And it's a compliment to those that are born and bred there. But to those that come from the outside, you've got a while to pay your dues. I was an interloper. To boot, I was a foreigner—a double foreigner, because I was actually born in England. If I were to do things again, I would do them a little differently for sure. I probably should have gotten more involved in the community.

### Kelly Leonard

[People worried] that he wouldn't be concerned with the art. He was Canadian, and we all made fun of Canadians. There was a lot of Canadian-American rivalry shit that we threw in there. But no one knew him. And actually, if you ask people, he's a pretty self-effacing guy, and he's shy. And he does love the work and the brand. Anytime someone says something about censorship at Second City, I'm like, "Are you fucking kidding me? You could not make the shows dark enough or mean enough for Andrew Alexander." He is obsessed with death. He has the darkest sensibility. You couldn't even reach the offending meter [limit]. So it's like, "Please, try. That's what he wants. That's what he finds funny." So we got along well.

### Paul Dinello, cast member

When I was there, I almost couldn't believe it. It seemed like Ken Kesey's Merry Pranksters. It seemed like we were all in a van and nobody was in control. I remember Amy [Sedaris] and I would scrape three dollars together and go, "Oh, great, we can get two hot dogs." We had no money, so we hung out at Second City all the time. Someone would be leaving, and they'd have parties, and Joyce would feed everybody. And we drank free beer there and hung out and performed. It seemed like there were no rules. I was never in a fraternity, but it seemed like getting paid to be in a fraternity somehow.

### Anne Libera

In the years between [the sale and Andrew's moving back to Chicago], there was a lot business-wise that was not handled well. There was a lot of going into the safe for money. It wasn't being run as a business. And even when I took over the Training Center, it was losing money, and within the first term we were showing a thirty-thousand-dollar profit. That had a lot to do with the fact that they weren't taking money from the students. And from an artist's point of view, when the business isn't being taken care of, you don't necessarily know that it's not, but you can feel it.

### Rose Abdoo

Andrew was taking Second City into the twenty-first century, making it bigger and more well-known and having the T-shirt sales and the drink sales. It felt to me like it was going from a cool little mom-and-pop theater that didn't have a cover charge to a corporation. That's the part that I found a little bit scary, and I'm kind of glad I got out when I did, because I really don't know what happened after that. But the fear of my era, or me certainly, was that it was going to be McSecond City, and that's what I didn't want to be a part of. Where all of a sudden there's one in Detroit and one in Cincinnati. And I thought, "It's got to lose something. It can't stay as special." As a businessman, he came in and made a lot of changes, and probably some of them were for the good. But that was the part that scared me. I loved the fact that it was this funky theater on Wells Street. I think that audiences from Chicago certainly felt like they were discovering this gem.

### Rachel Dratch, cast member

I think when I was there, that's when they started branching out to all these cities, which I hate. Sorry, Andrew, but it dilutes the specialness. And the other thing is, if you got on mainstage in Chicago, you really had to pay your dues onstage. But when they open it up in whatever town, it's someone with a lot less experience, so the show couldn't possibly be as good. I have spoken.

### Andrew Alexander

There was some method to all our expansion madness into smaller markets like Detroit and Cleveland. And it was good business. These were opportunities for directors and performers to create new shows without the media and community pressure of Chicago or Toronto. My sister, Lyn Okkerse, had opened a branch in London, Ontario, and it was a great training ground for directors and performers. Detroit became enormously important to our diversity program, and produced some terrific African American talent that went on to Chicago's e.t.c. and mainstage, and later to many notable TV shows.

### Fran Adams

He changed the colors of the logo, for God's sake! That is still the most appalling thing! It was red and black, red and black, red and black. Red and black! And he goes and puts up a bumble bee sign of yellow and black! I mean, hello, you get an F for corporate identity, you corporate loon! Good

God! Have you ever seen the golden arches being green? No! They're golden arches.

## Joel Murray

He was a good-looking guy with a gorgeous wife and a lot of money. He had a lot of respect there. He somehow figured out how to buy the place for a dollar, and that's a lot of respect on that one. He was the new guy. He was cool. He had great cars.

## John Rubano

It was kind of like, "Who's this guy and what's he gonna do and how's he gonna screw up Second City?" I think there was that, but he was enough of a businessman. He had enough savvy to leave it alone for the most part and let it be what it always was. I mean, you don't fix what's not broken. And then the franchising of Second City, riding the comedy wave of stand-up and stuff—he kind of rode on the coattails of that. I think he realizes now they might have gone too big, too fast. I don't know.

## Andrew Alexander

There was no health insurance [before]. And there wasn't that much of a management team, either. It was Joyce and Cheryl and some waiting staff. So we have health care. We have a pension plan. People have 401(k)s. To run a business and to build a business, you've got to make sure you're taking care of people.

In the summer of 1992, Alexander made an executive decision that would haunt him immediately and for years to come when he effectively removed the beloved Joyce Sloane from power and made her producer emeritus. Sloane's replacement, Kelly Leonard, was then a twenty-five-year-old former Second City dishwasher and host. He was also the privileged son of a Chicago radio icon. Yes, change was definitely in the air—and some thought it stank to highest heaven.

## Kelly Leonard

The guy who taught me how to host was named Chainsaw. And that exemplifies the level of service we gave at Second City. It was kind of astounding to me. The waitresses were rude to you, if they came to serve you at all. The hosts were mean. Customer service was not paid attention to and was held in disdain. And Joyce ran the theater—Andrew wasn't back here yet—but there was tons of shit going on. No one person could run everything. But there was no sense of having management around. Joyce ran everything. It was out of her head. Like, she kept the book that had all the benefits or the private shows and wouldn't let anyone else have them. And in many ways I think the reason she did that was she knew the brand was so important she didn't want to give up stuff in case someone would fuck it up, or say the wrong thing, or do the wrong thing, or not be Second City, because she knew what Second City should be. And unfortunately, when you get bigger as a company, you do have to surrender stuff. And that's been hard for me. Inheriting that mantle from her, you have a little bit of Stockholm syndrome—you're like, "This is the way it should be." ·

Joyce's health started to not do great. And for me it was also like, Wow, as much as I'm loving the shows, I know I was feeling like we've got to shake it up. We were getting a lot of press like we were a tourist trap. That's just the way it felt. Because I was now in the community, I went to all the other places and I was seeing groundbreaking work—and not seeing groundbreaking work at Second City with really good people. We weren't hiring the best talent at that point, either. And I didn't know why. And businesswise, the place was such a mess that it was like, "Wow, we could do more than just this."

In October of 1992, Andrew brought me to his office and said, "I want to offer you the job to produce." And I said, "What about Joyce?" And he said, "I've already talked to Joyce." And I was like, "I've got to talk to her first." And I did. I said, "So Andrew's talking to me." And she's like, "I know." I said, "Well, do you want me to turn it down? What do you want me to do?" Because she had taken care of me forever. And I don't know if I remember her exact words, but basically it was like, "If you don't do the gig, I won't know the person or trust the person who does it. I'd rather have someone I know." And she knew me. She knows me, warts and all. So I said yes. And I remember going home that night and telling my wife, and she didn't believe me. Literally. For a week. I think it was absurd for anyone to consider that Joyce wouldn't be running things, because she had just done it for so long. And I was a kid. And though she was still going to be here and participating, she's bigger than life, she's a legend.

### Anne Libera

Joyce was furious. She felt like she'd worked for a really, really long time and that she was owed something.

### Mark Beltzman

That was at the point when it went from a mom-and-pop organization to a business. And Joyce was mom, and she took care of everybody, and then when she wasn't taken care of the way everybody thought she should be taken care of, it just became uncomfortable. And we were all very protective of her, so I think there were a lot of people who had some animosity toward Andrew at the time for not doing the right thing.

## Ruth Rudnick, cast member

I felt awful for Joyce because I could tell she was so crushed. She was trying to be stoic, and I think she was still trying to figure out what she was going to do, so she didn't want us all to storm the castle or anything.

## Fran Adams

We were always so afraid for Joyce. We were all so protective of her. Everyone is still protective of her, and when Andrew came to town, he didn't respect her. It's really sad. She's fifty percent of each of us as a person. She built us as people. She built the directors. She knew the drink menu. She knew how many pretzels we were ordering. She knew all that. She knew every waitress's problem. She's fifty percent of everything in that building, and he came in and disrespected it, and it was so scary; it was hard to watch.

## Paul Dinello

Don DePollo died. He was sort of a Second City mainstay. And Bernie had less to do with the theater. Things were sort of changing, but I felt Joyce was still my boss and sort of a mother figure. I don't know how I feel about it now, but at the time I was sort of emotional when they let her go. And I was going to quit because of it, because I felt a loyalty to her. But it's hard to fully understand what the politics were there. It was such an actor's theater. We had this complete freedom, but you didn't really get involved with the machinations of how it ran from day to day. Even Joyce never was really boss-like. But you liked her there. It was like having your mom there and you can go talk to her, and she was fun to hang out with. And spiritually you felt like she sort of had her arms around the whole place. But from a business angle, I didn't really know—I was there to perform and for the free beer. So I had an emotional reaction to it, but in hindsight it's a little embarrassing just because I didn't really try to find out what the details were. I was just like, "Oh, they're letting Joyce go. I'm quitting."

## John Rubano

That was tough for me to see, because of what she had done for me. And I'm friends with Kelly, and I have no bad feelings toward him or anything, but I think that he knew enough to let the old guard pass and let that generation pass out of there, knowing what had gone before, and not mess with us that much.

## Mick Napier

It was actually really weird. I used to play pool at a place called Lakeview East. At that time a lot of people started coming there because they knew I was there, and they started talking about Joyce and that transition. And they did get me a little riled up about it. I wasn't sure about everyone's position at the time, and I was only getting it from one side. And I had been convinced that Joyce was being treated inappropriately, and I had always had an allegiance to her. While there was great talk of us all banding together to quit, I was getting ready to direct my first e.t.c. show. So I quit because I had the added urgency of going into a rehearsal process, and I didn't think it was a good idea for me or the cast or Second City to enter into a rehearsal process and then up and quit while you're standing up for a philosophical cause. So I quit early. And I think it really did shock everyone. And then I had a two-hour meeting with Andrew, but I stood my ground on it. And then things changed. People's outlooks changed.

### Andrew Alexander

I used to come into the theater and I was like a pariah. I don't know how much the alumni that had left here knew the circumstances of how Joyce had been treated by Bernie. My own opinion of it at the time was that I felt, "Okay, a lot of this anger is being directed at me and maybe should have been deferred to Bernie." Because I did take care of Joyce. I gave her a fifteen percent equity in the business regardless of her status as producer emeritus.

For many actors, to this day, Joyce is a second mother to them. So I completely understand the emotional connection. And I'm different. I don't have the same approach. It's just not who I am. That's not to say that I don't respect that approach. I was the daddy, I guess.

### Joyce Sloane

It was a little revolution. Bill Murray wanted to buy the place. I met with him in New York. He said, "It'll be good for everybody. We'll all come back and work."

### John Rubano

There were people who were just like, "Fuck that. I'm not going with the new people! You gotta dance with the one that brung ya!" Andrew was kind of hands-off with us, which I think was an incredibly shrewd move, and I think he told Kelly to be the same way. Because you come in and take out the queen, and the subjects are still loyal, and if you force the point, there will be the mutiny that you may have feared.

### Joyce Sloane

I had been sick. That's how it all happened. Pacemaker, three heart attacks, carotid artery surgery. It was sort of a rough thing to have the rug taken out from under you, to be told you won't have anything to do with the day-to-day running of the theater, a place where you've lived.

### Andrew Alexander

I had met with Joyce and written her a letter as well. I wanted to make sure that everything got out there in a sort of nonemotional way. Maybe that was not the best thing, because everybody got a chance to read it. Maybe I could have handled it better. It was very hard.

### Joyce Sloane

I still have the letter. It just says that I won't have anything to do with the day-to-day running of the theater anymore. It's hard to take in a letter. You would think that somebody would come in and sit down and talk to you about it. But it's all worked out. Everything's fine.

### Cheryl Sloane

That was a big day. It was Andrew's theater, and he had to take it in the [direction] he needed to take it, and you couldn't get in his way. And it's still here and doing quite well. A lot of people in the world of Second City may say things that maybe aren't completely complimentary, but you've got to trust the person who can carry the torch to carry the torch. And he grew the theater in a lot of ways. I think Andrew had a lot of foresight. Andrew saw the business potential for it and was able to grow into that potential. And I think we were doing things in small ways and he was able to take the money and put it toward growing all of those departments, which at first seemed crazy because there were all these people doing stuff that one person used to do.

### Andrew Alexander

If you're looking at investment or you're dealing with banks to expand the business, you have to have a certain order. And I would like to think that we kept a lot of that. A lot of what Joyce has contributed is still in play. I credit Joyce with the social responsibility of this organization. That started with Joyce—her work with charities and that investment in the community that Joyce has done her whole life. That is as important as the artistic contributions of Bernie and Del and Sheldon and Paul Sills and all those people—equally important to the fabric of who we are.

### Jeff Michalski

I thought Andrew was eliminating her because of her influence. She wanted to buy the company. She was going to make Andrew an offer. So she met with John Candy to work this thing out, and Candy, God love him, told Andrew. Made a joke about it at dinner.

### Cheryl Sloane

John wanted to buy the place. John wanted to buy everything. She talked to John. All these people wanted to buy it.

### Andrew Alexander

I do remember John mentioning that to me. I think John got a version of the events, and I think Joyce did speak to John. He wanted to know what was going on, and I kind of filled him in. John and I had talked at one point. We partnered up in the nineties for Pay TV, the comedy channel in Canada. And we had talked about him maybe becoming a partner in Second City, but it didn't go anywhere.

### Stephen Colbert, cast member

Not at first, but eventually Joyce had concern for you. She had been there a long time, and I think she could be encouraging. She'd come up to you and say, "That's a wonderful scene that you're doing." Or she would just talk to you about some story. Like, something you had done would have reminded her of something that Joe Flaherty or anybody from the past had done. And that gave you a sense of continuity and being part of a tradition and that you had something to measure yourself against, and it gave you hope that you weren't kidding yourself that you might have some facility for what you were doing, and there might be a future for you, or a place for you in the world. I don't want to be too grand about it, but that's what an older person does for a younger person, is they give them a sense that there's a place for them in the world, based upon their judgment or their shared perspective on what they've seen other people experience and what you're going through right now. And that's what Joyce provided. And so she could be an incredibly comforting figure, or a frightening figure if you upset her. You don't want to piss her off. She could fire you! And you'd worked so hard to get there.

### Ruth Rudnick

That's how she had her control, too. She could terrorize you. It's not like it was all sweet and light. She could kick ass. I remember once, somebody used the Second City charge card for something on the road. And she came back and was like, [*screaming*] "What do you think I am, the golden calf?" They still quiver when they tell that story.

### Anne Libera

It's a dysfunctional family. It's still mom. It doesn't matter what mom was like or what mom did. And it's easy to remember the cuddles and the ice cream and forget about the screaming. You'd get *screamed* at for something that was completely out of your control or a perfectly understandable mistake.

## Paul Dinello

It wasn't completely conscious, but Second City would really spoil you, because you got such a great response every night. So if one night it wasn't uproarious, if the audience wasn't ripping their heads off and throwing them at your feet, you'd be like, "Oh, this audience blows." So then it could get ugly. Stephen and I once did a show, and some high school bought, like, two hundred tickets, and they came to see the show. Colbert and I were out there improvising and we did this folk song. And they quietly, en masse, got up and started filing out—the whole audience. And we're like, "What the hell's going on?" So we changed the song to, "They're leaving, we can say 'fuck' now," as they were leaving. And so we did this whole song and it had about eighty "fucks" in it. They asked for their money back, so [Second City] had to give back two hundred tickets' worth of money, or however many people it was. And Joyce came barreling backstage. Colbert and I were still out onstage, and we could hear her screaming. And then my ears just pricked up when she said [*Joyce voice higher*], "And then who sang this song and said 'Now we can say fucky fuck'?" And I'm like, "Oh, fuck, we're gonna get fired." Joyce said, "I don't even wanna know!" And I'm like, "Oh, thank God!"

## Ron West, director

We were told to do a PG show for them. I think the chaperones in the group overreacted to our selections almost from the very start when we did this old blackout. Man and woman kissing onstage. Second man enters, saying, "Hi, honey, I'm home," surprising the couple. The second man says, "And what is *she* doing here?" Blackout. The chaperones—who were fairly near the booth—were like, "Oh, no, that's not what we asked for." They did this during other sketches, too, long before we did "Huck Finn," where I think Colbert dropped the "fuck" bomb. About half the audience left at intermission and Joyce gave them their money back.

## Anne Libera

Joyce came back and took each of them apart individually, describing Amy Sedaris as nothing but wigs and funny faces. And then she went up to the booth—Ron West was directing—and Stephen said, "You could hear the munching of bones and the sucking of marrow." It was scary.

Although Chicago's improv boom was still a few years away, Second City thrived in the early nineties. Mainstage and e.t.c. shows such as *Winner Takes Oil; Ameri-Go-Round; Truth, Justice or the American Way; Where's*

*Your God Now, Charlie Brown?;* and *Take Me Out to the Balkans* featured a number of future stars in training—including several of today's best-known performers. Among them were the two Steves: Carell and Colbert. The former was a generally reserved chap with a swell singing voice, from Concord, Massachusetts. The latter was a well-bred Northwestern-schooled thespian (also with a swell singing voice) from Charleston, South Carolina. A thea-tuh man through and through, he took a while to soften up. But once that happened, there was no turning back.

### Paul Dinello

I came from a blue-collar Chicago background, and Stephen had come from the South. And he got formal acting training at Northwestern, and I was just a drunk idiot. I think he thought I was a bit of a philistine, and I thought he was a bit of a dandy. His hair was in a pompadour, and he had, like, a red turtleneck on, and he held his chin in his hand. Rested his chin on top of his knuckles. And he was very dry. And I had never really followed any rules, nor did I really want to hear about the rules. I always sort of screwed around. I think Farley and I were closer, but oddly enough, Colbert and I hit it off more. I think initially we thought, "Boy, I bet it would be easy to hate this guy."

### Stephen Colbert

I was very actorly, because I had gone to theater school. And I was very controlled. I was all about planning. And Paul was sort of a wild, chaotic, impulsive energy comedically. Much sillier, much stupider behavior. And I'm happy to say he won that battle. He said my tie was tied a little too tight, and he was absolutely right. And he opened me up to a little bit of a wilder side, and so did Amy. And then the three of us became pretty inseparable, and I was very lucky and grateful to have those two people to love and be loved by, for the next few years, because it's not easy to be a lady-in-waiting there at Second City, while you're on the road all the time. You get to be on the road, which is great, but waiting for your work is an exhausting experience. Even waiting for a touring company. They keep you hungry.

### Paul Dinello

Stephen approaches things intellectually. Amy and I approach things emotionally. So when we started, he wanted to take the right road, and he wanted to hear what people had to say. And he wanted to intellectualize stuff and understand it, and sort of do things by the numbers. Amy and I were more the kind of people who would just jump in. And I remember when we first started, he had a thing: "I never laugh onstage." And we were doing this scene in the touring company and Amy put in these false icky teeth, which she wasn't supposed to have in for the scene, and smiled, and he started laughing. He just lost it, and he went backstage, and he was all upset about it.

### Stephen Colbert

I was so mad that we finished the song and then I fucking blew offstage and went and locked myself in the bathroom like a teenage girl, and banged my head against the wall with rage. And she and Paul, who were determined to get me to loosen up, were like, [*high mocking voice*] "Hey, are you crying?" Just mocking me mercilessly.

### Amy Sedaris, cast member

He was very serious in the beginning, and it was hard. But after that, he was all ours.

### Paul Dinello

By the time we got on mainstage, he had no problem showing up for a scene without his pants on. He did a three-sixty. He completely tossed the rules away.

### Stephen Colbert

They completely won. I'm forever grateful that they broke me.

### Nia Vardalos

He was always irreverent while remaining a gentleman. He gets this mischievous look in his eye and he knows he's done wrong, but oh, he'll do it again.

### Fran Adams

Stephen Colbert was always the Southern gentleman, and always very smart. But Stephen hung out with Amy and Paul, and they were a trilogy. If you could get Stephen on his own, he would be totally different, but he was very much under their influence. And Stephen and Paul was okay, but Stephen, Paul, and Amy wasn't a positive energy to the rest of the crew. They were positive to each other, but never to the rest.

### Paul Dinello

We were the kind of people that wouldn't really fit with the system, whatever it was, even though you could barely call it a system. But you still wanted to fuck with it.

### Nia Vardalos

There were definitely cliques. It's just high school all over again. This is what I always likened it to: it's six siblings that you didn't choose, and you have to share a bedroom with them, and for sure someone's always got stinky feet.

I reveled in that competition. The only time it's not good is when competition turns into grandstanding, because that is the exact antithesis of improv. So that was the only time I thought, "Oh, please, save it for the therapist's couch. Don't bring that here." And I did work with some people, who will remain nameless, who would come in and bring the days' problems into that tiny bedroom. And I just learned to avoid what I call the energy vampire.

### Mick Napier

Second City's formula for creating material is astounding. It's brilliant. When you direct there, having the show be not funny is not an option. You have to start with, "The show's got to be really funny," and then create from there. So how does that form an actor? It allows them this insane playground to try out everything good about themselves and everything bad about themselves to allow them to really find their voice. You try so many different scenes in the improv sets that you learn everything you need to know about yourself. So Stephen Colbert would be able to learn that it works really well when he has this high-status character that's a little bit quirky and a little bit weird. He learns time after time that it hits. Paul Dinello learns that if he plays this blue-collar rough character, the audience responds to that.

### Paul Dinello

Stephen always had the ability to play high-status idiots, because he's so well spoken and the intelligence oozes from every pore. He also had the ability to fuck with people and keep a straight face. In Chicago there were only a few agents. There was really sort of a limited situation. And the one that most of us used—I can't even remember their name now—but at one time they were a talent and modeling agency. And for some reason I had their cards with me. They said "modeling agency." And Colbert and Joe Liss and I, for some reason, went out to have a drink. And Colbert had red sweatpants on and a T-shirt or something. And each of us was going to go up to women and present this card and say, "We saw you dancing, and we're agents, and we're interested in you."

### Stephen Colbert

Not the proudest story in the world, but if you improvise a lot onstage, you end up doing it in your life. And the basic tenet is "Always agree, always go along, never deny, don't block." That kind of thing. So if a suggestion is made, you tend to follow the suggestions, even in your life, very quickly. It can lead to a sort of chaotic way of living. And we were out at some club, and we're downstairs. There were these beautiful girls on the dance floor, and we were like, "Aw, we would never be able to talk to those girls." And I said, "Yeah, but I bet if you were an agent, you could walk right up to one of them, and they would talk to you." I said, "I bet like this [*snaps fingers*], I could get that girl to talk to me." And they're like, "No fucking way." I said, "No, watch this." I forget what I said. "Hi, I'm from [whatever] agency. I just want to talk to you about your look." And she was like, "Oh, great." She came over and gave me the time. And I walked back over and said, "There, I did it. I had a conversation with her." In sweatpants. And I don't have the greatest physique.

Whether on the road or a resident stage, Second City actors often endured less than ideal conditions. Piper's Alley, the complex that Second City theaters have long shared with a handful of other businesses, was then notorious for its overall state of disrepair. The business next door was rumored to be especially atrocious.

### Craig Taylor

Piper's Alley was in terrible shape with the past owners. That Steak Joynt was in there for a while, and they closed down. That place was rat infested, and they had to go somewhere. And they came up where we were. I hated being the first one backstage.

### Rose Abdoo

People used to say the owner of the Steak Joynt's wife had a fur coat that was made from the rats.

### Nia Vardalos

I pulled out a costume, and it was wedged way into a cubby hole, and I was trying to decide if it was too garish. And I was pulling it out, pulling it out, and thinking, "What would Joyce say?" And a rat came with it, and I shoved it back and went, "Okay, I'm just going to go with this skirt."

### Stephen Colbert

The smell was just unbelievable. And there was thirty years of clothing piled on the floor backstage, because you'd finish the night and you'd be tired and you had a clown hat on or something. You just threw it on the floor some nights. And then the next night you didn't pick it up and another shirt went on top of it. And there were just great compost heaps of things. "God, the rats are living in there, I bet. I don't want to go through that." But then, "Oh, shit, I forgot. There's a priest collar in there someplace, and I need it!" And so you would dig through it just as quickly as you could, kind of shake it out, spray Lysol on it or something, and put it on. It was pretty raw.

### Amy Sedaris

There was a rat that galloped across the stage during a scene. And then you'd always smell them. You'd always smell a dead rat. It was just disgusting. So dirty back there. One time we lifted the couch up back in the greenroom, and we saw a rat eating out another rat's stomach.

### Craig Taylor

We hear this screaming, so we slide the couch out, and sure enough, they're both stuck there, and one was in the position to have dinner on the other one.

### John Rubano

Before the place next door to the Second City was called That Steak Joynt, years and years ago it used to be some kind of granary down below, so there were catacombs. The guy who killed the vermin in both buildings was in Second City one day, and I said, "Hey, is that place next door nasty?" He goes, "It's one of the worst places in the city. Don't ever eat there. The walk-in freezers are made out of wood, and the rats have chewed through the wood, and I've walked in there before and seen rats sitting on steaks."

We would have Mondays off in the resident company, and we'd do Tuesday through Sunday. So we came in on a Tuesday, and the greenroom just reeked. And I was like, "Goddammit! This is just ridiculous!" It's just foul with the smell of death. I go, "I've got to get to the bottom of this. We can't do the show with this." So we start tearing the greenroom apart. And there was this couch there. The couch itself was just a filthy, nasty thing. It was like a petri dish you could sit on. Just terrible. You could actually do an archeological dig through the layers, back to Nichols and May, perhaps. It was one of those things that if you lit it on fire, it would have burned for weeks like an oil well or something. Red Adair would have had to put the damn thing out. So we finally pull out this goddamn couch, and behind the couch is a glue trap. Now, a glue trap is maybe one foot by one foot square. And it's basically quicksand for a rat. It smells really good or tastes really good, and once they crawl on it, they can't get off. They're just stuck there. So I pull it out, and there on the glue trap are two rats. One is dead. The other is half-alive, and it has eaten the dead one. So I went ballistic. I was like, "Goddammit! How the fuck are we supposed to work in these conditions?" I just went nuts.

## Fran Adams

I've killed a mouse in my day. I think I was scared at how he snapped. And John's a very controlled person.

## John Rubano

So I got a piece of two-by-four and crushed the skull of the rat that was still alive. Then I got a pitchfork. We had a multitude of props backstage, one of which was a pitchfork. You can never have enough devil scenes or farmer scenes. So I got this pitchfork and scooped up the rats on the trap, and I took it into the box office and put it on the desk. And I just left it there and walked away. They asked who had done it, and I said, "I did. It's just revolting. We shouldn't have to work in these conditions." They had the exterminators there rather quickly after that. And I'm convinced that anybody who worked at Second City during that period on the mainstage has had five to ten years cut off their life from the poisons we had to encounter. It was truly appalling. Particularly the half-eaten rat. I didn't know that rodents were cannibals.

While disgusting vermin ran rampant, some far funnier human hideousness played out onstage. Prior to landing at Second City, Amy Sedaris had been a fan of *SCTV*. In the late eighties, her brother David (the bestselling humorist) was living in Chicago. Having already been introduced to Second City, he thought improv might suit his sister's talents and encouraged her to relocate. Soon she began taking Martin de Maat's improv classes at Players Workshop of Second City, where she met Stephen Colbert and Paul Dinello, the latter of whom she dated for several years. A keen observer of mortal foibles and life's grotesqueries, Sedaris had a penchant for getting ugly. Playing it pretty, she decided early on, just wasn't her thing.

## Amy Sedaris

I just don't find it interesting. I think there are enough girls out there who can do that, and look the part. I just didn't pay any attention to it. I don't remember wearing makeup onstage. I could do the different characters and wouldn't have to worry about that. I wanted a blank slate. You can just add one thing and you become that character, but if you've got cat-eye eyeliner on, then you're going to look like Sophia Loren in every scene.

## John Rubano

Amy, having come from the South, brought, like, this really weird dynamic that I had never known before, being a guy from the West. But the strange thing was that through her characters, I could see, "That's not too different from some of the trailer people I observed in Colorado." Her characters just happen to have a banjo in their mouth. Amy's not afraid to get ugly on you, and I think that's a big plus.

### Mick Napier

Amy always wants to adorn her characters with wigs or fuckin' Scotch tape. Beautiful woman who tries to make herself ugly every chance she has.

### Tom Gianas

Amy was the best I've ever worked with. There's no one funnier than Amy Sedaris. She can be hard to work with, though, and she had really specific attitudes about her comedy and what she wanted to do, and what she tolerated. And she could be tough on other people. But that's who you want. You want those people in that theater.

One of Sedaris's mainstage cohorts, Steve Carell, sometimes played her foil—as when he portrayed a polite serial killer named Chuck in "High Rise," from the 1992 revue *Truth, Justice or the American Way.* As they would in later years on screens big and small, his characters at Second City ranged from clueless to crazed. One of them would eventually spawn Judd Apatow's hit comedy *The 40-Year-Old Virgin.* Its gist: Carell—though nowhere near forty at the time—played a grown man who'd never had sex but attempted (poorly and hilariously) to convince his pals otherwise. Chest hair, it should be noted, remained intact.

### David Razowsky, cast member

I hung out a lot with Carell when we were in the touring company. Very ballsy onstage and very focused onstage and very present onstage. Offstage, still very present, but very shy. Not that he was scared of crowds. It was just he wouldn't necessarily turn to anybody and engage them in a conversation like other Second City people would. Certainly I would talk to anybody, and that has gotten me into trouble. Carell wasn't one that would go out and be the life of the party.

### Paul Dinello

We improvised a scene where he played a character who had never had sex. Like, an adult man who never had sex. It's a vague memory, but we were talking about what it was like to make love to a woman, and what it felt like. And then somehow the subject became what a woman's vagina feels like, and he said, "It's like feeding a horse."

## Stephen Colbert

I know I did it with him at least once. It was absolutely his idea. It was a guy who was however old Steve was at the time and a virgin, and couldn't reveal it to his friends because he's too embarrassed. The scene is we're all sitting around drinking. We'd actually go get beer from backstage and we'd bring it onstage and drink. We would mime all our props, except the beer. And we were all talking about sexual conquests. And Steve's examples were always a little suspect, like, "You know how breasts are so powdery?" We're like, "What do you mean?" "You know, how they feel like a bunch of grapes?" "What are you talking about?" And then it was slowly revealed that he was a virgin, and we helped him know what it was like to have sex with a woman. Scott Allman said, "Here. Grab my ass. Okay. This is like a really big breast. A little softer than that." Steve's grabbing his ass. "Stick your finger in my belly button. Okay, go ahead." So we would act it out for him, in a very loving way, like, "Man, you need to know what this is like." And obviously he made his own changes. But I was so happy when I saw that he was going to make that into a movie, because it gives me hope that all the scenes we never could quite make work at Second City someday might see the light of day.

## John Rubano

Steve and I would do these blackouts that would horrify the crowd every time. And we would have great joy in doing this. We would do one called "Shark Stomach." This involved me taking my shirt off and putting on a cleaner's bag. A clear, see-through cleaner's bag. I would pop a hole in the top and two arm holes, and I would wet it down so it would cling to me, and then I'd wet my hair. Carell would come out onstage in a sailor outfit with a big machete, and he would stand in front of the window, with the little seam down the middle. And he would say, [*sailor voice*] "That's the biggest great white we've had in these parts in a long time. Let's cut it open and see what's in it!" He would get the machete and start moving down the seam of the window like it was the belly of the great white, and then he'd get to the bottom and pull it out. I would kick open the doors with my hands and come flying out over the window and land on the stage. But while I was flying out, I would spit Pepto-Bismol onto the crowd and we'd go to black. Then the lights would come immediately back up. There would be no response from the audience. I mean, sometimes, like, "Oh, my God." Or a couple laughs here and there, but that was it. Steve and I would stand up, very proudly, and then bow. Then we'd say to the audience, "Do you want to see it again?" And they'd go, "No!" And we'd go, "Great, here it is again!" So I'd go backstage, Steve would come out, same thing. "That's the biggest great white we've had . . ." He would slice open the belly, I'd fly out, spit more Pepto-Bismol. Lights would go down, we'd stand up, proudly bow. "Do you wanna see it again?" "No!" "Great! We'll do it again!" We would do it three times. The rule of comedy three. It was almost like the stuff that Andy Kaufman would do. It was so weird. People would just start laughing at how ludicrous it was, at the end. That was never in a show. Remarkably.

On March 4, 1994, Second City and *SCTV* star John Candy died suddenly in his sleep on the set of his latest film, *Wagons East!* A heart attack was to blame. Andrew Alexander and Dan Aykroyd delivered eulogies at Candy's funeral service days later, and Los Angeles police shut down part of the San Diego Freeway for the short drive to Holy Cross Cemetery in Culver City.

Later that month, in the revue *Are You Now or Have You Ever Been Mellow?,* Colbert and Carell teamed up to perform a now classic scene called "Maya." It's the touching tale of a young white man who returns to his beloved Southern hometown—where people treat him like an elderly black woman.

### Kelly Leonard

Stephen was brought up in the moneyed South, and his father was involved in a civil rights situation in a hospital, and this is his worldview coming across on a Second City stage to transform it and create what I think was an incredible moment. It was one of the ways an all-white cast can deal with race in a way that's not embarrassing.

### Stephen Colbert

It wasn't that long after Clinton was inaugurated. And Maya Angelou had written and read a poem, ["On the Pulse of Morning"]. And I had started reading some of her poetry, and I had started listening to this group called Sweet Honey in the Rock that my wife—my girlfriend at the time—introduced me to. And I thought, "Ah, I wish I was an old black woman! They have so much character. I'm so characterless. There's no flavor to me. Who would be interested in me as a person?" I felt like I was a totally different person when I was back in my hometown in the South than I was in Chicago. Like, I had this split persona. I said, "I really would love to do a scene about what it's like to bring somebody home." But I also really wanted to do a scene where I was Maya Angelou. And so our director, Tom Gianas, said, "Why don't you try to do both somehow?" And so we thought about it, Carell and I. I don't actually think we even said, "When I'm home, I'll be a black woman." I said, "We'll just try to improvise a scene where those two things come together." And when we improvised it, that's what happened. That scene, as you hear it, is improvised almost exactly that way. Down to the song we sing at the end. It was the most complete improvised scene I ever worked on, and it was a group scene, which is a very hard thing to improvise and write if you give it all the time in the world. But we improvised it, and we went, "That's the second act opener. That's it." And we never changed a word of it. And that never ever happened again. The nice thing is it may be my favorite thing we ever did there, and also possibly one of the strangest things I ever did there, and yet somehow strangely sweet and sincere at the same time.

### "Maya," from *Are You Now or Have You Ever Been Mellow?*, 1994

LIGHTS UP ON CARELL AND COLBERT, DOWNSTAGE LEFT AND DOWNSTAGE RIGHT, RESPECTIVELY. THE SCENE IS PLAYED "STRAIGHT" THROUGHOUT—COLBERT DOES NOT AFFECT HIS VOICE OR MANNERISMS, EXCEPT FOR A SLIGHT SOUTHERN ACCENT.

**Carell:** This is great.

**Colbert:** Yeah, I love my hometown.

**Carell:** It is just beautiful.

**Colbert:** Yeah. I don't know if this happens to you, but when I come home I act differently, people treat me differently—it's a great feeling.

**Carell:** Yeah, it's the same way when I go home.

**Colbert:** You want to get something to eat?

**Carell:** Sure.

**Colbert:** That train ride just wore me out.

RUTH RUDNICK ENTERS STAGE RIGHT.

**Ruth:** Shirley! Shirley Wentworth! It's me, Missy!

**Colbert:** Missy Kensington! Oh, Lord, how you've grown! Missy!

COLBERT TWIRLS RUTH.

**Ruth:** Shirley, I have two kids of my own now and I named my girl Shirley and my boy Wentworth.

**Colbert:** Well, I'm twice blessed.

**Ruth:** You know, my mama—she passed away this fall.

**Colbert:** Oh, honey, I'm sorry to hear that.

**Ruth:** You were always like a second mama to me.

**Colbert:** This is my friend, Steve. Steve, this is Missy Kensington.

**Ruth:** Hi, nice to meet you.

**Carell:** Nice to meet you.

**Ruth:** Please come over to the house today and meet the children.

**Colbert:** Sure.

**Ruth:** I love you.

**Colbert:** I love you, too, darlin'.

**Ruth:** Bye-bye!

**Colbert:** God love you.

RUTH RUNS OFF STAGE RIGHT.

**Carell:** What was that all about?

**Colbert:** We're old friends.

**Carell:** Shirley Wentworth?

**Colbert:** Oh! I forgot to tell you. When I'm home, I'm an old black woman. Let's get something to eat. C'mon.

The transition of power at Second City was especially difficult for Joyce Sloane, but the much younger and greener Kelly Leonard had a rough go of it, too. After all, he was nudging out a beloved local legend—one who had begun her tenure at the theater years before he was born.

### Joyce Sloane

There were a lot of jokes, there were a lot of smear campaigns—until he developed his own people and his own group.

### Fran Adams

It just seemed so incredibly suck-up. I mean, here's this kid that we all like. We loved him because of who his father was, and he was a very polite young man, and very nice. And of course you want to see him succeed. There's no reason not to. But [the fact] that he's going to replace Joyce, as this kid? Andrew didn't bring in somebody from Toronto who had already done a thing or two.

### Anne Libera

Kelly was young and arrogant and thought he knew it all. On one level it was really exciting, because there was something about being in a place that felt really stuck, and all of a sudden, thank God, this stuff can happen.

### Brian Stack, cast member

I loved Joyce, but I didn't really get a chance to know her very well, because I came in kind of at the beginning of the time when Kelly was kind of overseeing the producer side of things. To Kelly's credit, he didn't pretend to know everything that was going on in the community. He actually asked people who he should see, what groups he should see, what kind of [stuff] might be around town that he might not already be aware of.

## Kelly Leonard

It was the new guard. And it was like, that's what it's got to be. And [cast member] Adam McKay was a good friend, so we were aligned philosophically on what we wanted to do. We had similar interests and we wanted to shake shit up. There are still people who are really pissed off about that. I remember when we changed the flag color. I had people in my office, furious, because we changed the color of the flag. Tradition is about breaking up tradition—that's what Second City should be. And I don't know that I ever articulated it as well as I could now, but you just had to fight your way through it. It was hard. And then you're firing people who worked here for twenty-five years, who everyone knows are incompetent or had some issue or whatever. But it was the right thing to do and you just had to brave it and do it. But then you also had to be prepared for people to hate you. I remember Andrew saying, "You can't have friends like you did before on staff. And you've got to know that people are going to talk behind your back and say awful things." And they did. Or do. I've been at it so long now it's like, "Who fucking cares?"

## Mick Napier

Kelly did get a lot of shit. He got a lot of heat. I personally tried to cut him a break because so many people were giving him so much shit. I guess they felt he was just kind of plucked from the box office [and put] into an executive producer position, and I think people were freaked out at the time. People are always freaked out over at Second City about something or another.

## Andrew Alexander

I think it was more centered on me, actually, than the person who was taking up the job. But we all lived to tell the story.

## Kelly Leonard

Because I was young and soon not married, I was out seeing shows all over the city. And there was a bunch of talent that we didn't hire, because they auditioned horribly, and sometimes they wouldn't even come to auditions. So [cast members] Kevin Dorff and Brian Stack and Adam McKay and David Koechner went out and hired them. These were all the big guns who were anti–Second City. And we basically said, "Come here. The place is changing. Be part of the change." And they did.

# 10

# Renaissance on Wells Street, Chaos in Canada, and the Falls of Giants

## 1995-2007

**Scott Adsit**
**Rachel Dratch**
**Tina Fey**
**Jack McBrayer**

KELLY LEONARD AND HIS COHORTS continued to buck the tried-and-true system. Their toil produced a critically lauded, fully improvised show called *Lois Kaz* in the e.t.c. theater, which laid the groundwork for a seminal mainstage revue dubbed *Piñata Full of Bees* in 1995. The rebels were aided by a thriving Chicago improv scene, as well as an ongoing urban renaissance that attracted an increasing number of young people (Second City's core demographic) with disposable income to work and live in the city—particularly in neighborhoods around the theater.

At first poorly attended and confounding to audiences (more than a few people walked out), *Piñata* ultimately became a modest hit that altered Second City's trajectory and imbued the place with a renewed sense of purpose and artistic pride. "Dump your lattes. Rip up your La-Z-Boy recliners. Shred your Blockbuster cards," began a *Chicago Sun-Times* review titled "2nd City Sheds Tradition, Finds Its Sting." "Second City's 80th revue, 'Piñata Full of Bees,' is a call for revolt against an America numbed by comfort." No blackouts, longer scenes, more props, and a hard-driving rock/rap soundtrack made it abundantly clear this wasn't your daddy's comedy cabaret. In an article headlined, "In 'Piñata,' Troupe Takes Daring Step, Breaks Out of Second City Mold," the *Chicago Tribune* praised the show's "unusual, memorable ensemble" and enumerated a handful of its "novelties," which included "a disabled basketball league, a homicidal ferret and an executive who's technically retarded (and given to similes, such as 'I could crush you like a cloud')."

### Kelly Leonard

Tom Gianas and I had been friends and were talking about what became *Piñata Full of Bees*. We put together a cast that was half old-school, half new-school. And we used to go to my health club and play basketball, and Adam McKay would come, and we'd talk about the kind of stuff we wanted to do. I remember the very first conversations were, "Let's do an all-improvised show." And it took a week to figure out that there's no way in hell we could do that and have it work. *Piñata* was a seventeen-week process. And it died during previews. You could hear a mouse shit.

### Tom Gianas

There was a month or so where it was not doing well in the previews, where, to their credit, they stuck with me on it and they let me continue to do it. Because why change something that's working as a business? And at the time, it was. We were selling out. In the previous shows, longtime fans of Second City weren't leaving and saying, "I don't want to go back there anymore. That's just bad." So what would motivate a businessperson to say, "Let's completely redo how we're doing shows and see what happens?" That usually comes out of financial straits, or business desperation. I felt like the form was dusty. It was stagnating. The one thing that's most important in comedy is the element of surprise, and there was none in those shows anymore. And, look, I directed a lot of them—shows that I'm proud of. But I also learned through doing the more conventional revues that it was time to do something different.

### Andrew Alexander

A journalist had written that Second City had become a haunt for beer-drinking tourists, the implication being that the best days were behind us. After watching a few of the previews, I knew that we were definitely saying goodbye to that audience, and wasn't sure who the new audience was going to be. This show exemplified the creative risks I knew should be taken, but that didn't make it any less nerve-racking.

### Scott Adsit, cast member

Rehearsals were exciting for me and Scott Allman, especially, because we had just come off a mainstage retrospective that was weak at best. Not that the material was inherently poor, but without its original context as a reflection of its audience, it lost its zing. We were doing scenes that had been created by brilliant minds to tap into the social and political mind-set of several different eras. But not ours. And, yeah, many themes transcend time, but style does not. And we were committed to re-creating the scenes as accurately as we could. Like a museum tour. And it would have been a great show if we had all the original creators from across the decades doing their material. It's all so personality-driven. But it was filtered through the seven of us, instead. And who wants to see that? We were pale, inherited imitations.

Anyway, we couldn't wait to go the exact opposite direction and do a show with no rules. No set, no accepted structure, no formal welcome, no hack characters lurking in the prop hat bin. The first thing we agreed on was no set. And that meant no doors, no window, no conventional way of entering a room. So, Gianas brought up the question of how a character would knock on the door to enter. I had the idea of hanging army helmets on bungee cords on either side of the proscenium so that when someone needed to knock, they would pull the helmet down onto their head, rap on it, and then let it snap back up. Funny, nonsense visual. Everyone said yes. Just that little thing thrilled me. That was my first indication that we would be taking the risk of looking foolish or "artistic" for the sake of moving forward. We wanted it to be art, and we weren't ashamed of that. It became very open and free. We felt a bit like Warhol's Factory—anything goes, no bad ideas.

### Jon Glaser, cast member

Comedically, it felt like things were changing a little bit. And I think the sensibility of a lot of the performers coming in was also different than the standard, especially with the blackouts where it's lights up, kooky joke, lights down. It wasn't that anybody didn't think that was funny or good. Maybe that was becoming a little old hat. People wanted to try something different, and also there was a movement of long-form improv going on at places like ImprovOlympic, and a lot of people getting hired at the theater were working at ImprovOlympic and were doing a lot of that kind of work and interested in it. So it was probably more of a timing thing than anything, just a certain group of people coming together at the same time who all wanted to do a specific kind of work.

### Adam McKay, cast member

We literally tore down the stage. We got sledgehammers and went and knocked down the stage. It was just an exposed brick wall. And there was no backstage. All the actors were onstage almost all the time, sitting in chairs. We used prerecorded music mixed with piano from Ruby Streak. We had hardly any lights out throughout the whole show. It was always just dimming and light changes. There were never blackouts. And there was a funny little musical number in there, but there were no big musical pieces. We did these kind of improvised story things using instruments. It was an aggressive show. We really went for it. And so I'm sure [the producers] had moments where they were freaking out a little bit, but it never came off to us like, "Pull the plug." And if it did, I didn't hear it.

### Kelly Leonard

They had this great idea that we all thought was hilarious to have a bit where they come out and tell the audience that the president had been shot and killed.

### Tom Gianas

I wanted to announce to the audience that Clinton had been assassinated. We had a conceptual idea. It wasn't just to shock the audience. And Scott Adsit's such a good actor. He's the one who made the announcement, and he really pulled it off. Because everything we did with the audience, we didn't declare as a piece of comedy right away. Before that, there was a long tradition of Second City scenes where they did use the audience. There would be plants, but they declared themselves as characters from the first line out of their mouths. It was broad and big and comedy. But we didn't do that. So during the improv set, we had Adsit come out and announce that the president had been assassinated. And it immediately sucked the air out of the room, the way it was orchestrated and the way he told it. When Adsit made the announcement, he cried actual tears because it felt almost like it had really happened by the way the audience reacted. I was in the middle of the audience, watching, and I felt it, too. It was chilling. Normally if you say something like that and they sense the joke, the partisan aspect of the audience will emerge. They would use it as a way to demonstrate their political affiliation. Well, there was none of that. There was just silence. So Adsit knew they really did buy it. He said, "We're going to bring out a TV and you can watch the coverage here with us or you can go home, but the show's over." So he rolled out a TV and [the tape] we had was cued up to sports bloopers, which were really popular at the time. And he turned it on and it's a dark theater and the audience is riveted because they're about to watch news coverage of the assassination of President Clinton. And on comes a tape of soccer and a referee getting hit in the nuts and people laughing and crazy sound effects. And Adsit's there and he's watching and he just starts laughing, on cue, as he's supposed to. And we slowly have other actors come out and watch the TV and really enjoy these sports bloopers. And the audience went from deeply saddened and grieving to confused and then angry. And then slowly they left the theater—it was absolutely full—until there was no one left. And it ends in dead silence. It was a joke that didn't declare itself clearly enough, and once it did, they didn't want it. They didn't like it. It was too dark. A lot of *Piñata* was about challenging the lack of appetite the country had for intellectualism, and this was an exploration of that.

## Rachel Dratch

I was so uncomfortable. I wanted to flee the building. It was so wrong in my mind. It was the most horrible thing I was involved with there. I hated every second of it. I guess we pushed the boundaries, and every so often you do something like that. There was a quote on the wall that Scott Allman said: "You could have heard a mouse shit." They didn't boo because they still thought it was real. They left thinking it was real. They were just dazed, confused, bewildered, angry.

## Scott Adsit

I remember just wanting to go out and find a truthful way to tell an audience that. I remember jumping at the chance because you don't get many opportunities to elicit anything more than laughter from that audience. So, yeah, we wanted to experiment with what we could get away with. Could we lie to them, betray them, then let them off the hook and still have their support? And so what if we didn't? If a hundred percent of them had laughed at the end, we would have been disappointed. Then it would have been just a skit instead of an experiment. So, I felt great going out there. The whole premise of *Piñata* was to get it wrong, even at the expense of an audience or two, on the path to something new. So, first I go out and interrupt a scene, which is an old, hacky device in a sketch show, the "scene breaking down" bit. I hate that because it's always so obvious that everybody's pretending to get angry at each other or whatever, and "stopping" the scene. Awful. So, we didn't want that, because nobody is ever fooled. I come out without entering the scene itself and trade close mutterings with Dratch, protecting the audience from what we were saying, instead of presenting it. We get the others offstage silently and she exits. I turn to the crowd and awkwardly tell them the news. It wasn't just a hush, but a pristine silence fell over them. That made me high. It was great. It was horribly selfish of us, but it was exhilarating and I was giddy because we were getting away with it. About two minutes into it, though, I felt like you do when you throw a fake punch at somebody and actually bust their orbital bone.

## Jon Glaser

It was definitely one of those things that I'm glad we tried. I think some people were pretty upset about it. Look, it was really fucking with the audience. Every time I tell someone that story, it makes me laugh so hard because it's so insane we did it.

## Adam McKay

Looking back on it, it was crazily irresponsible. Borderline mean. But also, in a way, kind of good, because we were just kind of screwing with stuff and trying different ideas. I had had good training from doing Upright Citizens Brigade, where we had plenty of shows where people were livid and mad and yelling, "That's not cool." The goal certainly was not to have someone scream in your face. But I also knew that if you went into that territory, you were going to find some really rich, original stuff.

## Chris Earle, Toronto cast member

[In Toronto] we felt fairly free of Chicago's influence [in the mid-nineties], and we had a very rich legacy in the original casts at the Firehall. I think it started to swing back again once *Piñata* happened in Chicago. I know Andrew was very excited by that, and there was a lot of excitement in Chicago, and I think he encouraged various Toronto people to come down and see that show. There was a deliberate move, I think, to try and get some of that looser, long-form style: a little bit less traditional lights up, lights down— more linking of characters in a show, some sort of overall structure—all the things that *Piñata* had. So people began to look toward Chicago again. And I think it was very back and forth. We tried going a little too far with that style and it wasn't really organic to us and we struggled a bit with that. I think we found a way to make it our own, to incorporate some of those stylistic innovations while at the same time doing it our way.

## Chris Jones, *Chicago Tribune* theater critic

In the eighties and very early nineties, the main action was in Toronto. That's where a lot of the stars came from. People like Mike Myers. Beginning in the mid-nineties, all of the energy of that company shifted back to Chicago. And I think it has stayed that way.

For his part in bringing *Piñata* to the stage, Leonard was praised in the press. That irked at least one cast member, who thought he was getting too much credit for their collective endeavor.

## Kevin Dorff, cast member

I'll just speak for myself, but I can also generalize a bit. We had no sympathy for him whatsoever. We had nothing but the highest expectations. For us, there was only one way for Kelly to go, and that was down from our level of expectation. I had no idea what he was up against. I had no idea what it was he needed to overcome or what he needed to do to make this happen. And I couldn't have cared less. I don't remember anyone expressing any sympathetic language at all for the position Kelly was in. Our attitude was he needed to get this done yesterday. We were very much young men in a hurry. And our attitude was, if anything, "Kelly's not moving fast enough."

### Tom Gianas

I just moved some stuff out of storage, and I saw this old poster that Scott Adsit did that was hanging backstage during the run. [The poster pictured Kelly Leonard in caricature and contained sarcastically glowing commentary about his heroic role in *Piñata*'s creation.] Adsit was an artist; he was always drawing caricatures backstage. [The poster] was an overt display of his resentment, of him feeling that Kelly was getting credit for *Piñata Full of Bees*.

### Scott Adsit

There was some article about the radical and bizarre new show being mounted at the Second City mainstage. It was a great bit of publicity because, generally, the press response for a Second City show at the time was essentially "Here's another one: Also quite good." So, to be recognized by the locals as being something more than just a tourist destination was an achievement for the mainstage. But the article only mentioned Adam, Tom, and Kelly as the instigators/innovators. As if the three of them got together, decided to change stodgy old Second City, and then hired some drones to fill out the cast and carry out their vision. The article just ignored the cast. Now, I know that that was not the intent of those three, but I was insulted and thought the rest of the cast should be, too. So instead of throwing a big hissy fit, I threw a subtler one. [The poster was] just a little sarcastic reminder to Kelly that he was not the only creative force at work.

### Kelly Leonard

Scott got mad because we did a version of *Piñata* at the Kennedy Center in Washington, D.C., [in 1996] and he wasn't in the cast because he was onstage in Chicago doing *Citizen Gates*. Adam McKay and Jon Glaser had left the company by then, so they were in the show, along with Steve Carell, Tim Meadows, Nancy Walls, Dave Koechner, and Theresa Mulligan. When we were in D.C., he put these flyers all over the theater. It was actually pretty funny, and I probably needed to be knocked down a few pegs in those days. I was getting a lot of good press personally.

### Beth Kligerman, director of talent and talent development

I like to say "we," and sometimes [Kelly] says "I." And as a young man, he was definitely saying "I" a lot during that time. And at times it sounded like it was Adam and Tom and Kelly doing something. So it was interesting. I was certainly there when Scott Adsit was putting anti-Kelly posters around the theater. That's a little bit of Adsit's demeanor, and Kelly deserved it.

Kelly is very creative and influential and can be very focused. And sometimes he can be bettered by remembering there's a team of people.

### Horatio Sanz, cast member

When I was there, we didn't win a lot of awards. Before that, I think people weren't thinking that Second City was where funny stuff is. It was more like, "Oh, that's that place that's been there awhile." And people started taking it for granted. I think Del putting Farley onstage and stuff like that—those were bold moves. But there was still a lot of complacency. I don't want to bad-mouth who was there, but they certainly weren't challenging the system. I think *Piñata* was the first time people were like, "Fuck it. If this show works or not, we're saying 'fuck you' to our home."

Fueled by new vigor, Second City Chicago continued to thrive both critically and commercially. After Tom Gianas and Adam McKay left to write for *Saturday Night Live* and Jon Glaser was hired by *The Dana Carvey Show,* Tina Fey stepped into Glaser's role for the rest of *Piñata*'s run. Eventually, *Piñata* gave way to *Citizen Gates,* Mick Napier's directorial debut on the mainstage. The celebrated and visually elegant *Paradigm Lost,* also under Napier's stewardship, followed. A decade later, several members of its cast would reassemble to shoot an NBC sitcom called *30 Rock.* One of them, Fey, would become a comedic icon of sorts—and as per *Vanity Fair* cover story verbiage of January 2009, an "American Sweetheart."

### Tina Fey, cast member

*Piñata Full of Bees* was definitely a huge turning point in the history of the theater, and I think the bulk of that credit goes to Adam McKay, because he has a way of shaking things up by inspiring people and making them want to get on board, as opposed to pushing them aside. He has a way of creating this enthusiasm. He really is responsible for that show in a lot of ways. It was a great cast and they all wrote it together, but he was the voice behind that show, and he was instrumental in changing the look and feel of those shows [that followed].

### Rich Talarico, cast member

The night that show premiered, there was suddenly a sense of awe around the place, as if some mighty gong had been rung. And it echoed in the months and years that followed. It was empowering, because the boundaries had been flung aside. And it was refreshing, because so many staples had been pulled out. On the downside, those inventive new things were maybe overused in subsequent shows—strobe edits, exposed walls, exposed everything—[and became] staples again, perhaps.

### Chris Jones

Mick Napier just came from a different world than the typical Second City world, which had always drawn heavily from sort of your academic, intellectual, slightly nerdy guy. And Napier wasn't that at all, because Annoyance Theatre, which is really where he came from, had been around by then and was well established, and was really doing a kind of intensely edgy Dada-like type of improv comedy, where they were saying "fuck" in every show, and they were playing with genres. They would do shows like *Co-Ed Prison Sluts,* for example. And they had sort of a "fuck you" attitude in the theater, so they never liked critics much. It was a much darker aesthetic. And he was a darker guy, and a different guy, and somebody not interested in what you would think of as sketch comedy. But the thing about Napier that worked well was that he changed his game enough when he got to Second City so that it worked in that format, but retained enough of his old self that it suddenly felt like he was throwing a lot of those old practices out the window.

### Mick Napier

I had just moved back from New York, where I had been working on *Exit 57* and I had just done a David Sedaris play. I met with Kelly, and he said, "Do you want to direct?" It was really hard, because I went to see *Piñata* with my girlfriend, and I looked at it and went, "Oh, my God, this is what I would do if I was directing the mainstage at Second City. I would do something this radical. This show is really amazing." I was impressed. And at the same time I was impressed, I was scared because I didn't know what the hell I could produce up there. They would say to me things like, "Don't worry. We don't expect you to create a show like this," trying to give me some solace. But it created more fear in me. It just made me crazier.

When it came time to cast a woman, I went to Scott Allman and I said, "What do you think?" And he said, "Hands-down, you should hire this woman named Tina Fey." I had never seen her. I got a tape of her in the tour co. show and she was okay on the tape, but I have to say, eighty percent of the reason I put her on the mainstage was because of Scott Allman's recommendation. He said that she was brilliant and that she's versatile and funny. And I said, "Is she crazy?" I try my best not to work with fucking crazy people. I'll take least talented over asshole guys or a crazy woman. At any rate, he said, "No, she's not crazy at all. She's extremely sane and talented." To be honest with you, I barely looked at the tape. I saw enough to know she was competent.

### Scott Adsit

Tina brought a mix of sober, laser-like truth to the show's opinions and a super-intelligent silliness that somehow was based in that same truth. Tina can suss [out] any situation immediately. She just sees through people and pretense right away, and that, mixed with her wit, is formidable.

## Kelly Leonard

Tina always did scenes on body issues, the feminine mystique. She was very attuned to what was different about women, especially in comedy, and she understood cruelty in a big way. I mean, she could cut people down big-time, and she's one of the nicest people I know.

## Scott Adsit

I remember Tina being a bit mousey in her big, puffy winter coat and these huge grandma hand-me-down glasses. But her ideas were great and she was a powerful member of the group pretty quickly. She and I got along great and ended up crafting a bunch of scenes together, most of which were just the two of us. We had to pick and choose which ones we wanted in the show because the show would be too heavy with two-person Scott and Tina scenes. It was painless to write with her because we had the same sensibilities and we just clicked.

In a scene called "Stripper," from the 1997 revue *Paradigm Lost,* Fey played a simultaneously indifferent and indignant "dancer" who was hired to strut her stuff in a cheap motel room audition for a bachelor party. It also featured Scott Adsit as the occupant of said motel room and the subject of Fey's scorn. With its deft dialogue and dearth of licentious crotch buffing, it was similar to Chris Farley's identically named scene in title alone—and side-splitting in its own right.

## Tina Fey

I've always been sort of fascinated with that stuff as a character, because it's so, so, so raw, and it's also a world that I just find creepy and don't understand. It's funny to play it in an improv context, where you're fully clothed pretending to be naked, and it makes people uncomfortable in a good way, I think—that whole topic. I like to portray how grim I think that job is. It's one of the grimmest jobs you could have.

## Mick Napier

When I directed my first show at Second City, I fired a guy so that I could bring in Jackie Hoffman to make three women and three men for the first time in the history of Second City. And when I did my first mainstage show, it was the first equal-gender cast in the history of Second City [Chicago]. It's gone to four [men] and three [women] before, but it stayed [gender equal] and I'm really proud of that. Because I think that alone allowed women greater options on that stage, because they're no longer just the counterpart to a male, which is what a lot of scenes were. When the touring company looks for women scenes in the history of Second City, it's slim pickins. The women at Second City never think about being a woman or what that is. They're just doing what they're doing. And the strongest woman at Second City never complained about always being a wife or a nurse or a whore. They just don't. There's this thing in the improv world on the Internet—endless discussions about how men treat women poorly in improvisation and how women have to stay strong and how women form improv groups and all this shit. And Tina Fey or Amy Sedaris or Stephnie Weir would have never ever formed a complaint about how men treated them onstage. What they would do instead is be wickedly fucking funny and strong and powerful with their choices on the stage. And be relatively silent otherwise.

**Andrew Alexander**

Toronto was always sort of gender-equal. I've really been a proponent of that. And I think it's been important. There have been some shows that were four and two, but overall if you look at the last fifteen years, it's been pretty equal.

**Tina Fey**

I had always felt that if a company is generating its own material, it was always preposterous to have this notion of "Well, if we have too many women, there won't be enough parts." I was very timid the first [rehearsal], but Mick was good. I didn't even really know how the process would work, and I remember Mick would be trying to make coffee on the breaks, and I would go over to him and be like, [*timid sounding*] "Well, I think, maybe I had an idea we could do something." He'd be like, "Okay, tell it. In the rehearsal. Bring it up in rehearsal." And I'd be like, [*timid voice*] "Okay." And then I'd go back into rehearsal and not say anything. But eventually I sort of found my way in that company. If I had to describe my role in that company, at that time, it was more of a writerly role and helping to come up with areas and ideas.

Back in Toronto, Second City had resided for more than two decades in the quaint but flawed Old Firehall at 110 Lombard Street. In the mid-nineties, Andrew Alexander decided the time was right to move his troupe into a slick new multimillion-dollar state-of-the-art venue at 56 Blue Jays Way. From the start it fell short of high expectations. Much interior reconfiguring and financial hemorrhaging ensued. While Toronto battled to get back on track with a string of generally well-reviewed shows such as *Sordido Deluxo* and *Psychedelicatessen,* Second City Chicago—already surfing the *Piñata* wave—stole more spotlight.

## Andrew Alexander

Len Stuart and I got very ambitious. We built an eight-million-dollar build-ing with two theaters, four or five hundred seats, and a restaurant. We were at the Firehall and the audience had disappeared—the young audience. And I felt I had to make some sort of dramatic change, to shake up the mar-ket. This was the mid-nineties. Things were great and the economy was strong and everybody was bullish, and I thought, "Okay, we'll just expand our experimental theater, with a Second City Training Center up there, and a cool restaurant." And it all made sense. But it was bad execution on the restaurant. And the theater had a design flaw that we eventually corrected. It took us years, though, to fix it properly, to make it work.

We had a hit show called *Last Tango on Lombard.* It killed. The new build-ing was ready to move into. We'd spent a year building it. So we move in and do the same show. Not one laugh. If I had a gun, I would have put it to my head that night. It was awful. I was sitting in the back row, and then I went down to the cast at intermission. I looked at them, and they were all white. And I said, "Don't worry, the second act will work." The second act didn't work, either. And it was like, "Oh, my God, we're fucking dead." I'd invested everything. I almost went bankrupt, actually. In fact, I had to sell my home in Chicago. I was just about bust. It was all losses.

## Bob Martin

There were so many problems with that space. Sight line problems, but mainly sound problems. And if there's one thing about comedy that is ab-solutely essential, it's that people hear you. *Last Tango on Lombard* was one of the best critically received shows in years for Second City, and it was run-ning for a long time. And then we took all this material that was really good and we put it on the [new] stage and it just failed. It was the same cast, same material, but the space was so terrible for what we were trying to do. So that was a miserable night. And it took a long, long time of trying to adjust the space and lowering the ceiling and considering using mikes, which every-body fought against. We never really got the space to work properly.

## Bob Derkach, musical director

We got it reasonable over the course of five years, but it was a lot of hard work. It was a difficult space to fill. For a while there, the first parts of the week were fairly small audiences.

## Lisa Brooke, cast member

Everybody was separated from each other at their tables. It was a very indi-vidual experience going to see that show. You really weren't picking up on the spark of laughter that was happening at different tables. It really wasn't what Second City was to me when I was growing up and so desperately wanted to be there. So I felt like I got there at this time when I lost. That's how I felt. I lost out on the real experience of Second City by being at 56 Blue Jays Way. Chicago was much more satisfying. It felt like doing the real Second City because the audience was right there and you felt like you were having a conversation with the audience instead of putting on a show.

Another pall fell over Wells Street and much of the comedy-loving nation in mid-December 1997, when Chris Farley died of a drug overdose at his Michigan Avenue condo, less than two miles from the theater that launched his career. Like his idol, John Belushi, he was only thirty-three.

### Andrew Alexander

Chris had shown up to our Christmas party and was in pretty bad shape, so when the news came about his death later that week, everyone was very, very sad, but not shocked.

### Cheryl Sloane

Chris was in town, and my mom was calling him to tell him to come over to the Christmas party, and for some reason he wasn't showing up. And my mom called him again and said, "Just come over, just come over." And he came up the steps and he had a drink in his hand and he had this girl with him. I was one of the first people to see him, and I said, like a friend, "Can I have a sip of your drink?" And he got this look of panic. I said, "I'm not gonna bust you, Chris. I'm just thirsty." And I took some of his drink—I don't even remember what it was—and I hugged him. And he said, "Is your mom pissed off at me?" I said, "No, nobody's pissed off at you. Everybody's fine. Come on in and have a good time." And I saw the girl he was with, and I went into my mother's office and I said, "Mom, I can't do this, but somebody's got to get this girl away from Chris, because he's going to die and she's going to be part of it." And my mother looked at me like I was crazy, as people do, and I said, "She reminds me of the girl who was with John [Belushi] when John died." And she just didn't say anything. That was Monday. And on [Thursday], my mom was supposed to meet Chris for lunch at the Pump Room and he didn't show up because he was dead. She said, "You called this one."

### Kelly Leonard

This is a place where, if you miss a show, you're gone. And [Chris's brother] John missed rehearsal. He lived with Chris at the John Hancock building. I called over there, and Teddy, who was the handler for Chris, was like, "I can't talk right now. The police are here." And he hung up. And I'm like, "Fuck you," and I call back, and I said, "I need John." Teddy said, "Kelly, I can't. This is serious. I don't know what to tell you." I said, "Is everything all right?" He said, "No, it's decidedly not all right. I'll call you later, okay?" And I hang up and I'm like, "What is going on?" I'm sitting here, and we had these phones with the lights. And suddenly everything lights up—every line at Second City, at once. And I see three television trucks coming here, taking pictures of the front of the building. And I just knew: "Chris is dead." And before anyone had told me, I called Andrew, who was in Toronto, and said, "I'm just telling you this now. I have a sneaking suspicion that Chris Farley just died." He's like, "What are you talking about?" I said, "This is what just happened." And I'm getting a call. I hang up, and it was John. He said, "Chris is dead. I don't know what to do. Can someone help me?" His touring company was at the theater, and Kevin Dorff was in that company, and Kevin and Chris were friends, so I had to go tell them. And everyone's crying and I said, "We've got to get John." We got him somehow and hid him out in the theater.

### Kevin Dorff

We were in rehearsal with Jeff Richmond for *Promise Keepers, Losers Weepers*. I had heard on the radio that morning that police had responded to a call at Chris's place, and assumed the worst. Later, Joyce walked into the main room, where we were working, and blurted out, "Did anyone ever doubt that this would be the way it would end?" Reporters had begun milling outside the building.

### Kelly Leonard

We barred reporters and I wrote up a statement. So Joyce and I went out front and I read a statement, and it was just weird. It was the first time I had been on *Good Morning America*. And I remember that some news reporter weaseled his way up here. He was pretending he came to get tickets and just walked into my office to interview me about Chris. I said, "Get the fuck outta here!" And people would call and yell and be like, "Why are you not talking to us?" And "We want an interview." I said, "No, we read a statement. This is the statement. I'll read it to you." I remember at that point saying to people, "Do you have any dignity whatsoever? I mean, I get you doing your job, but now you're yelling at me about this. I just lost a friend." Horrible. People were horrible. They forgot the human factor.

### Andrew Alexander

A bunch of us piled onto a bus I rented and drove to Madison, Wisconsin, for the funeral.

### Kelly Leonard

I just remember it being really quiet back and forth, and us being like, "What happened? How did we let this happen?" There was a lot of that. "I should have done this. We should have done an intervention. We could have stopped this." It's hard when you have a bus full of comedians who aren't in the mood to be funny. We got to Madison, and Lorne Michaels is there, and a bunch of people from *SNL,* and we're all saying, "Hi," and you're seeing a bunch of your old friends who have moved on and become famous, and your inclination is to high-five and hug. And instead you're crying and hugging.

### Tom Gianas

I was part of the bus trip. I just remember being smothered with sadness. You know how sometimes when you have a common friend or a family member who passes away, and you're not sure when it's going to hit you? I had that experience at the funeral in Madison. You get there and you see a common friend, and you guys hadn't spoken to or seen each other since the news. And then, for some reason, that connection makes everything come flooding out. Well, I happened to have that experience with Lorne Michaels. And so when I saw Lorne, I just lost it. I went to hug him, and it was the most awkward hug in the history of hugs. Intellectually, I know, "Wait, these arms don't do this. Arms, why are you doing this?" Because no one really hugged Lorne.

In late February 1999, a fatally ill Del Close decided he was tired of always being "the funniest person in the room." He died from emphysema on March 4—five days short of his sixty-fifth birthday and only one day after attending an upbeat living wake held in his honor at Illinois Masonic Hospital. Wearing a black, yellow, and red robe, oxygen tubes protruding from his nose and a bushy grayish-white beard sprouting from his face, the enfeebled but enthusiastic guru held court and talked briefly and proffered wisdom. There also were pagan blessings, poetry readings, white chocolate martinis (which Close gulped sans nausea despite his past and long-effective alcohol aversion therapy), and brief conversations with old friends. Among numerous Second City visitors was Close's former boss and sometime nemesis, Bernard Sahlins. While they'd mended fences years before, both continued to hold vastly different views of Second City's foundation and Close's life's work: improvisation. For the first time in their decades-long acquaintance, Sahlins conceded (albeit temporarily) that improv was indeed an art form—something of which Close had never been able to convince him. In a phone call one day before the gathering, Andrew Alexander conveyed similar sentiments. At long last, Close felt vindicated. Four months later his supposed skull—which would eventually be revealed as a fake—was donated to Chicago's Goodman Theatre for use in a future production of Shakespeare's *Hamlet.* Resting atop red silk under clear Lucite, it sits on a shelf in the office of Goodman artistic director Robert Falls, awaiting a big break that will probably never come. In the words of Second City alum Tim Kazurinsky, "Alas, poor Yorick, I knew him . . . Del?"

### Harold Ramis

I flew in from L.A. and went directly to the hospital from the airport. The party was held in the physicians' dining room in the basement. I remember seeing Bernie there and maybe Sheldon Patinkin, and I talked to a couple of other people while Del was being videotaped for the Upright Citizens Brigade cable show. Del was in a wheelchair, wearing pajamas and a robe, and had oxygen tubes clipped to his nose and looked surprisingly robust to me. We spoke briefly and not very pointedly, as I recall. Just small talk about the event. Del had invited a witch and warlock from some pagan coven— Del claimed to be a pagan, I guess—and Bill Murray was there and had hired saxophone players to provide music. Between the pagan ceremony and the sax solos, and the room full of improvisational actors from Second City and ImprovOlympic, it was a pretty unique experience.

### David Pasquesi

It was like a receiving line. Even then, when he's going to be alive less than twenty-four hours, he would be talking about how to keep improvisation going, that it's worth doing.

It was [hard] to feel out, because you were kind of making your pass past the casket, except in this case it was a guy in a wheelchair. And it wasn't really the old Del. He had oxygen on and he had a hard time breathing. And occasionally he'd laugh and it got kind of goofy. His brain's not getting a lot of oxygen, so he'd say some goofy things. What was really nice is to see how many people he affected—enough for them to come, some great distances, to be at this party.

### Bernard Sahlins

I came up to Del. He looks at me and says, "It *is* an art form." And I said, "Del, for tonight it's an art form." At which point he went into what I thought was a great chuckle, until somebody said to me, "You're standing on his air tube!"

### David Pasquesi

[*Jokingly*] Bernie gave him a pass for about six hours. That's it. That's all he was willing to give.

### Harold Ramis

I saw Del again near the elevators as I was leaving. I think he had had enough and was heading up to his room. This time we really talked, not for long, but seriously. I optimistically told Del that it wasn't over for him yet, that I expected to see him at some point out of the hospital. But I had no idea how dire his diagnosis was. He looked at me and shook his head and told me it was over for him, that he wouldn't last long. I can't remember what I said to that—just an awkward, poignant moment between us—and I left.

### Susan Messing, cast member

Del was my teacher, and he was one of my favorite people on the planet. I remember the night he died. Charna [Halpern, the owner of Improv-Olympic, where Del taught] called me and said, "Del has left the building." And I ran from home to Illinois Masonic and I touched a warm body, and knew that Del had left the building. And then I was on mainstage that night, and Kevin Dorff had taken a picture of Del and stuck it far up in the lights. As a matter of fact, I think that picture is still there.

### Bernard Sahlins

At the memorial service at Second City maybe a month later, everybody attacked Second City and me. They said that we had undervalued Del, denigrated him. I wasn't mad. One of the things that made people acolytes also made them dependent. And with the death of their hero, they looked for scapegoats. I didn't stay long. But I wasn't surprised. Nor was I offended. In fact, I felt rather sorry for them. They'd lost their leader. And now they were thrust out into the cold, cruel world.

Del Close wasn't the only improv guru to have left his imprint on Second City. Unlike Close, who was frequently blustery and often intimidating, Martin de Maat was introspective and eminently approachable. Like Close, he helped guide lives and careers. And in February 2001, after a long struggle with AIDS, he, too, passed away—but not before students and friends stopped by to say their farewells.

### Andrew Alexander

I flew in to see him at New York Hospital, and he was really critical. I was at his bedside and he was in very bad shape, struggling. He seemed very calm and sanguine in his life. He sort of had a spiritual side to him. So seeing him struggle in death was quite difficult for me.

### Tina Fey

When I first moved to New York, he had this awesome rent-controlled place in SoHo. I was moving here to write for *SNL,* and he was like, "Just use my place until you find one." It was very, very generous. He really had this sort of Zen approach to improvisation. Much more than anything to do with comedy. It was all about the rules of agreement and "Yes, and . . ." and almost spilling over as a life philosophy. I remember being in his class and writing down a list of all the things that he said that were so meaningful on several levels. His whole thing was, "Do it now. Do it too. Do it again. Put your head in your partner's bucket. The fun is on the other side of a 'yes.' " It was all stuff that was wholly true of beginning improvisation, but also sort of true in life. And he was just this very gentle person who made the classroom a safe place.

### Kelly Leonard

Anne and I dropped our kids off with my parents and we flew to New York. Tina Fey, Jeff Richmond, Rachel Dratch, and Kevin Dorff joined us in Martin's hospital room. We were completely unprepared to see him so thin and ill. He could only speak in a whisper. Anne brought along the plans for the new Training Center space in Chicago. She spread them out on his hospital bed and held his hand as she went through all the classrooms and offices on the blueprint. I honestly don't know how she held it together. Martin got tired and we hugged each other and said goodbye. He passed days later. If I have one regret in my time at Second City, it's letting my professional relationship with Martin lapse. We were always friends, but I didn't honor his contributions enough and I didn't find a way to take advantage of his gifts. He could be infuriating, erratic, and confounding, like all great artists. I let that get to me, and we really didn't resolve those issues by the time he died. It makes me sad to this day.

Mourning continued, but the shows went on. And as it had for four decades, Second City Chicago continued to draw celebrity visitors. Some were starrier than others. A year earlier, while in town filming *What Women Want,* Mel Gibson had dropped by to check out a show. Afterward, he stayed for some improv action.

### Kevin Dorff

Me and Jimmy [Zulevic] came up with an extended blackout about a Scots American dad making his son wear a kilt to school on the feast of Saint Andrew. The son, Zeus, was reluctant, so the dad—me—invoked Wallace himself.

### Rachel Dratch

The son was saying, "I'm not gonna wear my kilt today!" And the dad's like, "You will wear your kilt!" And it keeps going on, and out steps Mel Gibson in the wig and the kilt. "You'll wear your kilt in the name of William Wallace!" And the audience went nuts. They just were screaming for three minutes. It was the coolest way of introducing a star. He played the whole set. He was pretty good.

### Stephnie Weir, cast member

He was totally a "yes, and . . ." person, which made him a terrific improviser. And what was so great about him was, he really got the idea of ensemble. The only time he was thrust in the center was when we put him there. We were totally trying to show him off. I remember being backstage and calling my mother in Texas and being like, "I can't talk very long. But I just thought you should know I am about to be onstage with Mel Gibson."

### Kevin Dorff

The funniest thing about that night was Rachel and Stephnie repeatedly freezing Mel in the same position to get him to hold each of them in his arms.

In spring 2001, Second City's expansion continued with the opening of a new theater (now closed) at the Flamingo hotel in Las Vegas. Not long thereafter, on September 11, satire seemed small, irony irrelevant when terrorist attacks claimed thousands of lives and scarred a national psyche. Along with the country at large, Second City scrambled to comprehend what had happened. More dauntingly, they also had to find a funny but respectful way of addressing it. For reasons of timing (a new mainstage show was already set to open), the e.t.c. crew got called for duty. A couple of months later, as haggard rescue workers continued to comb through still-smoldering World Trade Center wreckage, *Holy War, Batman!, or, The Yellow Cab of Courage* was born. Some other title suggestions, such as *Hello Muddah, Intifada* and *Osama Sama Sama Sama Sama-Chameleon*, just didn't have the right ring.

### Joshua Funk, director

When Mick Napier came in to direct the mainstage the last couple of weeks, they took out anything that was suggestive of death or dying or terrorism and put up a very safe show that couldn't offend anybody. And the newspapers criticized us for that. I had been directing the e.t.c. show, so the producers came to me and said, "This e.t.c. show needs to be all about 9/11. Everything has to be about it." And that's when I realized that I had a pretty daunting challenge ahead of me.

### Beth Kligerman

The mainstage revue, *Embryos on Ice!, or, Fetus Don't Fail Me Now,* was scheduled to open on September 12. And I remember calling my guest list and inviting them not to come on September 12. Of course, we didn't have a show on September 11, but I remember being in the theater on September 12. I don't recall it being a full house, but there were maybe two hundred people in the audience, and everybody was so proud of each other. At the end of the show, Ed Furman said, "I want to pay tribute to all of you for coming out and being part of this." It was kind of a mutual standing ovation. It was a beautiful thing.

### Jack McBrayer, cast member

That was a bit of a rough time for me, and I really don't remember a whole lot of how it all came together. The whole theater was in a not great place, as was the entire country. It was very touch and go there for a while insomuch as would e.t.c. remain open as a theater. Shit was falling apart literally and figuratively.

The good news for us is that we did have the luxury of having a deadline for opening. It was a month or two after 9/11. So people were able to get back into some semblance of a routine of their daily lives, and we were able to get into some routine of our daily lives in terms of putting together a show. And very slowly we found things that were working in terms of addressing this terrible stuff, as well as being satirical and funny and making a statement that people could relate to.

Not only do you have the pressure of "Will the show be funny?" but, "Are we going to piss off people who come through these doors? Are we going to make people cry?" It was not a fun show for me. Plus, I was at a point where that was my third e.t.c. show. Every [Second City] performer has a shelf life, and I was entertaining ideas of moving on. Once we got that show up and running, I was definitely done.

### Andy Cobb, cast member

That irony-being-dead thing always felt like bullshit. The Holocaust didn't kill irony. Neither did World War II. Why would this? This was a shitty, tragic, horrible event in a human history full of them. Alan Arkin taught a workshop at the theater some months later. He said, "The world is a violent place. It just started getting violent for us. We've been lucky lately." That seems about right. It was a terrible time for the country, but in the end, terrible times are great for satirists. We're bottom-feeders, what can I say? Discussion was intense, passionate, and generally well informed. There were arguments—these are all passionate people and there are always disagreements in writing a Second City show. But this had some added pressure of wanting the material to live up to the amazing events we were experiencing. There was some friction when I gently objected to Second City's hanging an American flag in the lobby. I didn't feel any need to associate ourselves with a symbol that was then being used to suggest complicity with a Bush agenda. Not everyone liked that. It was a time when people's emotions were running very high.

### Keegan-Michael Key, cast member

It just was really somber. And the mainstage, they were reeling because they had already opened their show. And Kelly said to Josh, "There's an eight-hundred-pound gorilla in the room, and we can't not talk about it. We're the Second City. We're the temple of satire." And so that's a tall order. Make some satire out of the worst thing that's ever happened. So I tried to seek some solace from Joyce Sloane. I went to Joyce and said, "You've been here for forty-four years. Is this the worst thing?" "It's the worst thing, Keegan. It's the worst thing that has ever happened." Vietnam. "Worse." Kennedy being shot. "Worse." There was no way for me to compartmentalize it. It was the worst thing that had ever happened.

### Ron West

I think, in a strange way, the events made the show. People went to it because it's the satirist's job to give them a perspective on world events.

One of the show's most remarkable scenes featured Keegan-Michael Key as a Middle Eastern cabdriver who desperately tried to prove his American patriotism by bedecking his taxi in U.S.A. paraphernalia and repeatedly voicing his support for Uncle Sam and apple pie. Key later won a Joseph Jefferson Award for his overall performance.

### Keegan-Michael Key

One night my stage manager and I got into a cab, and the cabdriver had American flag stickers that were pretty [numerous] around this cab. My character's cab was bedecked with the Uncle Sam hat and the beard and the whole nine yards. But in this cab, there just all of a sudden seemed to be more American flags than I'd ever seen. And it was like, "Bing!" these big lightbulbs over the head of the cab all the way to Rogers Park. And I thought, since half our cabdrivers are of Arabic descent, what must they feel like right now? And that was the embryo that kind of was birthed into these scenes.

We were terrified. And then in the very first scene after our intro, where the couple gets in the car—my friend Samantha Albert is about the sweetest woman you'd ever meet in your entire life, and would never want to offend anyone for any reason ever, and she was the most courageous of all of us, because she was the person picked to be the super-progressive. "Don't we kind of deserve this in a way?" And we opened that show on November 11, 2001. I remember the first time we put that up in front of an audience, Andy Cobb and Samantha and I. I can't imagine our hearts beating any faster than they ever had in our lives. I was copiously sweating, and I was literally in my mind going, "Now, just as a contingency, think about what you're going to do if a bottle is thrown." I thought that that was a legitimate thought to have in my mind. Do I duck toward the wall? Where could it be coming from? And so half your eye is acting and the other half of your eye is scoping the angle that you're at, like, "Where could we duck?" And the first time we did it, it was just amazing. The release from the audience—not the laughter or the volume of the laughter, the energy of the laughter—just screamed catharsis, release. That lasted for probably four months. Maybe three months. And then it started turning into regular laughter. I'll tell you what, those first two months, it was like they were screaming at us.

### Andy Cobb

The coolest night I ever had at Second City was when a bunch of 9/11 New York City firemen and Governor [George] Ryan [of Illinois] came to watch. I was a big fan of Ryan for his work against the death penalty, and the firemen were very kind, self-effacing heroes. That was the most heartfelt ovation I've ever seen, when they took a bow after the show.

### Joshua Funk

We knew they were in the audience. There were about a dozen of them, and they came in uniform. And these guys looked like they had been through hell. And they came to the show and they laughed their asses off and came backstage with tears in their eyes and just said, "I cannot tell you guys how much we needed to laugh about this, because we spend twenty hours a day digging out bodies and digging through this horrific thing, and to be able to get out of New York and to see this show has brought us new life and made us feel so good." And then what happened after that was even more amazing. They started telling all the other firemen in New York working on Ground Zero to get away for a weekend and go see this show in Chicago, and they started coming all the time. And it was really powerful.

Finally in my life I felt like what we do is important. And it's so easy to think of comedy as that jester in the king's court, where this useless goofball is making people laugh and that's his whole existence. And I get that feeling sometimes when I look at myself in the big perspective. Is making people laugh really a valuable role in society, or am I just a joke? Especially in times like that, when you see people who are firemen and people who are going to war and people who are doctors and lawyers and saving lives and making huge differences. You second-guess it. Before 9/11, the shows had degenerated into a bunch of poop and fart jokes and just silly scene work. We were livin' life high on the hog. There was nothing that was pissing us off. We didn't feel the importance of social commentary. We were just going for laughs. And then when 9/11 happened, I think the paradigm of

Second City finally went back to where it was when JFK got assassinated and when the Vietnam War happened and when the civil rights era happened. And that is why Second City is what it is.

Especially in the months after 9/11—on newscasts, near watercoolers, in subway cars—discourse frequently turned to the topic of tolerance (or intolerance) and ethnic diversity. At the behest of Andrew Alexander, Second City had gradually begun that conversation internally several years earlier. As it long has, the theater prided itself on reflecting the beliefs, anxieties, and banalities of society at large. But society at large was black and white and Asian and Latino and openly gay, whereas Second City was largely straight and white and had been from the start. The theater's first black cast member, a workshop student named Bob Curry, joined the original touring company back in the late sixties. Aaron Freeman entered the fold in the late seventies, and future *Saturday Night Live* and film star Tim Meadows in the late eighties, to name some of the relatively few minorities on resident stages and in touring ensembles. Audiences, too, were—and still are—mostly white. It wasn't until the early to mid-nineties that resident stages, franchise locations (now-shuttered Detroit, in particular), and touring companies became noticeably more multiethnic. But while increased diversity broadened the base of scene-worthy subjects and lent authenticity to satiric send-ups of race and religion, some thought it smacked of affirmative action.

### Aaron Freeman

By the time I got to Second City [in the late seventies], I was the second Negro they had had in the history of the joint after Bob Curry. So certainly, if I wasn't funny, then it was going to be another twenty years before they had another one. That's how I felt about it. I mean, no one ever said that or anything. That was my own concern, because it was such a rare deal. I was so worried that I would just blow it for everybody.

Because I was a Negro, and they didn't have too many of those at Second City, I got a lot of leeway. People didn't bust my chops as much as maybe they should have. Although the whole skin color thing was pretty goofy at the time. For a while there I was not allowed to do any scenes where I was anyone's blood relative, because it wasn't credible. I wasn't gonna be anybody's father or son. They didn't think the audiences would buy it. But then Bernie found out about it and said, "No. I will not be a party to this blatant racism." That was it.

### Chris Jones

They made this effort to diversify themselves, to get away from three guys, two girls, and to have more women in positions of power, and more African

American performers, and that served them well. It didn't just create new avenues to find talent, but it also created better situations. Because you can do [scenes] about things better when you have a more diverse cast, and they were very bad at that in the early days.

### Hedy Weiss, *Chicago Sun-Times* theater critic

The one change that was most visible was, they started to make it more ethnic. But even that was formulaic. And I always got the feeling that you could only go so far. They never really took it to a dangerous point. I mean, is it really dangerous anymore to do a rap song? Wouldn't it be much more interesting to do Hyde Park blacks? Middle-class blacks? But they play it safe.

### Andrew Alexander

I was in L.A. during the riots. My wife and I lived through those seven days. And I remember flying out of L.A. When the plane took off, it flew over South Central, and you could see the fires. It was terrible. I came back to Chicago and was watching the set one night, and it was all these white actors struggling to deal with how to make a point about what was going on. And I realized they were having trouble with it. It was from a white point of view. To be authentic, you have to have a diverse group. That gives you permission to go places. That night was the beginning of a sincere effort to truly diversify Second City.

### Keegan-Michael Key

Our very first cast was integrated in Detroit. That's just Detroit. I think that if you're gonna have a theater in this city, come on, yo. You're not gonna have no brothers and sisters in the cast? I ain't seein' that. There's no such thing as a white neighborhood in Detroit. That does not exist. Now, it exists in the suburbs of Detroit. But there are not white neighborhoods in Detroit. The whitest neighborhood you're getting in Detroit is an integrated neighborhood. That's as white as it gets. And in Chicago, there are white neighborhoods and there are black neighborhoods and there are integrated neighborhoods. And Chicago was certainly a whiter city when it started than it is now. And that just was the case. I guess in Detroit we just never thought twice about it. And Andrew liked what we were doing there: color-blind casting and flipping roles and even gender stuff sometimes.

### Angela V. Shelton, cast member

Second City has a sorrier history of integration than the Catholic Church. I've only known of two openly gay people to be on a stage when I got there and after I was there. There may be some after I left Chicago [in the late nineties]. But I was the second or third black woman on a stage. They'd never had more than one minority on a stage [at a time] before, and by the time I got to e.t.c., we had the most integrated Second City cast in history. It was me and David Pompeii, who are both African American. Martin Garcia is gay, and Ali Farahnakian is Arab American. We called mainstage the big house and e.t.c. the plantation, the field. Whenever somebody from mainstage would come backstage to hang out at e.t.c., we'd be like, "You're coming to the fields to hang with the slaves, huh?"

### Ruth Rudnick

I remember when I was leaving. You have your "out" meeting, where you meet with Andrew and he asks you questions. "What do you think about this or that?" And I looked at him and I said, "You talk about how you want minorities in your companies. You've got Horatio Sanz in the touring company. Why don't you put him in a resident company? I don't understand it." I just went off. And I didn't tell Horatio that at all. But then, later, he came up to me and said, "Andrew told me what you said. Thank you." And Andrew put Horatio in a resident company. The fact that Andrew did that shows he was willing to listen and really try to make things better.

### Horatio Sanz

They needed my voice. At that time the place didn't have many Latino guys, and certainly didn't have anybody from my neighborhood. I grew up in the middle of Chicago, and there just wasn't a lot of presence in that building. Not that I'm this huge Latin pride guy, but I felt like a person from the middle of Chicago should be up there doing scenes about Chicago. I didn't do a lot of Latino-centric scenes at Second City. It was more about freaky shit that happened in the inner city as opposed to, "This is an injustice that's happening to these people."

### Andrew Alexander

There have been a lot of people who've felt that maybe there's been some affirmative action going on here, off and on. And it's a very touchy subject.

### Joshua Funk

There've been actors who have felt they needed to point to a reason why they didn't get promoted to the mainstage, and oftentimes they would use that excuse [of affirmative action]. I don't buy it. It had nothing to do with that. If you own a social and political theater, you have to represent society. There's no affirmative action there. That's just the nature of the beast.

### Angela V. Shelton

We were able to do material that had never been done on that stage. In Chicago we did this scene where I had everybody take out a dollar bill, and

I talked about the dollar bill and how the presidents on all of our money, most of them were slave owners—a little monologue about that. And then David Pompeii went around the room and started collecting all the dollars. And if there were black people in the audience, we would give it to them as reparations. The whole point of the monologue was, "If you think black people have a bad attitude, try giving them money." Some people would get pissed; some thought it was hysterical. What killed me was, I'm looking at a table of four who paid probably hundreds of dollars for this evening out. But what are they mad about? That one dollar. We gave the money away. We donated it.

## Joe Canale, cast member

I'll be perfectly frank. If you are a white guy, you go through the system and you pay your dues. And you perform for a long time. People take different paths. There are certain things they want to do here at Second City to encourage diversity, and yet the community of improvisers and sketch performers that they have to choose from is sixty-five percent guys, ninety-five percent white. I understand the way it works, and I understand that someone may be in town for two years and offer something that I certainly can't offer, and will get onto the stage. But that's the fact of the matter.

## Amber Ruffin, cast member

For me, it's easier to do a scene about being black to a theater full of white people. A black person who's watching can say, "No, it's not like that." But white people have to believe me. But, really, it teaches you how to convey something to people with whom you have very few like experiences.

While Second City grew more diverse, it also became less tolerant—of bad behavior, of actor-audience scuffles, of chemically impaired performances, of anger mismanagement. Good for business? Yes. But some thought the housecleaning also scrubbed away the theater's rebel soul.

## Ali Farahnakian, cast member

We were doing these prom shows, where about one o'clock in the morning you do shows on the mainstage for these prom kids. And they said basically, "You can't use the f-word in this show." And I was like, "We have a piece we created that we tour around the country where we say this word. It's not just thrown around flippantly. It has merit and value." They said, "Yeah, well, you can't." And at Second City, once you've been there for a long time, you kind of look for ways out and you start acting out in different ways because you just don't have the courage to walk away from something that good. And so a piece of me couldn't wrap my head around the fact that this place built on social and political satire, that was a rebellious kind of place where people speak their mind, was all of a sudden doing prom shows and telling people they couldn't use the f-word at one o'clock in the morning. So their handlers told the producers, and they told us. It was something that was difficult at that time, in my youth, to wrap my head around. So I was the one opening up the show, and I went out there and said, "Just so you guys know, we can't use the f-word in front of you, but that doesn't mean you can't." And all of a sudden they started yelling, "F-this! F-that!" [Second City] said I incited them to riot. That was the official decree.

### Stephnie Weir

By the time I left, there was a very familial composition on the stage. I think I was probably the matriarch and Kevin Dorff was the patriarch, and there were these siblings, and there were squabbles that were going on, and that's really how we behaved and treated each other, in the most fun way. And I wouldn't be surprised to learn that every cast has some of those roles. When I first came on, Rachel Dratch was definitely the matriarch. And Jim Zulevic was the very angry, bitter father. What I always found so humorous about our cast was, there were some drinkers, but we weren't like the legends before us, where there were the crazy parties going on backstage. Really wild group back then. I remember Susan Messing and Tami Sagher and I doing Tae Bo upstairs in Joyce's office in between shows. Or going for walks. Watching our weight and exercising.

### Angela V. Shelton

When I was on e.t.c., me and the other women on mainstage started exercising between shows. And then one day I remember thinking how lame that was. There was a time when people would be getting drunk or finding hookers—living life on the edge. And we're doing Tae Bo. We should be shooting up and having sex with each other!

### Kelly Leonard

The drug culture that existed when I first started here began dying off as people died. Did the fact that Chris Farley brought in cases of beer between shows make him a better artist? I would suggest to you no. And I would suggest you look at his body of work after he left here. It was not strong. And he limited himself when he was here, and his abilities to become a great artist. Physically hurting people [in the audience]? It's a litigious society. So let's say you break someone's arm, you get sued, and we have to go out of business. Is that what we want? I don't know. We've had people work here who've been really difficult, really out there, challenged us. Sometimes I felt it was worth it, and other times I didn't.

If there is a fear I've got, it's that I'm married, I've got two kids, I'm comfortable, I want to make money. And we're a business that's gotten bigger, and more people get insurance and there's other things that are at stake here that might make me or anyone less likely to make the dangerous choice. Andrew wants danger on the stage. It cannot get dark enough for him. And that's my sensibility as well—onstage. The true question is, was the work better when the institution was more permissive? I don't think there's any evidence that the work was somehow stronger then.

## Andrew Alexander

If you look back at fifty years and say, "Okay, who really exemplified that danger the most?" Farley did in a different way than Bill Murray. Bill Murray had a sort of intelligence and anger mixed up in his humor, and he's like that in life. Jim Belushi's danger was a little different. There was an anger behind Billy—this sort of brooding—that I think people responded to, whereas Belushi's was just a physical energy like Chris Farley's. It wasn't as dangerous. The danger thing with Del was just a game. He brought his life experience. [With Del and Chris], you're talking about people who have decided to live a life of "Am I going to die tomorrow?" That becomes their thing. That's implicit in their life. So you combine the Del Close story with the stories of his drug abuse and being in insane asylums, and it just blows the guy up to another proportion. And that's what we do in our society. Does that diminish Steve Carell, who is very levelheaded, funny, didn't kill his mother or hasn't got a needle stuck in his arm?

## Dan Bakkedahl, cast member

Jim Belushi lit a fire under me. He was like, "Where the hell is the anger? Nobody's punching anything anymore! How come nobody's in fights? How come nobody's getting fired? Kicked out! Burning the place down!" And I was like, "Got it." He said, "You go backstage. There's a huge hole in the wall in e.t.c. I put that there!" And we're like, "Yeah, yeah, I know." He said, "You know, Bill Murray knocked a guy out in the hallway 'cause he was talking during the show! This is ridiculous!" And I'm thinking, "Yeah! Yeah! I'll do that! I'll do that!"

## Lisa Brooke

Right after I left, I know the shit really hit the fan. Dan punched a wall and broke his hand.

## Peter Grosz, cast member

Sue Gillan [a cast mate] told me something amazing. She said Second City forces you to really be the person you are. You're put through some tests with other people, you have to question who you are, you have to create something. You have to both work and create with other people, you have to share, you have to be part of an entire building's business. You really have to go through a lot. And who everybody is really comes out, because while the stakes aren't that high, the amount of stuff you have to do is very personal and very interactive and it really runs the whole gamut of your personality. It puts you through a personality ringer.

The nice thing about Second City is, it's just enough pressure to make you creative and to fuel your engines, but it's not so much that you start being a dick. A real hard-core, Hollywood, smacking-lattes-out-of-your-assistant's-hand dick.

### Dan Bakkedahl

I had many times where I stopped in the middle of a scene and said [to an audience member], "Dude, shut your fucking mouth!" and then went back to the scene. And nobody ever said, "Hey, Dan, you gotta knock that shit off." Other than my fellow cast members, who were like, "It just makes me sick! It scares me! It's like my dad used to be!" And I'm like, "Hey, get over it." I thought it was all part of the thing, like I'm carrying the flag. What can I say? I was a dick.

Up north, more than dispositions turned sour when the SARS epidemic hit Canada in 2003. Not exactly a lure for travelers. Consequently, a tourism industry that was still feeling the effects of 9/11 tanked further, and with it Second City's box office receipts. Despite worries that the theater might close for good, however, it pushed on. After two more years at Blue Jays Way and a six-month hiatus, operations resumed in a smaller and far more comedy-conducive space at 51 Mercer Street, where the Toronto troupe still performs. Among revues staged there in the past few years, *Facebook of Revelations* brought steady sellout crowds, critical raves, and external proclamations of resurrection. "Four years ago, Second City almost ceased operations in Toronto," the headline of a *Toronto Star* feature declared in July 2007. "But now the resurgent company is getting the last laugh." A review in the same paper two weeks later gave *Facebook* four out of four stars. The show "will definitely make you laugh," Richard Ouzounian wrote, "but—even better—it will make you think."

### Klaus Schuller, Toronto executive director

In some ways, it's been kind of a reset for the theater. They did terrific shows in the building on Blue Jays Way, but the theater itself was not very intimate. The new place that we've moved into kind of took the best of our existing theaters and then just gave it a bit of a theatrical overhaul. In some ways people [thought it] spoke to a bit of an artistic renaissance in Toronto when we opened the new theater in 2005, but in many ways some of that was the fact that we were finally in a space that was appropriate to the art form.

## Bruce Pirrie

In Chicago, the shows [I directed] were sold out almost every night. They're booking people in; they've survived for fifty years there. And the power of Bernie [Sahlins] is now holding sway, which is "We have to brand this, we have to provide product, people have to know what it's about." A part of the whole process was to come up with a theme or to discover a theme within the sketches we were coming up with and have that fit into the title. I'm going, why do they want to do this? Because to my mind, if you come up with a theme first, whatever that might be, you keep scenes in that have something to do with the theme that maybe aren't that funny, and you start throwing out funny scenes that don't fit into the theme. I always find that you realize what the show's theme is at best a week after opening. I'm going, "Where's this coming from? Because this is counter to creativity." And I realized it's because it's commerce. Before, Second City's standard was, "You don't know what you're gonna get!" And now it's like, in ten words or less, tell us what it's about. Because then you can market it. So it's like, "Wow, this is a pyramid that's built upside down."

We did *Barack to the Future* in Toronto. We opened it in August [2008], going out on a limb that that's the way things were going to go in the States. And on election night, they already had a new scene that they were getting ready to put on if Barack lost. What had happened was, I'd done a show in Toronto two years [prior] that was a huge critical and financial hit, called *Facebook of Revelations*. The take-away from the success of *Facebook of Revelations* was: get a brand name in the title.

## Lauren Ash, cast member

The thing about that show was, people who had no clue about what Second City was came because they saw the title. As one women said to me in a Starbucks one day, "I saw your Facebook show! I had no idea what it was, but I love Facebook, so I went. It was hilarious! I'm coming back with more friends next week!" I think we managed to appeal to demographics that we hadn't appealed to before. In general, in Chicago people will go to Second City just because it's Second City, whereas in Toronto, the title of the show and the reviews about the show have a much larger impact.

# 11

## Offing Obama, Liberal Leanings, and a Still-Beating Heart

### 2007–present

EARLY IN 2007—after a year that saw yet another young and talented Second City actor, Jim Zulevic, die of an apparent heart attack, at age forty—*Between Barack and a Hard Place* opened on the Wells Street mainstage. Shows before it generally had fared well critically and commercially, but this one was different in that it centered on the biggest political superstar since JFK—and a resident Chicagoan to boot. Hailed by critics and crowds alike, *Barack* sold out for weeks in advance and garnered glowing ink—including a Sunday cover story in the *Chicago Tribune Magazine.* The e.t.c.'s inventive *Campaign Supernova* made waves, too. When a floored Sheldon Patinkin stopped backstage one night to give notes, cast members recall, his eyes were not dry.

Toward the end of 2007, Second City Chicago hosted a $750 per ticket fund-raiser benefiting Senator Obama's presidential campaign. Obama himself even showed up to press flesh and talk briefly and view his satirical skewering. In a surprising flash of dark humor, witnesses say, he seemed amused by a scene that featured Molly Erdman as Hillary Clinton plotting the assassination of her sainted Democratic opponent. When Obama formally accepted the nomination in late August 2008, Second City was invited to perform scenes from the show in Denver. Roughly two months later, the distinguished gentleman from Illinois crossed historic boundaries to become the most powerful person on Earth.

## Matt Hovde, director

*Between Barack and a Hard Place* opened in January 2007, long before Obama was any sort of lock to even be nominated for the Democrats—let alone on the cusp of possibly winning the election. Even back then, I think we felt like it was an exciting time politically. And there were a couple of things we did with *Barack* that resonated with people. The point of view of that show was actually kind of optimistic. And I think for a while, the shows at Second City had been very pessimistic, or at least dark. The Bush regime had made Second City a little angrier as a theater. The message at the beginning and end of *Barack* was, "There's actually somebody out there that people like, that people are rooting for. And he's from Chicago."

## Joe Canale

That's the first time they really started to realize the impact a title could have. Every time we pitch titles, I pitch *The Second City Sells Out,* because it's a double entendre. But they're very conscious now of getting a good title because they think that can help them out a lot. And the show ran for a long time, because Obama became more prominent. We could have run it for six more months.

## Ithamar Enriquez, cast member

He was still very new. He was still very mysterious. We made fun of the fact that we were really excited about him and everyone was really excited about him, but we really couldn't point to why we were so excited. It was like, "He's mysterious, he's charming, he's charismatic. But where does he stand on the issues? Who cares? He's mysterious, he's charming, he's charismatic." The opening of the show was all six of us saying we were Barack Obama, and we had monologues [describing] different walks of life. Because he was appealing to everyone. He was half-black, he was half-white, he was this, he was that. In a way we couldn't pinpoint who he was, because he was so many different things.

## Brian Gallivan, cast member

I think Brad Morris watched him, especially during the scene Molly and I wrote and performed where she's Hillary trying to get me to assassinate Obama, and I won't do it because I'm so attracted to him. Brad told me that sometimes it seemed like Obama would turn around, like, "Can I laugh at that? All right, everyone's laughing at that, so I guess I can."

## Brad Morris, cast member

He even laughed at the scene about him being assassinated. I wouldn't have fun with that if it were about me, Brad Morris, being assassinated. It would be much worse to be a black guy running for president. So he definitely knows how to laugh at himself.

### Molly Erdman, cast member

I was really nervous about it. Michelle Obama had come to the show months before that with some of her family, so at least we knew that he knew about it. My thought was that if there were anything objectionable, Michelle would have put the kibosh on it somehow.

I think I was the one who introduced Obama after we finished our twenty-minute version of the show. And he came out and he gave us all hugs and he said something to me like, "I'll even hug you, Hillary."

### Amber Ruffin

While Barack was there, all his Secret Service men were cold and serious. I was scared of them. After he left, while all his Secret Service men were filing out, one of them grabbed a prop knife that was sitting around backstage and said, "What in the world is this?" We all froze, and then he started laughing. Secret Service knows funny.

### Chris Jones

In the last few years, Second City shows took an overtly lefty trajectory. If you looked at Second City in the eighties, it was somewhat equal-opportunity political humor. It was poking fun at power in a traditional satirical way, but without a particular point of view. And then, beginning [in the mid-nineties], the shows had inherent points of view and themes. In the last five years, those themes got more and more political. And so you got to the point where you could discern not only the political affiliation and the liberalism of the show, but they were these point-of-view shows. Their jabs changed from everybody to one side, so that you now had this liberal trajectory going on. And then, lo and behold, they get their own president, who is like them: post-racial, liberal, smart, put-together, ambitious. Obama's their perfect doppelgänger.

A far less beloved Illinois politician was the subject of Second City's skewering in early February 2009. Shamed governor Rod Blagojevich, then accused of trying to sell Barack Obama's Illinois senate seat (among numerous other alleged crimes), was mercilessly lampooned in a speedily written show called *Rod Blagojevich Superstar!* Premiering on normally off nights in the e.t.c. theater, it quickly sold out an initial six-week run, garnered rave reviews, moved to a larger venue, and was featured on several national media programs, including the *Today* show on NBC and National Public Radio's *All Things Considered.*

Second City began life as a largely provincial, fiscally faltering, anti-establishment underdog. With international name recognition, annual revenues in the tens of millions, and a homegrown president it helped champion now in the White House, it is no longer that. But one thing hasn't really changed: the theater on Wells Street. A half century on, it is still the heart that pumps lifeblood into ever-extending tentacles, and the key to Second City's longevity.

### Chris Jones

I think that they are now the establishment. They're going out there every night as the brand leaders of what they do, and to some degree they have raised their game accordingly. They're very flashy shows, and they're very flashy people who do them, and there's a very high emphasis on polish. It's not as raw as it once was.

### Hedy Weiss

I would say that some of the casts at e.t.c. have been very, very strong. And actually, technically [strong] in their ability to sing, to dance, the way they move the ensemble spirit. That's all on a very high level. But it's the material. And in a way, if you take your material off TV, that's what you're going to get. To me, it's like, instead of looking at real life, they look at television's version of real life, and so it's plastic. They don't go back to the source. I think you have to go back to the street.

They have to do what nobody does: they have to read more. And I think they also have to take many, many more risks. And you know what? Maybe they would have a less polished show, but maybe they would have something more adventurous. I think they're too worried about being slick and packaged and safe and dependable.

### Megan Grano, cast member

I brought in a scene about women in the United States who are so obsessed with being skinny and actually starve themselves and have anorexia. I said I wanted to juxtapose that with women in Afghanistan who are actually starving to death, and how bad it is. And everybody was like, "Ooh, you're so dark." And I'm like, "Oh, God, I don't think that's dark. I think that it's an important subject." One night a woman pulled me aside and was like, "That scene was so dark, so racist." And I said, "I feel that you missed the point, then, and I'm sorry that you thought it was dark." She yelled at me, and they left the theater and tried to get their money back. And I walked away, because I didn't want to get in a fight with her about it. But I'm like, "I feel so sad, just deep sadness, that that's what you thought the scene was about. I pity you because that makes me think you're really dumb."

### Bruce Pirrie

There's a whole different culture in Chicago than there is in Toronto. Canadian culture is more amorphous. But Chicago is where it started, and the sense of history in connection with the past is palpable. Bill Murray and John Belushi were *in that building.*

### Ruby Streak

Basically, it's a miracle that there's still the tiny little work going on and the tiny little shows and little lives, and there's a huge corporation wrapping around it. But I think everyone's smart enough to know that you don't mess with what this place is really here because of, and that's the actors and shows they write. That's the gold mine.

### Rob Belushi, cast member, and son of Jim Belushi

There's nothing like being on Wells Street. You can smell spilled beer from generations. I remember being a child there. I was just kind of thrown on whoever was around while my dad was there. And so that place is very much a part of how I grew up. Now Second City is a corporation and even a bit of a factory these days, but it's really still the same idea. It's an idea based in performance, so if you take it to Vegas or you take it to Detroit or Toronto or any of these places, it's still the same formula or structure, and you feel part of a legacy.

# EPILOGUE

INEVITABLE GROUSING and lingering bitterness notwithstanding, Second Citizens are generally a gracious and grateful bunch when it comes to their shared alma mater. Even the starriest ones—in several cases, especially the starriest ones—readily give credit where credit is due. For as competitive and political and ego crushing as comedy college at Second City can be, many consider it the purest and most fulfilling creative experience of their lives. After all, it's what taught them teamwork and honed their humor. It's what strengthened their skills and embraced their eccentricities. It's what drove them to win and dared them to lose. To varying degrees and in various ways, it's what made them who they are today.

As for the bosses—Bernard Sahlins, Andrew Alexander, and Kelly Leonard, in particular—it's only natural that they get a heaping helping of grief along with the glory. But while their number crunching and corporatizing and reorganizing didn't (and don't) sit well with everyone in the Second City family, the theater would almost certainly not have survived—much less thrived—for this long without their support and guidance. After all, talent needs stability and opportunity to truly shine.

**Richard Kind**

Whenever anybody says, "Oh, I saw you in Chicago," I go, "Oh, back when I was good?" I was smarter then, I was so well read. And I listened well. I would walk down the street and you had to pay attention to what people were saying, you know? It's something I don't do nowadays, especially in L.A. You let the world go by. At Second City, oh my God, I listened and I reacted and I wasn't self-centered. All I was worried about was the world.

I think anybody who goes to Second City because they want to advance their career is both a fool and a jerk. If you don't give a hundred percent to your work and only your work and use it as a stepping-stone, I think you're doing yourself not only a disservice, but I think you'll find that you're not getting all that you can out of it. The one thing that I like to say is "Enjoy the journey." When you go on your road to stardom or fame in this business, the journey turns out to be a lot more fun than you ever think it will be. That's only in retrospect, but the journey is a blast. Take your journey at Second City, enjoy it, stay with it. They'll be the best years of your life.

### Shelley Long

I found out that I could be funny professionally. I had been sort of a comedy geek as a kid at times. But I didn't even think about, "Would that translate on a professional level?" And I found that it did. At that time, being someone from the Second City meant something. I think it probably means more now. But it meant something, even back then. More than I realized. When I went to L.A. and I went to New York—especially in L.A.—people knew about the Second City, and they knew people that had come from the Second City and what that meant about their talent and their experience.

### Betty Thomas

We did the show out in California. And I realized after it was over and I went to do some stupid TV show that my life could end. I could have a motorcycle accident or anything like that, and I would have achieved more than I ever thought I was going to. I thought, "I don't have to do anything else in my life. I've already done what I think is a pretty fucking big deal."

### Dan Aykroyd

Anyone who had the skills and talent to be accepted by Second City will surely relate that their experiences in the program were among the most satisfying of their lives. For me, I met my best friends there. We used the techniques to do good, honest work, and took them with us into later careers. The type of hyphenate writer-actor produced by Second City and its imitative groups dominates the entertainment industry today.

### Joe Flaherty

When you look at the stuff you've done since then, no matter what the quality of it is—I mean, God, you could win Academy Awards—there was still that little theater that we would go to every night where we had a chance to do funny sketches that we created. I look back on it and I think, "Geez, I wasn't paid much money when we were doing that show, but I never seemed to be poor." I got by, and had so much fun, and loved that work so much. Maybe you look back and it's a little too golden. Maybe there's a little bit too much of an aura there, but I don't think so. In one way, I could have done that stuff for the rest of my life.

### Jeff Garlin

I look back at my time at Second City and it wasn't really that pleasant. But I learned everything I know. There would be no *Curb Your Enthusiasm* if it weren't for Second City. Because of Second City, I became a better comedian.

## Jim Belushi

Second City was a dream realized. Not only did I feel like I was in a family, but I had purpose and meaning in this family, and there's been no other family like it since—including the one I was raised in. I was connected, I was alive, I was needed, I was wanted. I was at one hundred percent every show. I had a place among this family of misfits. We were no longer misfits—we were powerful and funny and we belonged and were recognized for our worth.

## Alan Arkin

It's just a very deep emotional connection between everybody I've ever met who's been there. It's a subconscious brotherhood that's very strong. It's kind of a reverential feeling and a deep love for the training we got, the people we met, and the opportunities. It's like being part of a fraternity, a very deeply felt and life-changing fraternity. It's kind of an unspoken thing. You show your ring and you do the little fraternity dance, and then you go about your business. But it's always there. It's always there.

# ACKNOWLEDGMENTS

In late 2007, shortly before Christmas, I was hoisting a few with veteran *Chicago Tribune* scribe and WGN-AM radio host Rick Kogan. Not long into our barside chat, talk turned to recent Chicago-centric books that were penned by out-of-towners. From a posh turn-of-the-century cathouse to a World's Fair serial killer, we'd overlooked some great stories that were right under our noses. And that's when he said it: "You should write a book about Second City." Being that the legendary comedy theater was right under my nose—not to mention a subject about which I'd written so often I took it for granted—it was an idea I hadn't seriously pondered. So a huge debt of gratitude goes to Rick for his inspired idea and his ongoing support of my work.

As an aspiring first-time author, I needed an agent. Fortunately, Ken Wright of Writer's House literary agency in New York stepped in and was immediately passionate about the project. Without his vast knowledge of the publishing industry and his sharp negotiating, *The Second City Unscripted* would have remained just that—unscripted. Over at Villard, thanks to my first editor, Bruce Tracy, for having faith in my ability to serve up what he rightly termed "a tall order." Bruce's exceedingly able and always buoyant successor, Jill Schwartzman, was an excellent adviser and receptive sounding board who made innumerable improvements to the manuscript—to its wording, its pacing, its overall structure. A salute also goes to assistant editor Ryan Doherty, who was with this book from its infancy and whose smart editorial input enhanced the final product. Assistant editor Lea Beresford's thoroughness, optimism, and helpful direction made the whole process inestimably smoother. Eagled-eyed copy editor Bara MacNeill, associate copy chief Beth Pearson, and proofreaders Kate Norris and Kenneth Russell mended screwy grammar, kept the narrative flowing, caught gaffes great and small, and in general made the words—mine and others'—more readable than they would have been otherwise.

Of course, nothing would have come to fruition were it not for the early and steadfast support of those who run and once ran The Second City. Proprietor and executive producer Andrew Alexander and vice president Kelly Leonard—both longtime bosses there—gave generously of their time, resources, historical knowledge, and wealth of contacts. With a phone call or an email, they often were able to hook me up with alumni whose fame is such that requesting an interview through traditional channels would have been futile, or taken weeks of wrangling I couldn't afford. As she has for decades, exalted producer emeritus Joyce Sloane continues to hold court (and cheer on the Cubs) in her memorabilia-stuffed corner office. I'm grateful to have spent time with someone who continues to be such a vital part of the theater's evolution. I'm equally indebted to Bernie Sahlins, Second City's original owner, producer, and driving force. Like Joyce Sloane, he's among an increasingly small number of people who helped transform the Old Town comedy cabaret from locally revered gem to internationally known funny farm. Thanks to Bernie for being so accessible and responsive in person and otherwise. Another Second City veteran, former director and current artistic consultant Sheldon Patinkin, was an invaluable resource, too. His keen and colorful memories of people, places, and events helped shape the narrative and informed my conversations with others. Second City and its actors are lucky to have his continued creative support. When it came to plundering the Second City Rolodex, wedging me into sold-out shows and arranging in-house interviews, production coordinator Monica Wilson always came through. So did Chris Pagnozzi, who unearthed classic photographs and hard-to-find articles, tracked down long-lost photographers, and steered me through Second City's amazing digitized archives.

And I was thrilled beyond measure that the scores upon scores of Second City actors, alums, and outside observers I spoke with—far too many to name individually, and including those whose contributions were regrettably lost in the final edit—had so many fantastic tales to tell. Their honest, detailed, and sometimes emotional recollections made the story of Second City come alive for me and on the page.

My journalistic mentor and big brother from another mother, Bill Zehme, championed this endeavor from the idea stage on. A bestselling author and celebrated celebrity profiler whose work I admire greatly, he's long been a tremendous adviser on writing and the invariably arduous task of bookmaking (the literary kind). Eternal thanks, pally, for the ongoing edumacation. Top-notch scribe and editor Josh Schollmeyer combed through chapter after chapter, giving astute counsel on everything from content to cadence. He, too, was an ardent advocate from day one, and I'm enormously obliged for his talents and zeal.

At the *Chicago Sun-Times,* where I've been a staff writer for nine years, thanks to editor in chief Don Hayner and former editor in chief Michael Cooke for temporarily springing me to finish the book. Additional hat tips to veteran *Sun-Times* theater critic Hedy Weiss and the many other colleagues and former colleagues who provided insight, offered assistance, and expressed interest. Thanks also to former *Chicago Tribune* theater critic Richard Christiansen and current *Tribune* theater critic Chris Jones.

When it came to transcription, the bionic Sara Baum brought her A-game. For many months she transplanted scores of interviews and more than a million words from tape to page at lightning speed. I'd say Sara's hands should be bronzed, but that would probably make it hard for her to type.

For some weekly respite from the daily grind, I often bellied up at my favorite joint on earth, Twin Anchors Restaurant & Tavern, in Chicago's Old Town neighborhood. A round of plaudits to owners Paul Tuzi, Gina Manrique, and Mary Kay Cimarusti and their always congenial staff for the Sunday night suds, solace, and sustenance.

Over the years I've been incredibly blessed to have the backing of many family members—both immediate and extended. As ever, my parents, Sam and Paula, are ceaseless fonts of advice, encouragement, and unconditional love. And they never seemed to worry about what I'd do with an expensive English major. I owe them much more than words can express. My sisters and their respective mates have been great boosters, too, so thanks to Lisa and Brady and Sarah and Joe. The same goes for my always supportive in-laws and countless relatives—from grandparents and cousins to aunts and uncles—who've cheered me on along the way. And props to my good friends Kirsten Bedway and Simeon Peebler for their unwavering enthusiasm.

Last but farthest from least, the three loves of my life: my wise and wondrous wife, Sandy, and our treasured daughters, Grace and Audrey. Even more than the legally binding contract I'd signed, they were (and are) powerful motivation to keep on keeping on. This one's for them. Everything is for them.

# SELECTED SHORT BIOGRAPHIES
## OF SECOND CITIZENS

**Scott Adsit** Cast member 1989–98. Numerous TV appearances include *Friends, Curb Your Enthusiasm, MADTV, Mr. Show with Bob and David, The Office,* and as the voice of Clay Puppington on many episodes of the stop-motion animation series *Moral Orel.* Currently stars as Pete Hornberger on NBC's hit comedy *30 Rock.*

**Andrew Alexander** Current CEO and executive producer. Owner of Second City Toronto since 1974; owner of Second City Chicago since 1985. Co-founded *SCTV* in 1976. Co-production deals have included partnerships with MGM Television, Imagine Films, Disney Studios, and United Artists. Alexander has developed television programming for ABC, CBS, NBC, Fox Television, Comedy Central, HBO, Showtime, A&E and the Canadian Broadcasting Corporation.

**Alan Arkin** Cast member, Chicago and New York, 1960–63. Has starred on Broadway and in scores of films, including David Mamet's *Glengarry Glen Ross; Grosse Pointe Blank;* and *Little Miss Sunshine.* His role in the latter won him an Oscar for best supporting actor in 2006.

**Dan Aykroyd** Cast member, Toronto, 1973–75. Starred in first few seasons of *Saturday Night Live.* Numerous movies include *The Blues Brothers* with John Belushi, *Ghostbusters* with Bill Murray and Harold Ramis, and *Driving Miss Daisy* with Jessica Tandy and Morgan Freeman.

**Jim Belushi** Cast member 1976–78 and 1980–81. John Belushi was his older brother. Was a featured player on *Saturday Night Live* and starred in such films as *About Last Night . . . , K-9,* and *Salvador.* Also starred in the now syndicated sitcom *According to Jim,* which ran from 2001 to 2009.

**John Belushi** Cast member 1971–72. Starred in first four seasons of *Saturday Night Live* as well as in *Animal House* (co-written by Harold Ramis); *The Blues Brothers* with Dan Aykroyd; *Continental Divide;* and *Neighbors.* Died on March 5, 1982, in Los Angeles.

**John Candy** Cast member, Chicago and Toronto, 1973–76. Starred on and wrote for *SCTV* between 1976 and 1983. Popular movies include *National Lampoon's Vacation; Splash; Uncle Buck; Planes, Trains and Automobiles; The Great Outdoors;* and many more. Died in 1994 while filming the posthumously released *Wagons East!*

**Steve Carell** Cast member 1988–94. Appeared on Comedy Central's *The Daily Show with Jon Stewart.* Stars on NBC sitcom *The Office.* Films include *The 40-Year-Old Virgin, Little Miss Sunshine, Bruce Almighty, Evan Almighty,* and *Get Smart.*

**Dan Castellaneta** Cast member 1982–87. Voice of Homer Simpson, Groundskeeper Willie, Mayor Quimby, and Krusty the Clown on Fox's long-running hit *The Simpsons.* Has also appeared on numerous sitcoms and in several films, including Jeff Garlin's *I Want Someone to Eat Cheese With.*

**Del Close** Director, Chicago and Toronto, 1972–82. Widely known as America's guru of improvisation. Taught such stars as John Belushi, John Candy, Bill Murray, and countless others. Helped create *SCTV* in Toronto. Worked briefly as "House Metaphysician" on *Saturday Night Live.* A former carnival fire-eater, Close did early stints on Broadway and as a stand-up comic. Memorable movie roles include Reverend Meeker in *The Blob,* a corrupt Chicago alderman in *The Untouchables,* and a deathly boring high school teacher in *Ferris Bueller's Day Off.* Died in 1999. Willed his skull to Chicago's Goodman Theatre for use in production of *Hamlet.* Skull later discovered not to be his.

**Stephen Colbert** Cast member 1988–94. Earned national notice as correspondent on Comedy Central's *The Daily Show with Jon Stewart.* Starred with former Second City mates Amy Sedaris and Paul Dinello in Comedy Central's *Strangers with Candy* and its later film version. Currently Emmy-winning host of *The Colbert Report* on Comedy Central.

**Melinda Dillon** Cast member, Chicago and New York, 1959–61 and 1964–5. Films include *Close Encounters of the Third Kind; The Prince of Tides; To Wong Foo, Thanks for Everything! Julie Newmar;* and *Magnolia.* Has also appeared on the TV shows *Law & Order: Special Victims Unit* and *Picket Fences,* among others.

**Paul Dinello** Cast member 1987–93. Notable TV shows and appearances include *Exit 57, Strangers with Candy,* and *The Colbert Report.* Also starred in the movie version of *Strangers with Candy* with fellow Second City alums Stephen Colbert and Amy Sedaris.

**Brian Doyle-Murray** Cast member 1969–71. Appeared on numerous episodes of *Saturday Night Live* and *SCTV.* Scores of film and television shows include *Caddyshack, National Lampoon's Vacation, Scrooged, JFK, Wayne's World, King of the Hill, Seinfeld,* and *Family Guy.* Co-wrote (with Harold Ramis) the hit comedy *Caddyshack,* starring brother Bill.

**Rachel Dratch** Cast member 1995–98. Appeared on *Saturday Night Live* from 1999 to 2006. Other TV shows include *30 Rock, The King of Queens,* and *Frasier.*

**Chris Farley** Cast member 1988–91. Starred for five years on *Saturday Night Live.* Movies include *Black Sheep, Tommy Boy,* and *Beverly Hills Ninja.* Died on December 18, 1997, in Chicago.

**Tina Fey** Cast member 1995–97. Appeared on *Saturday Night Live* from 1997 to 2006. Was the show's first female head writer. Films include *Mean Girls* and *Baby Mama.* Created and currently stars on NBC's hit sitcom *30 Rock.*

**Joe Flaherty** Cast member and director, Chicago and Toronto, 1969–79. Starred in and wrote for all six seasons of *SCTV* as Count Floyd, Guy Caballero, and many other popular characters. Has also appeared on such shows as *Freaks and Geeks, Frasier, The King of Queens,* and in many films.

**Jeff Garlin** Cast member (sort of) 1985–86. Gained notice as a successful stand-up comic in 1980s. Played for several seasons on hit sitcom *Mad About You.* Currently stars in and co-executive-produces hit HBO comedy *Curb Your Enthusiasm,* with Larry David.

**Michael Gellman** Cast member 1973–76; Toronto director and Edmonton resident director 1980–84. Has long worked at the Second City Training Center in Chicago, where he's a senior faculty member.

**Tom Gianas** Director 1990–95. Wrote for *Saturday Night Live* from 1995 to 1998. Also penned episodes of the Jack Black HBO comedy *Tenacious D* and MTV's *Human Giant,* which he also executive-produced and twice directed. Executive-produced many episodes of *The Man Show* on Comedy Central.

**Valerie Harper** Cast member 1960s. Gained fame as Rhoda Morgenstern on *The Mary Tyler Moore Show.* Also starred in the spin-off show *Rhoda.* Stage work includes *The Tale of the Allergist's Wife* on Broadway and the title role of Golda Meir in *Golda's Balcony.*

**Barbara Harris** Founding member of the Compass Players. Second City cast member, Chicago and New York, from 1959 to early sixties. Tony Award–winning, Oscar-nominated actress has starred in numerous Broadway productions, hit TV shows, and popular films, including *The Seduction of Joe Tynan, Peggy Sue Got Married, Dirty Rotten Scoundrels,* and *Grosse Pointe Blank.*

**Bonnie Hunt** Cast member 1985–90. Has appeared in several films, including *Rain Man, Dave,* and *Return to Me,* the latter of which she also co-wrote and directed. Once a frequent guest of late-night host David Letterman, Hunt has also starred on several talk shows of her own, including the currently airing *The Bonnie Hunt Show.*

**Fred Kaz** An accomplished jazz pianist, Kaz joined Second City as musical director in 1964. He stayed with the company until 1989, nurturing comedic greats such as John Belushi, Bill Murray, and many others.

**Tim Kazurinsky** Cast member 1977–79. Starred for several seasons on *Saturday Night Live.* Perhaps most recognized for his role as Carl Sweetchuck in the *Police Academy* movies. Co-wrote hit films *My Bodyguard* and *About Last Night . . . .* Has appeared on TV in *According to Jim* and *Curb Your Enthusiasm,* among other shows.

**Richard Kind** Cast member, Chicago, 1983–87; L.A., 1988–89. Has appeared in many television shows, including the long-running *Spin City* with Michael J. Fox, *Mad About You,* and *Curb Your Enthusiasm.* Kind's numerous film roles include one of the main character voices in Pixar's hit *A Bug's Life.*

**Robert Klein** Cast member 1965–66. A legendary and bestselling stand-up comedian, Klein has also appeared in scores of films and television shows. They include the Mike Nichols–directed *Primary Colors,* the TV series *Sisters,* and Jerry Seinfeld's documentary *Comedian.*

**Kelly Leonard** Vice president, the Second City; president, Second City Theatricals. Tenure began in 1988. Oversees all the company's live theatrical operations. Produced such seminal stage productions as *Piñata Full of Bees, Paradigm Lost,* and *Holy War, Batman!* Brokered deal that brought Second City to the high seas in a partnership with Norwegian Cruise Line. Currently, Second City maintains seven full-time ensembles aboard NCL ships.

**Eugene Levy** Cast member, Toronto, 1973–75; cast member/writer, *SCTV,* 1976–84. A mainstay of Christopher Guest's mockumentaries (*This Is Spinal Tap, Waiting for Guffman, Best in Show, A Mighty Wind*), Levy starred in all six seasons of *SCTV.* Other popular movie projects include the *American Pie* films.

**Shelley Long** Cast member 1976–77. Best known as Diane Chambers on the long-running ABC comedy *Cheers,* Long also starred in the popular *Brady Bunch* movies and has made guest appearances on Kelsey Grammer's hit sitcom *Frasier,* among many other shows.

**Roberta Maguire** Cast member 1969–71; director of Chicago touring company 1972. Trained under improv master Del Close. Has taught and performed improvisational theater all over the United States and at such schools as the Cornish College of the Arts and the University of Washington in Seattle. Is also a founder of Chicago's Tony

Award–winning Victory Gardens Theater, where she produced, directed, and performed for many years.

**Andrea Martin** Cast member, Toronto, 1974–76; cast member, *SCTV*, 1976–84. Has starred in numerous plays, TV shows, and films including *Innerspace, Wag the Dog,* and *My Big Fat Greek Wedding.* Voice work has appeared on countless cartoons, including *The Simpsons* and *Jimmy Neutron: Boy Genius.* Won Tony Award for 1992 Broadway debut in *My Favorite Year,* and starred in Mel Brooks's *The Producers* on Broadway in 2005.

**Jack McBrayer** Cast member 1997–2002. TV shows and films include *Arrested Development, The Colbert Report, Talladega Nights: The Ballad of Ricky Bobby, Walk Hard: The Dewey Cox Story,* and *Forgetting Sarah Marshall.* Currently stars as Kenneth Parcell on NBC's hit comedy *30 Rock.*

**Adam McKay** Cast member 1993–95. Wrote for *Saturday Night Live* in the late nineties, and went on to direct several popular comedies, including *Anchorman: The Legend of Ron Burgundy, Talladega Nights: The Ballad of Ricky Bobby,* and *Step Brothers.*

**Tim Meadows** Cast member 1989–91. Starred for several seasons on NBC's *Saturday Night Live.* Films include *The Ladies Man, Mean Girls,* and *Walk Hard: The Dewey Cox Story.*

**Bill Murray** Cast member 1972–74. Spent several seasons on *Saturday Night Live* in the seventies before embarking on one of the most successful movie careers in comedy. Films include *Stripes, Caddyshack, Ghostbusters, Groundhog Day,* and *Scrooged.* Dramatic works include *The Razor's Edge, Rushmore,* and *Lost in Translation,* for which he was nominated for an Oscar.

**Joel Murray** Cast member 1985–89. Younger brother of Bill and Brian Doyle-Murray. TV projects include co-star roles on the ABC sitcom *Dharma & Greg* and the A&E drama *Mad Men.*

**Mike Myers** Cast member, Toronto, 1986–87; Chicago 1988. During Myers's highly successful stint on *Saturday Night Live* from 1989 to 1993, his film career took off with the 1992 hit *Wayne's World,* which he followed up with a sequel. Other blockbusters include the *Austin Powers* films and the animated *Shrek* movies for Disney.

**Bob Odenkirk** Cast member 1991. Spent several seasons writing for *Saturday Night Live.* Also wrote and starred in the HBO hit *Mr. Show with Bob and David,* appeared on HBO's critically acclaimed comedy *The Larry Sanders Show,* and directed Jeff Garlin's stand-up special *Young and Handsome: A Night with Jeff Garlin,* which was filmed at Second City in 2008.

**Catherine O'Hara** Cast member, Toronto, 1974–76; cast member, *SCTV,* 1976–78, 1981–82, 1983–84. Has performed in scores of films and television shows such as *Home Alone* and *Six Feet Under.* Perhaps best known for her roles in Christopher Guest's mockumentaries *Waiting for Guffman, Best in Show,* and *A Mighty Wind.*

**Sheldon Patinkin** Began as general manager of Second City in 1960. Went on to direct numerous shows in Chicago and Toronto. Helped establish *SCTV* and edited many early episodes. Chaired Chicago-based Columbia College's theater department from 1980 to May 2009 and is now chair emeritus. Currently serves as artistic consultant for Second City and Steppenwolf Theatre Company.

**Gilda Radner** Cast member, Toronto, 1973–74. Standout member of *Saturday Night Live* cast from 1975 to 1980. Married actor/director Gene Wilder and starred with him in 1986 film *Haunted Honeymoon.* Her bestselling autobiography, *It's Always Something,* was published shortly after her death from ovarian cancer in 1989.

**Harold Ramis** Cast member 1968–74; cast member/writer, *SCTV,* 1976–77. One of the world's foremost comedy directors and writers. Films include *Animal House, Caddyshack, Stripes, National Lampoon's Vacation, Ghostbusters, Back to School, Groundhog Day, Multiplicity, Analyze This, Analyze That,* and *The Ice Harvest.*

**Joan Rivers** Cast member 1961–62. A legendary stand-up comedienne, she was also a popular guest host on *The Tonight Show Starring Johnny Carson* and has appeared on such TV shows as *Nip/Tuck* and *Boston Legal.* Known for her red carpet Oscar interviews and cosmetic surgeries.

**Eugenie Ross-Leming** Cast member 1971–73. Has written and executive-produced such popular TV shows as *Supernatural, Lois & Clark: The New Adventures of Superman,* and *Scarecrow and Mrs. King,* which she also co-created.

**Bernard Sahlins** Co-founded Second City in 1959 with Howard Alk and Paul Sills. Sold the company to Andrew Alexander in 1985. A playwright, producer, and director, Sahlins also founded Second City's Toronto branch in 1973 and helped launch *SCTV.*

**Paul Sand** Cast member, Chicago and New York, in the early 1960s. Studied with famed French mime Marcel Marceau. Appeared in numerous stage productions on and off Broadway. Won Tony Award in 1971 for *Paul Sills' Story Theatre* on Broadway. Scores of television roles include Robert Dreyfuss on the 1975 CBS sitcom *Paul Sand in Friends and Lovers* and guest turns on *Bewitched; St. Elsewhere; Magnum, P.I.; Dharma & Greg; Joan of Arcadia;* and *Curb Your Enthusiasm,* among many others.

**Horatio Sanz** Cast member 1992–98. Starred on *Saturday Night Live* from 1998 to 2007. Also appeared in the TV series *Fillmore!* on USA Network and in the film comedy *Step Brothers,* directed by fellow Second City alum Adam McKay.

**Amy Sedaris** Cast member 1987–93. A favorite guest of late-night host David Letterman. Well known for role as Jerri Blank in *Strangers with Candy,* a Comedy Central show co-starring Paul Dinello and Stephen Colbert. Films include *The School of Rock, Strangers with Candy,* and *Shrek the Third.* Her brother is bestselling author David Sedaris.

**Martin Short** Cast member, Toronto, 1977–78; cast member, *SCTV,* 1982–84. Appeared on *Saturday Night Live* from 1984 to 1985, and starred on *The Martin Short Show* and *Primetime Glick.* Films include *¡Three Amigos!, Innerspace, Father of the Bride,* and *Captain Ron,* among others.

**Paul Sills** Called "the godfather of modern improvisational sketch comedy" by *The New York Times.* Co-founder and director of the Compass Players; co-founder and first director of Second City. Went on to found Game Theater, *Story Theatre,* Sills & Co., and (with Mike Nichols) the New Actors Workshop in New York. Died in early June 2008.

**Joyce Sloane** Producer emeritus. Has been associated with the Second City since 1961. Served as associate producer and executive producer, and is now retired from the day-to-day operations. Along with founder Bernard Sahlins, produced Second City shows in Toronto, Los Angeles, New York, and abroad. Also founded the Second City national touring companies and the Second City e.t.c. Co-founded Second City in Toronto in 1973.

**Jim Staahl** Cast member 1970–74. Co-starred with Robin Williams in many episodes of the hit sitcom *Mork & Mindy.* Has appeared on several other sitcoms and penned numerous animation scripts with writing partner and former Second City cast mate Jim Fisher. Also had roles in the film comedies *Night Shift, Airplane II,* and *Spies Like Us.* Had a recurring role in HBO's *Curb Your Enthusiasm* in 2002.

**David Steinberg** Cast member 1964–66, 1967 (brief stint). A popular comedian, talk show host, and director. Appeared numerous times on *The Tonight Show Starring Johnny Carson* (which he also guest hosted); starred in his own talk show in the seventies; recently hosted *Sit Down Comedy with David Steinberg* on A&E. Directorial projects include *Newhart, Seinfeld, Friends, Mad About You, Weeds,* and *Curb Your Enthusiasm.*

**Len Stuart** Shareholder and co-chairman of Second City since 1976. Began financial involvement with *SCTV* in 1978.

**Betty Thomas** Cast member 1973–76; director, Chicago, 1988. Began directing career after starring for several seasons as Officer Lucy Bates in the critically acclaimed television drama *Hill Street Blues.* Directed films including *The Brady Bunch Movie,* Howard Stern's *Private Parts, Dr. Dolittle,* and *28 Days.*

**Dave Thomas** Cast member, Toronto, 1975–77; cast member/writer, *SCTV,* 1976–82; guest appearances 1982–84. Achieved superstardom with *SCTV* co-star Rick Moranis as beer-swilling, back-bacon-snarfing duo Bob and Doug McKenzie. Took act to the big screen in early eighties film *Strange Brew.* Numerous TV shows include several seasons of the sitcom *Grace Under Fire, King of the Hill, Arrested Development,* and *The Simpsons.*

**Nia Vardalos** Cast member in Edmonton and Toronto, 1987–90; cast member, Chicago, 1990–94. Breakout film role was in the blockbuster comedy *My Big Fat Greek Wedding* in 2002, which she starred in and wrote. Also wrote and produced *My Big Fat Greek Life,* a TV show based on the film.

**George Wendt** Cast member 1974–80. Best known as the lovable barfly Norm Peterson on long-running ABC comedy *Cheers.* Married to fellow Second City cast mate Bernadette Birkett. Starred as Edna Turnblad in *Hairspray* on Broadway in 2008. Other stage work includes *Art* and *Twelve Angry Men.*

**Fred Willard** Cast member 1965–66. Another staple of Christopher Guest's mockumentaries. Has also appeared in episodes of the hit sitcoms *Roseanne, Friends, Everybody Loves Raymond,* and *Mad About You,* and in scores of films ranging from *Waiting for Guffman* and *Best in Show* to the Oscar-winning animated feature *Wall-E.*

*Sources: SCTV: Behind the Scenes; the Internet Movie Database; Second City archives; www.secondcity.com.*

# BIBLIOGRAPHY

## Books

Belushi Pisano, Judith, and Tanner Colby. *Belushi: A Biography.* New York: Rugged Land, 2005.

Coleman, Janet. *The Compass: The Story of the Improvisational Theatre That Revolutionized the Art of Comedy in America.* New York: Alfred A. Knopf, 1990.

Farley, Tom, Jr., and Tanner Colby. *The Chris Farley Show: A Biography in Three Acts.* New York: Viking, 2008.

Griggs, Jeff. *Guru: My Days with Del Close.* Chicago: Ivan R. Dee, 2005.

Johnson, Kim "Howard." *The Funniest One in the Room: The Lives and Legends of Del Close.* Chicago: Chicago Review Press, 2008.

Klein, Robert. *The Amorous Busboy of Decatur Avenue: A Child of the Fifties Looks Back.* New York: Touchstone, 2006.

Nachman, Gerald. *Seriously Funny: The Rebel Comedians of the 1950s and 1960s.* New York: Pantheon Books, 2003.

Patinkin, Sheldon. *The Second City: Backstage at the World's Greatest Comedy Theater.* Naperville, Ill.: Sourcebooks, Inc., 2000.

Sahlins, Bernard. *Days and Nights at the Second City: A Memoir, with Notes on Staging Review Theatre.* Chicago: Ivan R. Dee, 2002.

Shales, Tom, and James Andrew Miller. *Live from New York: An Uncensored History of Saturday Night Live.* Boston: Little, Brown and Company, 2002.

Spolin, Viola. *Improvisation for the Theater: A Handbook of Teaching and Directing Techniques.* Third Edition. Evanston, Ill.: Northwestern University Press, 1999.

Steinberg, David. *The Book of David.* New York: Simon & Schuster, 2007.

Sweet, Jeffrey. *Something Wonderful Right Away: An Oral History of the Second City and the Compass Players.* New York: Avon Books, 1978. Pompton Plains, N.J.: Limelight Editions, 2004 (reissued).

Thomas, Dave (with Robert Crane and Susan Carney). *SCTV: Behind the Scenes.* Toronto: McClelland & Stewart, Inc., 1996.

Woodward, Bob. *Wired: The Short Life and Fast Times of John Belushi.* New York: Simon & Schuster, 1984.

Zoglin, Richard. *Comedy at the Edge: How Stand-Up in the 1970s Changed America.* New York: Bloomsbury, 2008.

## Video/DVD

Belushi, Jim. *Second City Presents . . . with Bill Zehme.* Directed by John Davies. Brad Gray Television and John Davies Prods. Bravo TV, 2002.

Murray, Bill. *Bill Murray Live from the Second City,* VHS. Produced by Bill Murray. RKO Home Video, 1980.

*SCTV: Volume 1—Network 90,* DVD. Shout! Factory/Sony Music Entertainment, 2004.

*The Second City: First Family of Comedy,* DVD. Acorn Media, 2006.

## Newspaper and Magazine Articles

Adler, Anthony, "Love & Money: Second City at a Crossroads." *Chicago Reader,* November 12, 1993.

Barnes, Clive, "Revue in New Version of Eastside Playhouse." *The New York Times,* October 16, 1969.

"Belushi Joins Lemmings." *Chicago Daily News,* November 16, 1972.

Bommer, Lawrence, "Second City's Second Rate Second Look." *Chicago Reader,* December 23, 1994.

Bridges, Les, "Theater of the Elusive Reality: At Second City on Wells Street, the Search Goes On." *Chicago Tribune,* June 7, 1970.

Burleigh, Nina, "Chicago's 'Regular Guy' Actor Is More Complex Than You Think." *Chicago Tribune Sunday Magazine,* August 9, 1992.

Caro, Mark, "Analyzing Harold; Now That He's Back Home, Ramis Has a New Film—and a Renewed Outlook," *Chicago Tribune,* March 14, 1999.

Christiansen, Richard, "Bad Break for Good Talent: Second City Sells Short." *Chicago Daily News,* October 16, 1969.

Christiansen, Richard, "Bernie Sahlins, Mr. Second City." *Chicago Daily News,* December 13–14, 1975.

Christiansen, Richard, "Is Bernie Sahlins Going to Be a Big Man?" *Chicago Daily News,* September 23, 1967.

Christiansen, Richard, "Onward and Upward with John Belushi." *Chicago Daily News,* February 17, 1973.

Christiansen, Richard, "Personal View of Troupe's Rise to Fame." *Chicago Tribune,* April 15, 2001.

Christiansen, Richard, "The Plans Are Big for Second City." *Chicago Daily News,* November 19, 1966.

Christiansen, Richard, "Second City Enters New Era with Some Old Standards." *Chicago Daily News,* August 3, 1967.

Christiansen, Richard, "Second City's Founding Father Comes Home." *Chicago Tribune,* September 21, 1980.

Christiansen, Richard, "SNL Raid Will Close 'Jubilee.' " *Chicago Tribune,* August 31, 1982.

Christiansen, Richard, "Success Is Sweet: Homegrown Playwright's Career Turns into a Hit." *Chicago Tribune,* March 8, 1981.

Christiansen, Richard, "A Theater Dies, but a Director Lives." *Chicago Daily News,* December 9, 1967.

Cocks, Jay, "Messages from Melonville; SCTV Is the Funniest Show on the Air and Maybe the Best Too." *Time,* November 6, 1981.

Colander, Pat, "Second City Marks 25 Years of Laughter." *The New York Times,* December 16, 1984.

Collins, Glenn, "John Candy, Comedic Film Star, Is Dead of a Heart Attack at 43." *The New York Times,* March 5, 1994.

Corliss, Richard. "End of a Samurai Comic; John Belushi: 1949–1982." *Time,* March 15, 1982.

Donner, Ted A., "Del Close: An Uncensored Oral History," *Chicago Reader,* March 12, 1999.

Ebert, Roger, "Steinberg—He's Short but Hustles." *Chicago Sun-Times,* September 3, 1967.

Ebert, Roger, "Wired" (book review). *Chicago Sun-Times,* June 17, 1984.

Elder, Sean, "The Funniest Graduate of 'Saturday Night Live' Has Made an Art Form (and a Career) out of Insincerity and a Blank Stare." Salon.com, February 6, 2001.

Emmerman, Lynn, "Blues Brothers Take a Dive for Privacy's Sake." *Chicago Tribune,* August 9, 1979.

Entertainment Brief (no title). *Chicago Sun-Times,* November 26, 1967.

Entertainment Brief. "First Second City Film to Roll Jan. 3." *Chicago Daily News,* November 25, 1967.

Entertainment Brief. "Second City Troupe to Play in New York." *Chicago Tribune,* April 4, 1966.

Entertainment Brief. "Signed by Second City." *Chicago Sun-Times,* November 25, 1963.

Esterow, Milton, "Second City Troupe Opens New Show." *The New York Times,* September 14, 1963.

Esterow, Milton, "Second City's New Revue Is Off to Hilarious Start." *The New York Times,* January 24, 1964.

"Five Actresses Show Fashions at Second City." *Chicago Daily News,* June 10, 1963.

Folkart, Burt A., "Film Comedian John Candy, 43; Began on 'SCTV.' " *Chicago Sun-Times,* March 5, 1994.

Friend, Tad. "How Harold Ramis's Movies Have Stayed Funny for Twenty-five Years." *The New Yorker,* April 19, 2004.

Gallo, Hank, "James Belushi Takes the Time to Listen to His Own Success." *Chicago Tribune,* May 11, 1989.

"Garrick Arches Find a Home in Theater." *Chicago Sun-Times,* February 24, 1961.

Gerard, Jeremy, "Bill Murray Is Still the Second City's Loyal Son." *Chicago Tribune,* June 21, 1981.

Gold, Aaron, and John Rebchook, "Comic Star's Death Stuns Relatives and Friends Here." *Chicago Tribune,* March 6, 1982.

Green, Larry and Laura, "Chicago Happening: Successful Child Pacification Program Produced at Old Town's Second City." *Chicago Daily News,* July 12, 1969.

Harris, Sydney J., "Second City: Mellower, but Still Pert." *Chicago Daily News,* March 24, 1972.

Heffernan, Virginia. "Anchor Woman; Tina Fey Rewrites Late-Night Comedy." *The New Yorker,* November 3, 2003.

Helbig, Jack, "Friends and Coconspirators Recall the Crazed Career of an Improv Olympian." *Chicago Reader,* March 12, 1999.

Helbig, Jack, "The Mysterious Martin de Maat." *Chicago Reader,* February 23, 2001.

Helbig, Jack, "The Powers That Be Have Shaken Things Up and Made Things Better and Funnier the Second Time Around." Chicago *Daily Herald,* August 1, 1997.

Helbig, Jack, "Revolving Door Policy." *Chicago Reader,* August 3, 2001.

Helbig, Jack, "Turning the Big '4.0' Second City Hits Four-Decade Mark—Still a Funny Farm of Comedy." Chicago *Daily Herald,* December 10, 1999.

Hevesi, Dennis, "Gilda Radner, 42, Comic Original of 'Saturday Night Live' Zaniness." *The New York Times,* May 21, 1989.

Houston, Gary, "The Man Who Gets High Watching 'The 43rd Parallel' at Second City." *Chicago Sun-Times,* April 2, 1972.

Jevens, Darel, "Holy War, Batman! Or the Yellow Cab of Courage." *Chicago Sun-Times,* November 13, 2001.

Jevens, Darel, "The Second City: Comic Sages for the Ages." *Chicago Sun-Times,* December 12, 1999.

Johnson, Allan, "On the Laugh Track: Reliving 40 Years of Second City Through Performers' Eyes." *Chicago Tribune,* December 12, 1999.

Jones, Chris, " 'Between Barack' Funniest Second City Show in Years." *Chicago Tribune,* March 24, 2007.

Jones, Chris, "Did the Compass Point to the Birth of Improv?" *Chicago Tribune,* July 10, 2005.

Jones, Chris, "Second City's e.t.c. Finds Laughs in Stressful Times." *Chicago Tribune,* November 23, 2001.

Jones, Chris, "Tina Fey Moves to Prime Time, Bringing Second City Along." *Chicago Tribune,* October 8, 2006.

Kart, Larry, "Andrew Alexander Ready to Direct the Second Advent of Second City." *Chicago Tribune,* April 14, 1985.

Kart, Larry, "Brilliant 'Cows on Ice' A Must for Laugh Lovers." *Chicago Tribune,* November 11, 1983.

Kart, Larry, "Center of Comedy Culture Is Settlement Called Second City." *Chicago Tribune,* May 7, 1978.

Kart, Larry, "1st-rate reunion for Second City." *Chicago Tribune,* December 16, 1984.

Kart, Larry, " 'Freud' Didn't Slip, but Not the Best Revue." *Chicago Tribune,* April 18, 1979.

Kart, Larry, "From Corn Chips to Comedy, Schreiber Is the Old Master." *Chicago Tribune,* August 6, 1978.

Kart, Larry, "Second City: Critical in '59, Cozy in '79." *Chicago Tribune,* December 9, 1979.

Kart, Larry, "Second City Has a Winner with a Play on Mamet." *Chicago Tribune,* February 25, 1978.

Kleiman, Carol, "Shelley Gets a Challenge of a Very Different Sort." *Chicago Tribune,* August 6, 1976.

Kurson, Robert, and Bill Zwecker, "The Wild Last Days of Chris Farley." *Chicago Sun-Times,* December 21, 1997.

Lavin, Cheryl, "Falling Star." *Chicago Tribune,* May 23, 1982.

Leonard, William, "Dog Gone! The Second City Is 10 Years Old." *Chicago Tribune,* December 7, 1969.

Leonard, William, "Second City Opens Its New Theater Wednesday." *Chicago Tribune,* July 30, 1967.

Leonard, William, "Second City's 'Viper' Doesn't Have Very Much Venom." *Chicago Tribune,* February 6, 1967.

Lesner, Sam, "Gifted Newcomer Dominates Revue." *Chicago Daily News,* January 22, 1964.

Lesner, Sam, "Second City Revue Spouts Political Bile." *Chicago Daily News,* November 30, 1967.

Mark, Norman, "Steinberg Returns to Second City." *Chicago Daily News,* July 26, 1967.

McCarthy, Ellen, "Ben Stiller Isn't Funny. Or So He Says." *The Washington Post,* December 22, 2006.

Mnookin, Seth. "The Man in the Irony Mask." *Vanity Fair,* October 2007.

"Old Comedies Shown Outdoors." *Chicago Daily News,* August 8, 1963.

Ouzounian, Richard, "On Target with Urban Life." *Toronto Star,* July 20, 2007.

Ouzounian, Richard, "Second to None; Four Years Ago, Second City Almost Ceased Operations in Toronto. But Now the Resurgent Company Is Getting the Last Laugh." *Toronto Star,* July 7, 2007.

Patinkin, Sheldon, "My Five Years at Second City." *Chicago Daily News,* December 12, 1964. Panorama section.

Petersen, Clarence, "Second City's Don DePollo Is a Stark Raven Madcap." *Chicago Tribune,* March 18, 1977.

Pouteau, Jacques, "London Greets Revue by Second City Players." *Chicago Tribune,* August 18, 1965.

Reich, Howard, "Fred Kaz, House Pianist: For 17 Years, Adding Shine to the Second City Stars." *Chicago Tribune,* May 30, 1982.

Roeper, Richard, "Nothing to Brag About for Farley's Party Pals." *Chicago Sun-Times,* January 8, 1998.

Sahlins, Bernard, "Cum Grano Sahlins." *Chicago Daily News,* December 11, 1971.

Sahlins, Bernard, "Second City Scores a First." *Chicago Sun-Times,* November 20, 1999.

"Satire in Chicago." *Time,* March 21, 1960.

"Second City Troupe Moving to Its New Quarters Aug. 2." *Chicago Tribune,* July 16, 1967.

Sharbutt, Jay, "Second City Aims for the Stars with Blasts at Popular TV Shows." *Chicago Tribune,* September 2, 1977.

Siskel, Gene, "The Blues Brothers: Belushi and Aykroyd: An Odd Couple Live in Perfect Comic Harmony on TV, Record, and Film." *Chicago Tribune,* June 29, 1980.

Siskel, Gene, "A Quality Act—On, Off Stage." *Chicago Tribune,* March 7, 1982.

Siskel, Gene, "Wild Bill Murray: A Big-Time Clown Puts on a Serious Face." *Chicago Tribune,* June 10, 1984.

Siskel, Gene, " 'Wired' Transforms John Belushi Story into Harrowing Tragedy." *Chicago Tribune,* May 27, 1984.

Smith, Sid, "In 'Pinata,' Troupe Takes Daring Step, Breaks Out of Second City Mold." *Chicago Tribune,* June 23, 1995.

Smith, Sid, "2nd to None; How America's Most Renowned Improv Club Keeps Its Long Winning Streak Alive." *Chicago Tribune,* May 20, 2007.

Solomon, Alan, "Taking a Swig of 'Canadian Export' at Second City." *Chicago Tribune,* August 16, 1974.

Spitznagel, Eric. "The Devil's Comic." *Chicago* magazine, September 2003.

Spitznagel, Eric. "Playboy Interview: Steve Carell." *Playboy,* June 1, 2008.

Starr, Mark, "Second City Proves First Rate Success." *The Wall Street Journal,* June 17, 1974.

Steinmetz, Johanna, "Second City at 15 Looks Ahead." *Chicago Sun-Times,* October 6, 1974.

Sternbergh, Adam. "Stephen Colbert Has America by the Ballots." *New York* magazine, October 16, 2006.

Stoneman, William H., "Critics in London Acclaim Chicago's 'Second City.' " *Chicago Daily News,* April 24, 1963.

Sweet, Jeffrey, "Brothers, Sisters, Black Sheep: An Alumni Scrapbook." *Chicago Tribune,* December 9, 1984.

Syse, Glenna, "A First-Rate Show from Second City." *Chicago Sun-Times,* June 5, 1971.

Syse, Glenna, " 'The Mother to Us All': Second City's Joyce Sloane Nurtures Chicago Theater." *Chicago Sun-Times,* August 27, 1989.

Syse, Glenna, "2nd City Message Comes Up Cold." *Chicago Sun-Times,* May 8, 1969.

Syse, Glenna, "Second City's New Faces Promising." *Chicago Sun-Times,* October 16, 1969.

Syse, Glenna, "Second Helpings." *Chicago Sun-Times,* August 25, 1969.

Thomas, Mike, "Alan Arkin's Second Wind: 'Sunshine' Boy Overcame Self-Doubts During Chicago Improv Stint in '60s." *Chicago Sun-Times,* February 22, 2007.

Thomas, Mike, "Comedian Gives Props to City That Launched His Career." *Chicago Sun-Times,* September 25, 2005.

Thomas, Mike, "Jim Belushi Looks Back at Anger: According to Comic, It's a Sign of Manhood." *Chicago Sun-Times,* May 14, 2006.

"Time Listings." *Time,* December 1, 1961.

Tresniowski, Alex, Giovanna Breu, Cindy Dampier, Luchina Fisher, Lorna Grisby, Kelly

Williams, John Hannah, Craig Tomashoff, Ulrica Wihlborg, Rodd Gold, Vickie Bane, Mary Green, and Cynthia Wang. "Requiem for a Heavyweight: Pratfalls, Pain and Laughter Marked the Short, Reckless Life of Funnyman Chris Farley." *People,* January 12, 1998.

Tucker, Ernest, "Gianas Helps Keep Second City Vibrant." *Chicago Sun-Times,* August 17, 1990.

Tucker, Ernest, "It's Busy Backstage at Second City." *Chicago Sun-Times,* September 25, 1992.

Tucker, Ernest, "2nd City Sheds Tradition, Finds Its Sting." *Chicago Sun-Times,* June 23, 1995.

Weiss, Hedy, "E.t.c. Goes from Barack to Broke in Blink of an Eye; Satire Always Topical, Often Uneven." *Chicago Sun-Times,* December 9, 2008.

Weiss, Hedy, "The Revelation Will Not Be Televised." *Chicago Sun-Times,* January 8, 1999.

Weiss, Hedy, "Right on Target: Second City's Latest Revue As Topical As Ever," *Chicago Sun-Times,* December 23, 2005.

Williams, Michaela, "Second City Shows New Quarters." *Chicago Daily News,* July 13, 1967.

Williams, Michaela, "They Made the Movie in Chicago (and Avery Got the Girl, Too)." *Chicago Daily News,* March 30, 1968.

Ziomek, Jon, "The Dinosaur of Improvisation." *Chicago Tribune,* November 5, 1978.

# INDEX

# ABOUT THE AUTHOR

**Mike Thomas,** a staff writer for the *Chicago Sun-Times,* has interviewed numerous renowned comics and comedic actors—several of them Second City alums—including Jerry Seinfeld, Robin Williams, Carl Reiner, Bill Cosby, Tom and Dick Smothers, Chevy Chase, Sarah Silverman, Richard Lewis, Phyllis Diller, Bob Newhart, Rodney Dangerfield, and Jon Stewart. Thomas's national magazine work has appeared in *Esquire, Smithsonian,* and *Playboy* and on Salon.com. He lives in Chicago with his wife and their two daughters.